Chicken Soup for the Soul.

The Empowered Woman

Chicken Soup for the Soul: The Empowered Woman
101 Stories about Being Confident, Courageous and Your True Self
Amy Newmark. Foreword by Joi Gordon

Published by Chicken Soup for the Soul, LLC www.chickensoup.com
Copyright ©2018 by Chicken Soup for the Soul, LLC. All Rights Reserved.

The publisher gratefully acknowledges the many publishers and individuals who granted
Chicken Soup for the Soul permission to reprint the cited material.

Front cover photo of woman courtesy of iStockphoto.com/GlobalStock (©GlobalStock)
Front cover photo of beach courtesy of iStockphoto.com/Szepy (©Szepy)
Back cover and interior photo of Joi Gordon courtesy of Dress for Success
Interior photo of running woman courtesy of iStockphoto.com/lzf (©lzf)
Photo of Amy Newmark courtesy of Susan Morrow at SwickPix

Cover and Interior by Daniel Zaccari

Distributed to the booktrade by Simon & Schuster. SAN: 200-2442

Publisher's Cataloging-In-Publication Data
(Prepared by The Donohue Group, Inc.)

Names: Newmark, Amy, compiler. | Gordon, Joi, writer of supplementary textual content.
Title: Chicken soup for the soul : the empowered woman : 101 stories about being confident,
      courageous and your true self / [compiled by] Amy Newmark ; foreword by Joi Gordon,
      CEO, Dress for Success.
Other Titles: Empowered woman : 101 stories about being confident, courageous and your true self
Description: [Cos Cob, Connecticut] : Chicken Soup for the Soul, LLC, [2018]
Identifiers: ISBN 9781611599817 (print) | ISBN 9781611592818 (ebook)
Subjects: LCSH: Self-esteem in women--Literary collections. | Self-esteem in women--Anecdotes. |
      Self-actualization (Psychology) in women--Literary collections. | Self-actualization (Psychology) in
      women--Anecdotes. | LCGFT: Anecdotes.
Classification: LCC BF697.5.S46 C45 2018 (print) | LCC BF697.5.S46 (ebook) | DDC 158.1082/02--
      dc23

Library of Congress Control Number: 2018935474

PRINTED IN THE UNITED STATES OF AMERICA
on acid∞free paper

25 24 23 22 21 20 19 18   01 02 03 04 05 06 07 08 09 10 11

The
Empowered
Woman

101 Stories about Being
Confident, Courageous
and Your True Self

Amy Newmark
Foreword by Joi Gordon
CEO, Dress for Success Worldwide

Chicken Soup for the Soul, LLC
Cos Cob, CT

Chicken Soup
for the Soul

Changing the world one story at a time®
www.chickensoup.com

Table of Contents

❶

~Who Am I?~

❷

~I Found My Courage~

❸

~Doing What's Right for Me~

❹

~Going It Alone~

❺
~I Stepped Outside My Comfort Zone~

❻
~Walk the Talk~

❼

~Sticking Up for What's Right~

❽

~Time for Me~

❾

~Figuring It Out Myself~

Foreword

Twenty-one years ago, Nancy Lublin had a very simple idea — that $5,000 could change the world. Since Nancy's initial investment in 1997, Dress for Success has grown from a church basement to a global enterprise that has empowered more than 1,000,000 women in thirty countries.

In the many years since I joined Dress for Success I have been fortunate enough to connect with some remarkable women — strong, independent and courageous — as they have first walked through our doors and then gone on to open doors for others. They have broken barriers, triumphed over adversity, shared their stories with the world and now give back to Dress for Success and their communities as donors, mentors and volunteers.

I've watched women do what seemed to be impossible, overcome the unthinkable and transform right in front of my eyes. At Dress for Success, we build a woman's confidence from the inside out. Many of these women have been survivors of domestic violence, the prison system, poverty, debt, homelessness, health battles, traumas and heartache. They have the opportunity to experience a broad range of programs — from job training to financial education to leadership courses — and these programs help fulfill our mission of empowering women to achieve economic independence.

When Chicken Soup for the Soul approached us regarding their new book about "The Empowered Woman" we knew it was the perfect partnership. The thought of 101 powerful stories from women sharing their personal, revealing stories with each other was exciting. And now that we've seen the manuscript, we are even more excited. A portion of proceeds from the book sales will go towards funding various Dress for Success programs available to the women we serve, but what's even better is how much these stories will empower, energize, and even entertain the women who read them.

Sometimes, becoming an empowered woman means going outside your comfort zone and facing your smaller fears, even something as simple as picking up a dead animal you found in the back yard. That's what Jennifer Kathleen Gibbons tells us in her story in Chapter 2, which is all about "finding your courage." But sometimes, finding your courage is way more scary, as B.B. Loyd tells us when she describes packing up her kids and flying back to the U.S. from the military base in Germany where they were living with her abusive husband. Miraculously, the skin ailment that had been mystifying her doctors for nine months cleared up within one week of her arriving at her safe new home.

It can also be scary to take a stand and advocate for yourself, and the women who do that deserve to feel very proud, as you'll see in Chapter 7, about "sticking up for what's right." April Knight was a forty-five-year-old widow who really needed her job working in a store, but when her boss told her she would be fired if she didn't let him engage in inappropriate behavior, she filed a lawsuit against him. Her co-workers shunned her and her family was not supportive, but April won five years' worth of wages, plus what she really wanted -- a letter of apology and a letter of recommendation so she could get another job.

Feeling empowered doesn't always mean that you have to right a wrong. You can be perfectly content with your life, but realize *that's* the problem — you're content, but stuck in a rut. In Chapter 5, which is all about "stepping outside your comfort zone," you'll meet Tonya Abari, who is a plus-sized but fit woman who always loved dancing but was afraid to be seen in a Zumba class wearing her exercise clothing. Not only does Tonya get up the nerve to join a class, she ends up becoming the instructor.

Stepping outside your comfort zone can also mean learning how to do things on your own, and in Chapter 4, you'll be inspired by the women who resolved to do things alone, including traveling around the world. Wendy Ann Rich was one of them. She decided to make a list of all the things that she was reluctant to do by herself after a friend of hers refused to even enter a restaurant alone. That led Wendy to travel from Canada to Japan on her own, where she says, "I found myself good company for a whole month's worth of memories."

Going it alone doesn't have to mean foreign travel. It can be something simple, like learning to fix your car, or put up wallpaper, or light a fire in the fireplace. Malinda Dunlap Fillingim tells us that she was reluctant to change an unusual light bulb in her home, but her ten-year-old daughter thought that was ridiculous, as Malinda needed that light to read. She said, "You are setting such a bad example for me." Malinda figured out how to change the bulb, and she did feel pretty good about herself after she did it. She's one of the many role models in this collection of success stories that run the gamut from tiny victories and changes, to huge life changing ones. You'll find they are all an inspiration, and you'll undoubtedly find yourself doing something differently, or bigger, or better in the coming weeks.

We have our own collection of success stories at Dress for Success as well. Tracy Anne is an example. She escaped with her two children from an abusive husband, taking her crucial first step toward empowering herself and becoming self-sufficient. We helped her get back on her feet, and she believes, "Dress for Success is a sisterhood; we're all on a level playing field when we are there. You're there to share with a circle of friends, not to feel like you're less than anyone else."

We provided Tracy with career counseling and she says, "I realized that I was letting other people write my story and I needed to write my story myself. When you get out there and hear about other people's lives, you feel so connected to them and no longer embarrassed about what happened to you. I feel like I lost myself to life's circumstances and Dress for Success helped to get *me* back."

Another client, Roxanne from Los Angeles, was laid off from her job and then diagnosed with a terrible, rare disease. She was referred to Dress for Success and she remembers, "I was surrounded by positive women — the more I took action and found the confidence, the more opportunities started presenting themselves, and the more determined I became to win them. I started getting interviews and was able to get beautiful suits from the organization. I felt confident, even with half a smile. They assisted me with my résumé, gave me an Armani suit and I nailed the job interview." Roxanne says, "Dress for Success was the lighthouse, the beaming light that said 'we're here' as I was going through the storm."

And here's one more story for you, from Shannon in Portland, Oregon, who ended up at Dress for Success after her husband's business was burglarized and he lost the equipment that he needed in order to make a living. Shannon realized she needed to get a job if they were to survive. She had a college degree and she'd gotten plenty of jobs before. But this time it didn't happen, so she took someone's advice to go to her local Dress for Success chapter. She says, "When I stepped through the doors of Dress for Success, I felt such a positive energy and hope. They saw right away what I had forgotten that I still possessed. The first time they suited me, they gave me clothes that made me look more poised and charming than I remembered myself being. I looked at myself in the mirror and thought, 'Wow. I'm a beautiful woman and I'm going to be successful and it's starting right here.' It was more than a new outfit. It was an inside-out experience."

These impactful stories bring so much joy to my life. I am proud to see hundreds of thousands of women around the world taking control, finding their voices, supporting other women and inspiring others with their success.

Today I want to thank you for picking up this book. I know you will finish it a different person than you were when you started it. The power of women sharing their best advice, their disappointments and triumphs, and their growth process with each other is truly astounding. What makes us successful is that we recognize we are in this together. When we actively help and appreciate each other, we are unstoppable.

~Joi Gordon
Chief Executive Officer, Dress for Success Worldwide
March 1, 2018

The Empowered Woman

Chapter 1

Who Am I?

Changing Destiny

From our ancestors come our names,
but from our virtues our honors.
~Proverb

hen I was born, my mother named me Linda Pearl Davison. My mother was feuding with her sister-in-law, and she named me "Linda" to spite her sister-in-law, who had planned to name her baby Linda. I was born first (by a week), but my mother's sister-in-law refused to be cheated out of the name she'd chosen and also named her baby Linda. Now there were two "Linda Davisons" in our small town. My mother and her sister-in-law never spoke to each other again, and I never met the cousin who shared my name.

The name "Pearl" was given to me because my mother owed several months' back rent to a woman named Pearl. She hoped if she named her baby after her landlady, she wouldn't evict her. It didn't work. I especially hated the name Pearl when I discovered it was a growth inside a mollusk. I never pictured a pearl as a precious jewel. To me, it was a tumor in the slimy stomach of a shellfish.

So my first name was given to me in spite. My middle name was given to me to avoid eviction and was gross. And my last name, Davison, was given to me reluctantly and grudgingly by my father, who was separated from my mother.

When my mother was angry, which was often, she screamed my name "Linnn-daahh," making it seven syllables long. In my mind, I heard "Linnn-daahh disgusting-growth-inside-a-mollusk Davison!"

In school, the popular kids had nicknames like Rocky, Candy and Sunny. My nickname was Zipper — because I was so skinny. If I turned sideways and stuck out my tongue, they said I looked like a zipper. So there it was — another unwanted name.

When I got married, my last name changed to Stafford. First, I had my father's name; now I had my husband's name. When I lost my husband, I was no longer "Mrs. Stafford," and it didn't feel right to still use his name.

I had been given names that I didn't want and didn't like, and I felt like I was going through life wearing hand-me-down clothes that didn't fit.

I was an artist but seldom signed my paintings because I felt like I was giving the credit for my work to someone I didn't know.

When women marry, they usually change their names. I wasn't going to get married again, but why couldn't I change my name anyway? For once in my life, why couldn't I be called whatever I wanted to be called?

I discovered it only cost $150 and took three weeks to change one's name in the state where I lived. Why hadn't I done this twenty years ago?

I bought a name-your-baby book and made a list of the names I liked. I practiced saying and writing them. After going through about fifty names, I chose April Knight.

I was born in April, a month of spring, flowers and new birth. I was a freelance writer, and many of the courageous knights in history were "free lancers" whose loyalty was not to the king, but to their own sense of honor and chivalry.

Three weeks later, I became April Knight.

I changed my name and changed my life. I felt re-born. I hadn't realized I was carrying so much emotional baggage from my unhappy childhood. My name was a big part of that baggage.

I was surprised at people's reaction to my new name. My family was scandalized! How could I turn my back on the family name? My ancestors must be spinning in their graves!

Other people thought I was having a mid-life crisis or had "gone peculiar," and who knew what I'd do next?

It only took about a month for people to remember to call me April, and soon they forgot I'd ever been called anything else.

My real friends knew it was a big step in healing myself, putting the past behind me and becoming a new stronger, better person. Since I changed my name, I felt empowered.

For thousands of years, people have believed "nomen est omen"—your name is your destiny.

I'm my own person now. I'm not my parents' daughter, someone's wife, or that shy, nervous, frightened child anymore.

I take pride in boldly signing my paintings "April Knight." They are my paintings, and I'm not sharing credit with any ancestors.

I am painting better than I have ever painted. My art has taken a new direction. No more bland paintings of flowers and deer walking through the peaceful forest. Now I paint pictures of knights in shining armor riding magnificent, wild-eyed horses as they charge into battle. My paintings have passion, power and romance, and colors leap from the canvas in ways they've never done before. The knights are a symbol to be fearless and noble, and have the courage to slay the dragons in our lives, whatever they might be.

Changing my name was one of the most powerful, proud moments of my life. I declared myself 100 percent *me*, not pieces and parts and leftover scraps of other people. I felt free at last.

When I reach a different stage of my life, I might change my name again. It's up to me and only me what I am called.

Hello, I'm very happy to meet you. Please let me introduce myself. My name is April Knight.

~April Knight

Writing the Road to Myself

*Every secret of a writer's soul, every experience
of his life, every quality of his mind,
is written large in his works.*
~Virginia Woolf

I had gone from being a daughter in my parents' home to marrying and being a wife. Within a year of marrying, I had a child and a new role: mother.

It seemed that I was always defined in relation to someone else. I was somebody's daughter, somebody's wife, somebody's mother. So, where was Jane? More importantly, *who* was Jane?

In between having four more children, supporting my husband as he started a business, and serving in our church and community, I looked for Jane. Sometimes, I wondered if there was anyone to look for. Did I exist outside my relationship to others? I didn't know.

And then I wrote a story. It was a short story aimed at children. Before I could talk myself out of it, I typed it (these were pre-computer days) and sent it out. To my astonishment, it was accepted.

I wrote more stories. Some were accepted; many were rejected. Still, I kept writing. And, in writing, I found my voice. I also found that people listened.

I wrote of mothering. I wrote of living with chemical depression. I wrote of living on ten dollars an hour (with five children to support) while my husband's fledgling business struggled to survive.

And thus I became an independent person, looking for and finding the words inside me. I shared those words with others. I knew that I could make a difference through those words.

An introvert by nature, I am reticent about speaking in public. However, through my writing, I can free those words. I can touch others by sharing my thoughts and feelings, my experiences and struggles.

"I didn't know you suffered from depression," one friend said after reading my article on living with depression.

That opened a dialogue between us on how depression can be as debilitating as any physical disease. We laughed and cried together as she shared her own experiences. Our friendship deepened. At the same time, my confidence grew along with my newfound independence. I had a sense of empowerment that was all the sweeter for knowing that I was helping someone else.

Independence and identity mean different things to different women. For me, they mean giving voice to the words that swirl through my mind and heart, praying they will touch someone.

Ironically, that form of *independence* re-confirms my *connections* to others, and makes my life richer and all the more fulfilling.

~Jane McBride Choate

Color Me Fabulous

My real hair color is dark blonde.
Now I have mood hair.
~Julia Roberts

The whole thing started when I heard through the always-accurate-and-completely-reliable family grapevine that my brother-in-law thought I looked like Julia Roberts. Never mind that what he actually said to my sister was, "Do you ever look at Deb and see something there that sort of reminds you of Julia Roberts?" And never mind that the only feature I possess that is even remotely similar to her is my loud, obnoxious laugh. All I knew was that my self-confidence had just received a major boost. As far as I was concerned, he practically said, "Wow, have you ever noticed that Deb and Julia Roberts are practically twins?"

I happily tucked this lovely compliment away and pulled it out whenever I needed a little pick-me-up. Then came the fateful day when I needed more than just a pick-me-up. My husband had been out of the country for almost a month, and I was run down and worn out from handling our six children by myself. I felt antsy and in need of a change — specifically, something fun that had nothing to do with being a mom and housewife. Something along the lines of a pick-me-up-and-put-me down-as-a-completely-different-person.

And who better than Julia Roberts?

It just so happened that this little epiphany occurred at the exact same moment I found myself standing in the hair-color aisle of the store.

So there I was, staring at boxes of hair dye that ranged from dark blonde to light brown — shades that were safe and subtle and very similar to my natural dishwater brown color. I could have easily chosen any one of these and been fine, but no. I wasn't in the mood for "fine." Instead, my eyes drifted off to the right, down to the bottom shelf that held several boxes of the most beautiful auburn shades.

A spark flickered inside, and for the first time in weeks I was excited about something. In that moment, I knew this was exactly what I needed. I stood for a few more minutes, biting my nails and contemplating what box to buy, trying to decide which one would look best with my fair skin and blue eyes. And all the while, my excitement grew. This was the best idea I'd had in a while, and I wondered why I hadn't thought of it a long time ago.

I finally chose a box that showed a picture of a gorgeous woman with glossy, copper-colored hair. It was a change, and a drastic one at that, but my hair philosophy has always been Go Big or Go Home (a motto that served me well in the 1980s). I hugged the box against me and headed for the checkout.

I had just enough time to get home, tuck in the baby for his nap, and color my hair before the kids got home from school. Enough time, I figured, to transform myself into a new woman. I got straight to work, reading the instructions much faster than I should have, and skipping over that part where I was supposed to cut off a small section of hair and test it first. Before long, I was in front of the bathroom mirror, a towel draped over my shoulders and plastic gloves on my hands.

The "transformation" happened with alarming speed. One minute, my hair was wet and dark brown; the next minute, it was… pink. Pinkish orange, actually, with a sickly yellow foam mixed in. I blinked at my reflection, which bore an unsettling resemblance to a human matchstick. *I'm sure it's supposed to look like this,* I told myself. Not that there was anything else to do at that point. The solution was on my head, apparently already working its magic. I set the timer and waited.

After twenty minutes, I peeked in the mirror again. My hairline had turned a neon coral that reminded me of undercooked salmon. But hope springs eternal, so I stepped in the shower, tipped my head back, and rinsed.

Streaks of bright red splashed the shower walls and glass door, running down my arms and legs. "It looks like a Stephen King movie in here!" I shrieked to no one in particular. I took comfort in seeing that the color flowing down the drain was a most definite red, not orange or pink. At last, my hair was fully rinsed clean (along with the walls and shower floor), and I stepped out and wrapped my head in a towel.

It was time for the Big Reveal. I stood before the mirror and pulled off the towel. As my hair fell to my shoulders, my mouth hit the floor. My hair was red. Really red. Not a rich auburn red, but more of a flaming stop-sign red. The irony of the whole situation hit me like an icy splash of water: I had wanted to look like a celebrity, and now I did. The only problem was that my look-alike celebrity happened to be Ronald McDonald, *not* Julia Roberts.

The straw that broke the camel's back came later that afternoon when my kids got home from school. They piled in the door and filed right past me, dumping backpacks and shoes as they went. At last, my first grader walked in. He stopped two feet from my chair, looked around in confusion and said, "Where's Mom?"

I burst into laughter and couldn't stop for quite some time. There was nothing I could do but wait a few weeks and then recolor my hair back to its normal, boring shade. Until that happened, it took a rather insane amount of courage to go out in public. I'm proud to say I did it. And no one asked where the rest of my clown suit was.

And after a few weeks passed my hair color faded to a very attractive strawberry blonde, which I was happy to keep. As painful and embarrassing as this lesson was to learn, I figured it out eventually: I'm better off with a little less Julia Roberts and a lot more me.

~Debra Mayhew

Saving Town Hall

Start by doing what is necessary, then what is possible,
and suddenly you are doing the impossible.
~St. Francis of Assisi

One February evening in 2001, my husband Jimmy came home from work and said, "Our Board of Selectmen voted to demolish Ashland's historic 1855 Town Hall and replace it with a brick imposter." I'd never noticed the building in our downtown before, but Jimmy is an architect and he was concerned, so I asked for more details. "It's a simple but elegant Greek Revival building with ornate details that disappear into the all-white color scheme," he said.

That weekend, we drove over to Town Hall and walked around the two-story antique's perimeter. He pointed out its classic but neglected gable, frieze, pilasters and windows. "See how the old windowpanes distort the reflected trees, clouds and sky, creating a wall of tiny, ever-changing abstract paintings?" he said. "It means they're the original windows."

His praise of the architecture triggered something in me, something almost motherly, something so fierce I could not stop it. I saw the building in an entirely new light and knew this defenseless beauty of yesteryear needed someone to save it from destruction. That someone, I decided, would be me.

The next week, I hurried down to a Historical Commission meeting where I asked for the committee's plan to stop the demolition.

The elderly members looked at each other with puzzlement. Then the chair said, "It's not practical because of the large expense. You'd have to hoist it up on girders to shore up the foundation." He continued, "We don't have the resources for such a project."

At first, I felt dejected, even silly for having such a crazy idea. But later I became emboldened, eager to push myself in ways I didn't think possible. I was determined to save this building even if the Historical Commission wasn't going to give me any help. Then, in what was to become the first of many firsts, I wrote a letter to the editor of the local paper decrying the demolition. I contacted another person who wrote a letter to the editor, and we formed a tiny group called "Save Ashland Town Hall." That led to phone calls from other residents wanting to help. Every week, our group got a little bigger. As it turns out, a lot of residents wanted the building saved, but didn't have any idea how to do so.

Neither did I. But I took on the challenge anyway, deciding I'd figure out what needed to be done along the way.

I went to my first Board of Selectmen meeting in the basement of Town Hall and asked the intimidating men sitting in front of me to save Town Hall. "No. We need a new, larger one," they said. "Besides, it's not even historic. It's not like Abe Lincoln ever slept here."

Their responses made me rethink the cultural norm of destroying something small, unique and handcrafted to build something large, generic and mass-produced, of disowning something that had local but not national value, of denying the historical significance and markers of everyday people.

The selectmen spoke of progress. But what exactly was my town progressing *toward*?

I spent my Wednesdays and Saturdays at the Historical Society going through microfiche and newspaper files, discovering my town's rich history and how much of it had taken place within the hallowed rooms of our old Town Hall. The building had also served as a jail, a high school, a community center, a Cub Scout headquarters, a movie theater, and a ballroom. Ironically, I discovered that an Abe Lincoln had slept there one night, albeit a resident and not the one who was our sixteenth president.

I spoke at more Board of Selectmen meetings as a way to reach out to the residents watching the meeting on cable at home. "Men who fought in the Civil War — at Gettysburg, Spotsylvania and Fredericksburg — danced above us upstairs during Grand Army of the Rebellion balls," I said. "If that isn't historic, I don't know what is."

A small group of us held community meetings, hosted cable shows, gave speeches, enticed newspapers to do stories, distributed posters, spoke at town meetings and got the school-age kids involved. But, most importantly, we re-discovered a long shuttered, second-floor ballroom behind a locked door. I managed to get a town employee to let us in.

At the top of the aged oak stairs, I found a cavernous hall with seventeen-foot ceilings, an intact stage, a rosette in the ceiling and ornate plaster molding surrounding the edges — all in need of repair. It was hidden away from the modern world, a place where time stood still. Images of the room's old-fashioned beauty spread like wildfire. People wanted to see it, to keep it, to have a say in the way their town looked, to celebrate the loveliness that already existed. The grassroots effort to save the building quadrupled in size.

During one of my daily walks around the neighborhood, a guy drove by and shouted, "Save Town Hall." People stopped me all over town and said, "I saw you on cable. Thank you," and "I wish I had the courage to stand up for something I believed in."

But it wasn't all municipal wine and roses. The folks who wanted to raze the building spread mistruths about the building's historical and physical integrity. They said the second floor was likely to fall down. They said the building could not be rehabbed. They said it would never be on the National Register of Historic Places. And those unkind remarks spread to the folks trying to save it. My neighbor said they were saying terrible things about me, like "Who is this girl? She's trying to sabotage the government." Other folks in our group received calls saying, "You don't know who you're up against."

The opposition proved formidable.

To counter any self-doubt, I trained myself to imagine the renovated, registered historic structure standing tall and proud in our town. I imagined children climbing the wide, antique staircase to gaze up at the intricate rosette. I imagined proud residents taking pictures out front and inside during the grand opening celebration.

Even my boss noticed a difference in me. He said, "You seem really alive, excited about life." Honestly, the most surprised person in town during these months was me. Never before in my life had I given anything my "all." I didn't know I possessed such persistence.

> *Never before in my life had I given anything my "all."*

In the end, my fellow citizens and I battled for Town Hall and won. The people of the town voted to issue a $4 million bond to renovate the building. I saw the project through by serving for three years on the renovation committee. Once finished, our Town Hall became a downtown jewel and the first building in Ashland to be placed on the National Register of Historic Places. The new Town Manager reported that citizens and vendors who visited the Town Hall proclaimed it "one of the prettiest in Massachusetts."

As for me, I became a woman who stood up for what she believed in and saw it through. Since saving Town Hall, I've encouraged others to stand up for what they believe, to take that first step into the limelight, to challenge authority. And although I didn't realize it at the time, by stepping up to save the Town Hall, I actually saved myself, too. I rediscovered the power within me that had been there all along.

~Giulietta Nardone

Finding Mai

*To forget one's ancestors is to be a brook
without a source, a tree without a root.*
~Chinese Proverb

I don't remember exactly when it happened, but I do remember exactly how I felt when it did.

I was about seven years old and a relative was driving me somewhere. Suddenly, a car pulled up next to us. The two boys in that car yelled two words at us that would change my life.

"F*cking gooks!" they called out, taunting us with their diabolical smiles.

At first, I didn't understand what those words meant, and I certainly did not understand why the boys seemed to be so angry. With fervor, the boys continued the profanities.

I felt humiliated, ashamed. The blood rushed to my face as I began to understand that I was a "gook," and that was a very bad thing. Eventually, they drove off, leaving me feeling completely insignificant.

Before this incident, I had a general feeling that I did not belong in the country in which I lived. Being a foreigner, I simply did not fit in. I was terribly different from the kids who attended my elementary school. I was often teased or misunderstood.

As I sat in the car, I put two and two together. I decided that those boys had delivered a message from the rest of the world, and I should be ashamed of who I was.

From that point on, I was.

I started to loathe being Vietnamese. I hated the weird sound of my name, Mai. I hated the sound of my native language. I hated how different my food was. I hated my greasy black hair, unflattering jaundiced skin, and narrow eyes that seemed to taunt me whenever I smiled.

During this time, I often accompanied my mother on trips to grocery stores. These stores frequently carried personalized items such as mugs with first names imprinted on them. Many times, I looked for a "Mai" mug. There were plenty of "Mary" mugs, but "Mai" mugs did not exist. Sometimes, children have a way of overly dramatizing events, and I was no exception. Whenever I failed to find a mug with my name on it, I assumed it meant that I wasn't good enough, that I didn't belong, adding further fuel to the fire already lit by those teenage boys.

Years passed. Although my general confidence grew, my sense of cultural identity did not. All my friends were Caucasian. I only spoke Vietnamese when absolutely necessary. Ninety-five percent of the food I ate was American, for good reason. Once, someone quipped that the *bánh cuốn* (rice noodle roll) I ate resembled a "translucent turd." Being the outsider was so embarrassing that I overcompensated, trying to fit in even more. One man commented that I spoke like the quintessential "valley girl." Mission accomplished!

In high school, I finally obtained U.S. citizenship. At long last, I had the chance to discard my birth name, Mai.

Prior to the citizenship ceremony, I had pondered many new names — the more American-sounding, the better. I entertained several candidates, finally selecting Kristen. Kristen just happened to be a popular, blond, blue-eyed cheerleader who ruled her high-school class, along with her prom-king, football-playing boyfriend. She was the epitome of *everything* I wanted to be.

With my new name, I could officially begin a new life, a new identity, a new me. I was ecstatic. I began to introduce myself as Kristen. Enthusiastically, I left the "old" Vietnamese me far behind, in favor of a new and "improved" American me — who would finally fit in. Surprisingly, something indiscernible lingered. Something felt strangely incomplete.

Soon after I gained U.S. citizenship, I met a new friend. She was lively, confident, and definitely Vietnamese. I remember the first time I heard her speak Vietnamese in the midst of American classmates. She spoke without an ounce of embarrassment, but rather with a sense of pride. I marveled at her. Over the next few months, we spent a significant amount of time together. I observed her closely, much like a student observes her teacher. She balanced both of her worlds comfortably, living in the present, but honoring her past. With each interaction, her sense of self-love rubbed off on me and nourished me like a salve to my parched skin.

With her help, I made other Vietnamese friends. While I already had many kind American friends, my Vietnamese friends provided me with a new sense of empathy. They understood the emotional complexities of being a refugee in a world that wasn't always trying to understand exactly what it meant to be a refugee. They accepted me for everything I was and everything I wasn't. Finally, I truly belonged to a community that made me feel completely understood.

My new friends took me on a journey where I was reminded of the beauty of my birthplace, as well as the tremendous resilience, strength, and perseverance of my people. I dined at Vietnamese restaurants and listened to Vietnamese music. I even started to speak Vietnamese again. Gradually, the sound of my native language became comforting. The taste of my native food became sumptuous. The sound of my native music became ethereal. The knowledge of my ancestors became fascinating. My eyes were re-opened to a mystical world I had left behind, years ago, sitting in that car.

I no longer felt like I had to fit inside someone else's world. Finding mugs with "Mai" imprinted on them wasn't important anymore because I finally knew I belonged. Being different was no longer a reason to be ashamed. Now, it was something to embrace.

Because I had legally changed my first name and all my official documents reflected it, everyone I met called me Kristen. Ironically, the new name I had waited so long for now sounded oddly unnatural.

One night, I met a teenage boy at a high school party. He introduced himself and asked me what my name was. Proudly, I said, "Mai."

Years after I allowed two complete strangers and two vile words to redefine my sense of self-worth and identity, I had finally taken the power to love myself back into my own hands.

Today, I introduce myself as Mai. I am proud of who I am and what I am. Like many explorers, I uncovered a buried treasure I never expected to stumble upon. The person I had lost years ago was finally found. And I will make sure to never lose her again.

~Kristen Mai Pham

How about Italian?

Our self-respect tracks our choices. Every time we
act in harmony with our authentic self and
our heart, we earn our respect. It is
that simple. Every choice matters.
~Dan Coppersmith

"I t's our six-month anniversary," Rich said. "Why don't we go out tonight? Where would you like to eat?"

Immediately, I thought *Italian food*, but I said, "I don't know. You choose."

"Okay, we'll have Mexican."

Mexican again.

I waved from the window as he backed out of the driveway, and then collapsed into a chair and let the tears flow. Here I was, still a newlywed, but feeling completely alone.

I had willingly relocated to Cincinnati from the small town of Marshall, Michigan, after our wedding, but the adjustment had been more difficult than I'd imagined. I was terrified of getting lost in the huge city and equally afraid of the fast-moving, multi-lane traffic. But more importantly, I was afraid to share my thoughts and fears with my new husband.

My relationships with men had never been comfortable, but when I met Rich, I knew he was the man for me. I loved his quirky sense of humor, intelligence and strong faith. After only eight months of dating, we married.

I basked in his love — yet I felt as if I had to be on my best behavior, as if one wrong move on my part would ruin our relationship. I found it difficult to reveal my thoughts to him. As considerate as he was, when he arrived home from work, I expected to be scolded for something I had done or not done. I was afraid to express my opinion about the most insignificant things — even picking out a restaurant for dinner! I was behaving exactly like my mother.

Mom enjoyed spending time with her children when Dad wasn't around. She'd play cards with us, tell stories about her childhood, and sing old songs with us. Sometimes, we'd try out new craft projects. But at five o'clock, we children fled to our rooms while my mother nervously tended to the meal she was preparing. Dad expected to eat at precisely 5:30.

> **I realized that a marriage in which I couldn't be myself wasn't really a marriage at all.**

We never knew what Dad's mood would be when he came home. Occasionally, he seemed light-hearted, but usually he walked through the house yelling about something. We couldn't predict what would set him off.

When I was fifteen, I found someone in whom I could confide all my hopes and fears; my friend Patty. I had relied on her ever since. She was the one I cried to now.

Patty finally suggested, "You're depressed because you're not being yourself with Rich. Why aren't you telling him how you feel instead of telling me?"

"I can't do that."

"What's the worst thing that could happen?"

"He would be disappointed in me. Or he might get mad."

"Would he leave you? Would he beat you? Would he murder you?"

"Of course not," I laughed.

"Would you be any worse off than you are now, sitting around crying?"

I wasn't sure. I had to think about that — and pray. Rich wasn't anything like my father, yet I desperately feared his disapproval. The idea of sharing my inner thoughts with him terrified me.

Still, I didn't want the kind of marriage my parents had. Mom tiptoed around Dad to avoid his anger, but as hard as she tried, she couldn't make him happy. He scolded her when she was too playful, and he criticized her when she was too quiet.

One time, he came home early. Mom was demonstrating a gymnastics trick with a glass of water balanced on her forehead. The door swung open, surprising us and causing Mom to spill the water. "What's this foolishness?" Dad demanded.

"I… I was showing the kids something I learned to do in high school," Mom stammered.

"When are you going to grow up? You act like one of the kids." She didn't respond, but was quiet the rest of the day. Later, Dad berated her. "What's the matter with you? Quit moping around." She couldn't win.

And there I was, following in Mom's footsteps, tiptoeing around Rich, mentally rehearsing everything I said to him, even jumping up when he arrived home so he wouldn't catch me watching TV or doing something equally frivolous. I thought, *I can't win in this relationship if I'm afraid to be myself. I will end up just like Mom.* I had to make a choice — spend the rest of my life being lonely and miserable, or face my fears in hopes of developing the kind of relationship I longed for.

I decided I had to share my thoughts and feelings with Rich no matter how difficult, and I had to begin that night before I lost my resolve. Voice quavering, I asked, "Couldn't we go for Italian food to celebrate our anniversary?"

"I thought you wanted Mexican."

"No, I really want Italian."

"Okay, Italian it is."

As we pulled out into heavy traffic, I took a deep breath and forced myself to say, "I hate to admit this, but this city intimidates me."

"I didn't realize that."

"I'm afraid to leave the house on my own, afraid of getting lost… and being stuck in the house is making me depressed."

"Oh, baby, I didn't know. I can help you figure out how to get around." He put his hand over mine and squeezed.

And as simply as that, I began sharing my feelings with Rich.

When he didn't scoff at my fears, I began to disclose more. Little by little over the next months, it became easier to be open with him. I shared things with him that I had only told Patty. Eventually, I was even able to talk to him about how hard it was to talk to him!

The change didn't happen overnight, of course. Responding in a new way took effort and practice. I'd take a step forward and then would find myself slipping back into old patterns, which caused me to feel depressed again. But I had learned the warning signs. Whenever I started withdrawing, I reminded myself of the kind of marriage I wanted. I realized that a marriage in which I couldn't be myself wasn't really a marriage at all.

One afternoon, Rich found me curled up on the couch engrossed in a novel. I hadn't started supper, but I didn't jump up at his arrival. Instead, I simply smiled and said, "I'm on the last chapter — it's too exciting to put down. I'll be finished in fifteen minutes."

These days, Rich and I share laughter, tears, and even opinions. Learning to ask for what I want and to share my innermost feelings not only gave me the marriage of my dreams, but made me a more confident person. And in the process, I found a new best friend.

~Diana L. Walters

A Storyteller Is Born

Inside each of us is a natural-born
storyteller, waiting to be released.
~Robin Moore

ne hundred pairs of eyes are fixed on me as I stand on stage performing a humorous story. Waves of laughter from the audience wash over me. I am halfway through when the story pictures in my head that roll out the plot suddenly stop. My mental screen is devastatingly void of content. Empty!

Fear rises from my gut. I have seen other beginner storytellers succumb to that fear and leave the stage humiliated and defeated. I am, for the first time in my very short career, experiencing the dreaded nightmare of "The Blank-Out," the bane of all actors who perform live and without notes.

Looking away from the audience, I take a deep breath and let the silence settle into my bones. Then, like magic, the rest of my story suddenly reappears. I smile triumphantly and pick up where I left off. An almost imperceptible breeze flows over my face as one hundred people heave a great, collective sigh of relief. Their storyteller is back on track!

The spinning wheel of my story begins again. My yarn stretches out and winds around every person, pulling them together into a unity of delight. The room once more rings out with laughter, a sound that is music to my ears.

***

My story really began in October 2015. My husband and I had retired and moved to the scenic, seaside city of Nanaimo on Vancouver Island, where I was looking forward to quiet, creative activities like writing and painting. Prior to this, I had led a fairly sheltered life and was quite shy. In every social occasion, my outgoing husband took the lead, striking up conversations with strangers.

We heard about an upcoming storytelling event and decided to attend. As the storytellers on stage wove their magic, the audience laughed and wept and sang. Like everyone else, I fell under their spell. Somewhere in the middle of the third story, a brilliant rocket of excitement exploded inside me. I had an epiphany. "I love stories! These are my kind of people! I want to be a storyteller!"

No matter that storytelling necessitated getting up on a stage under bright lights and addressing strangers. Storytelling also required using a microphone and tons of memorization. Let's not forget self-confidence and the ability to act that were also needed! Where was I going to get the talent, memory, and courage needed to become a storyteller?

Next to dying, public speaking was my greatest fear. *I must be out of my mind!* I thought to myself. *My memory isn't that great. What if I get up there and forget my story? I don't want to fail!* But negative self-talk had no effect on me. I had never felt so alive before that moment.

So when they announced there would be a storytelling workshop in a few months, I registered and persuaded my husband to sign up as well. I needed his support, as I was too shy to enter a roomful of strangers by myself.

I also signed up to tell a story on stage a month after the workshop because I wanted to push myself to jump into this new world before I lost my nerve.

The main reason motivating me to do this utterly out-of-character, crazy thing was that I was sixty-six years old, and already my memory was starting to slip. My late mother had dementia, and I had read that one of the ways to help prevent memory loss was to keep the brain active by learning new things.

I detested memorization, but the opportunity to give the gift of laughter or touch people's hearts with heartwarming stories meant more to me than the pain of self discipline it would require to become a storyteller. All I had to do was grab myself by the neck and march forward through my wall of fears.

The first night I was scheduled to go on stage, I felt like I was being led to the guillotine. My stomach was churning, my hands were icy cold, and my knees trembled as I walked down the steps to our car. Nothing improved once I was in the hall. I had imprinted my twenty-minute story into my memory through a month of hard, focused studying. Once on stage, I fell easily into my story, describing the scenes without stumbling or faltering. I finished to a thundering wall of applause, and later hearty congratulations from the other storytellers and several audience members. A thrill of exhilaration (and relief) blasted through me. I was hooked!

And so my adventure began. I started to tell stories every month, sometimes on stage and sometimes in my living room. With my newly found self-confidence, I started a story circle for beginners, and we shared stories and the learning process together.

Eventually, I even made friends with the microphone, an object that terrified me in the beginning. Within a few months of beginning to tell stories, my memory started to improve noticeably. It was remarkable.

Strangers began coming up to me in the street, telling me how much they enjoyed my storytelling. At first, I was shocked that anybody would remember me and I was shy about accepting their praise. Recognition was not common in my life before this. My self-esteem began to rise, and I became more comfortable talking with new people.

Overcoming my fears made me stronger and gave me a lusty appetite for trying even more new, fun activities. I started playing the ukulele and even tried Zumba exercise classes. I joined three choirs and took up pickleball, badminton, carpet bowling and kayaking.

Everywhere I went, people were friendly and welcoming. Over

time, my shyness just faded away. To my happy surprise, I found that I was good at each new thing I tried, and my self-confidence continued to grow.

Today, I am a different woman from the timid one who moved to this city two years ago.

All these wonderful changes in my life came about when I listened to my heart and ploughed through my fears. And the Blank-Out? I learned it happens to all storytellers once in a while, even the professionals, so I'm taking my blank-out in stride and won't worry if it happens again.

I'm already looking forward with excitement to my next new pursuit, which starts up in a few weeks. Bollywood dancing anyone?

~Christine Clarke-Johnsen

Lord, Make Me a Babe

*An empty lantern provides no light. Self-care is the fuel
that allows your light to shine brightly.*
~Author Unknown

I recently found out that my soon-to-be-ex-husband is dating someone. He and I were sitting outside of our son's classroom door at the middle school, waiting for our parent–teacher conference. At school events where parents are present, it's easy to spot the divorced parents. They look kind of stiff and surly. Generally, they are not talking to each other. They can be spotted at soccer games, too. One doesn't need a graduate degree in psycho-therapy, which I happen to have, to figure out which couples are together now only by the necessity of parenthood.

Down the school hallway, a lady I did not recognize flounced by. "Hii-yii," she sang out in a lilting, singsong voice. She was not talking to me. The soon-to-be-ex turned beet red. Like a character straight out of a time-machine movie, I instantly morphed into a high school junior.

Harry's teacher came to the door and invited us in. Thankfully, I morphed back into my middle-aged-parent self. The focus shifted to Harry, our adolescent, soon-to-be-from-a-broken-home son. I survived the conference and walked to my car alone afterward.

As soon as I got home, I picked up the phone and called the soon-to-be-ex. "Are you dating?" I asked.

"Howdja know?" He never did know when to lie.

I don't know why, but it hit me like a kick in the stomach. Truly, this was the end to an eighteen-year marriage, where no one on the face of the earth could have tried harder than I did to save it. Several years earlier, my girlfriends had an intervention with me. "Linda," they said at a lunch meeting, "you're in an emotionally abusive marriage."

"I know," I said, "but it's still better than the alternative." The alternative is what I am now facing: the Big D. I still can't bring myself to say it.

So, there is no use crying over spilt milk or going into the maudlin details. Like the flaming co-dependent that I am, I tried to move heaven and earth to save my marriage. In fact, to borrow a phrase from a twelve-step program, I used to refer to it as rearranging the chairs on the deck of the *Titanic*. With icebergs rearing their ugly heads in the distance, I did everything I could and more.

And now, I am facing the D-word. He filed. Not only that, but now the other D-word is being thrown out there. He is *dating* someone. After eighteen years, he is not dating me.

So, if I explain that I woke up one morning several days ago with butt-kicking depression, one would understand why. This depression was like moving slowly underwater with a boulder on my back. I wanted to break into tears at the drop of a hat. I rehearsed calling a psychiatrist friend and telling her that it was time to sign me up for antidepressants. Through some serious hard times, I have resisted that option.

Friday morning, I trudged off to work. Keeping cash flow was a necessity at my stage of life. I sat down in my office. My client came in. I noticed a change from her previous appearance. She looked terrific! Her hair was natural and pulled back, instead of heavy and long. Her eyes looked wide open. This woman really knew how to put on make-up. Instead of winter brown and black, she was wearing pink and white with matching pink socks. She was getting enough sleep, and it showed in her complexion.

I marveled at the difference in her, especially the make-up. Then it hit me like a voice from God, like a bolt of lightning, like a revelation from above in a low, thunderous voice: "Linda, you can do this, too."

"What, God?" I asked the voice in my head, meanwhile listening empathetically to my client. (Only really experienced psychotherapists can listen to God and their clients at the same time.)

"You can do this, too." It was God's voice again.

Finally, the revelation came through loud and clear: "You can become a babe."

"A babe," I gasped internally. "But, Lord, what about the flab under my arms and my thighs?" No use arguing with God. The revelation was unequivocal. The still, small voice had delivered the message loud and clear. My calling, at this juncture, was to become a babe — a fifty-six-year-old babe.

> *Finally, the revelation came through loud and clear: "You can become a babe."*

Who am I to argue with God? My course is set. Whatever it takes — a trainer-diet-make-up consultant. I know what I've got to do.

My final court date is several months away, and what sweeter justice than to show up in divorce court having morphed into a veritable babe. Not for him, but for me, and for my girlfriends who will be cheering me on every inch of the way.

So, I'm on my way to Babedom. And you know what else? My depression mysteriously evaporated. Poof. Like the parting of the Red Sea. I am a woman with a mission.

Whenever I begin to mourn the past or even ponder the thought of my soon-to-be-ex with someone else, I say this little prayer, "Lord, make me a babe."

It's working. I'm looking better already.

~Linda Hoff Irvin

9

Fear of Rejection

Everything you want is on the other side of fear.
~Jack Canfield

ne fine Sunday morning, I sat in front of the television with my coffee and turned on Oprah's "SuperSoul Sunday." On the screen, I saw a radiant woman talking to Oprah. I learned that she was Arianna Huffington, who had written a new book called *Thrive*. I connected with her story of overworking and trying so hard to live a successful life. Okay, maybe my life wasn't just like Arianna's, but I was also a woman who worked two jobs, a single mom, a writer, and a person who felt drained, emotionally exhausted and broken inside. I was on the verge of a breakdown.

Honestly speaking, I had no clue who Arianna Huffington was. I had read numerous articles on the Huffington Post website, but was never curious enough to research where that name came from.

I watched the show and cried all the way through it. I felt like God or some kind of higher power was talking to me. He was telling me to stop and thrive. I wasn't alone; many women like me had gotten up and changed their lives, and so could I.

I was so inspired that I went on Arianna's website to buy her book and found out about the California Women's Conference. The ticket was expensive, but I needed to feed my soul and, ironically, it was to be held on my forty-fourth birthday. If I bought the ticket, it would mean no Starbucks morning coffee for about two weeks and four extra hours of tutoring work, but I decided to just do it!

I woke up the morning of the conference feeling excited and energized. It felt like it was the best thing I had *ever* done for myself! There were so many inspiring speakers, including Jack Canfield, Lisa Nichols, Immaculée Ilibagiza, Sekou Andrews, and Arianna Huffington herself.

Toward the end of the day, it was time to get books signed by Arianna Huffington. I was the very last person in line, but eventually I got to Arianna, and when our eyes met, the kindness in her made me feel like I was about to meet a friend. I sat down slowly on the chair next to her and started to talk. With tears rolling down my face, I told her how I had always wanted to be a writer, but it was hard for me to pursue my dream while raising my kids. As I spoke, she put her hand on my shoulder and turned to get something from her purse. She pulled out her business card and handed it to me. I went silent and looked at her, and then at the card.

"Write to me, honey," she said with a smile.

Slowly, I picked up my signed book and business card, and got up from my chair. I had no clue what she meant by "write to me." Arianna Huffington had given me her business card, but what was I supposed to do? Could she really have meant it? Did she really want me to write to her?

I went home that night with a lot to think about. I could go back to being the same old Tami, who just allowed life to happen while permitting others to make decisions for her. On the other hand, I had just left a twenty-year marriage and I was taking baby steps toward becoming the woman I knew was somewhere inside me.

That night, as I sat in front of my laptop, I felt like a child who had lost her way and had no one to guide her. What should I say to Arianna Huffington? And why would a busy woman like her even respond to me? I wished someone would tell me what to do, but I reminded myself that I had already made the choice to be a strong, independent woman.

I decided to write something anyway. Later I could decide whether to send it to Arianna. So, I wrote about myself and my dream of writing.

I hoped to touch people's hearts through my words, and tell them what I had learned from all my years of pain and being disconnected from myself. I wrote a few drafts (eleven to be exact), and then the most difficult part came: Should I send it or not? It was 2:00 a.m. by then, and my finger kept avoiding the "Send" button. The fear of rejection seemed so much bigger than it should be. I finally told myself that even if I never heard back from her, I couldn't live with the regret of not trying. At 2:48 a.m., I finally hit "Send." Afterward, I fell asleep immediately from the mental exhaustion.

I woke up around 7:00 a.m. and found several notifications on my phone. As I lay in bed, I started to scroll through them — and then jumped out of bed. I had received an e-mail back from Arianna Huffington! She wanted me to become a blogger for the Huffington Post, and she connected me to the editors!

It's been over three years since that wonderfully stressful day that was filled with the fear of rejection and ended up changing my life. Today, I have published three books and written numerous articles for the Huffington Post, Thrive Global (Arianna's new website), and Mind Body Network. I also run my own website called Detoxthesoul. com. I have gone back to school to get an MFA in Creative Writing at Chapman University. And, most importantly, I learned that rejection only means that I tried to do something outside of my comfort zone, and it is by going outside my comfort zone that I continue to make progress.

~Tami Shaikh

10

Welcome to New York

Life is not about waiting for the storms to pass.
It's about learning how to dance in the rain.
~Vivian Greene

y husband had already been working at his new job in New York for a few weeks. Back home in Texas, the kids and I waited for the relocation company to start the process so we could make our big move to follow him. But, as it turns out, we were waiting for a hurricane at the same time: Hurricane Harvey. And on Friday, it hit.

Alone in our home, the phone blasted alerts around the clock of potential flash floods and tornadoes. What did I do? First, I turned off the news. My rattled nerves could only handle knowing about our individual, immediate danger, not what was going on all over the Houston area. Then, we waited, for four grueling days.

Once the worst of the storm was over, we breathed a huge sigh of relief. Our home was completely intact. Many were not so lucky.

The rain continued, along with the potential for flooding. All the airports were shut down, with no news about when they'd reopen. I decided we would drive to New York, instead of waiting. Our relocation started, despite the many closed and treacherous roads.

Driving from Houston to New York on my own with our three kids and a dog was not initially well received. My friends and family were extremely concerned about our safety. I did what I knew was best for our family. One of the many reasons I wanted to get to New

York soon was because I wanted my kids to have the most seamless transition possible; I wanted them to start school on the first day.

We left on Tuesday and drove north to escape the storm. Our first stop was to see our family friends in Dallas. They opened their doors to us, and their three kids greeted our kids like long-lost cousins. Everyone played, and they fed us comfort food. With soothed nerves and full bellies, we piled back into the car. Now sunny skies beckoned us on the open road, and we drove and drove.

We kept in touch with my mom in Los Angeles, and she willingly became our remote travel agent and navigator. She was a lifesaver. Over the phone, we worked out how far I'd be able to drive for the day, and she'd book us a dog-friendly hotel. We spent the first night in Muskogee, Oklahoma. Safely checked in before dark, we grabbed a quick dinner and then fell fast asleep. We rose early the next morning and started our second day.

> **There have been many times when I've wondered who I am now that I'm a mom.**

Stopping only when absolutely necessary to go to the bathroom or eat, the kids were upbeat and surprisingly well behaved. Normally, we have epic meltdowns at Target or even walking the dog in our neighborhood, so the fact that they never complained or fought was beyond my comprehension. I will be forever grateful for whatever mysterious force pulled them from the depths of their everyday antics and bestowed on them the ability to behave, listen, and help me.

The second night, thanks to my trusty mom, we ended up in Terre Haute, Indiana. It was a beautiful, historic college town, and we were able to walk around with the dog. The kids loved watching the sun set and rise from our fifth-floor hotel room, and they played silly games in the room. They were able to make every new hotel room and every new nook and cranny into a wonderland of imagination and adventure.

By our second night, I expected my adrenaline to wear off and fatigue to set in. But no, I kept going like a machine. I never once felt exhausted or incapable of continuing. I also knew that the more we drove, the sooner we'd arrive safely at our final destination. Determination was my driving force.

On the third day, my mom booked our hotel. It was eight hours away, and I wasn't sure if I could make it. We stopped in downtown Columbus, Ohio, and picnicked in Capitol Square. We saw the beautiful Ohio Holocaust and Liberators Memorial and met friendly people. Everyone wanted to stop and pet Bonzo, our lovable two-year-old Cocker Spaniel.

Eventually, our scenery changed, and the cool weather blew over the mountains and trees. The roads started to wind, and Hennie, especially, gushed over the views from her window. We stayed our final night in Bedford, Pennsylvania.

We hadn't seen Steve in weeks, so our last morning we ate breakfast and eagerly headed to New York. Over bridges and through tunnels, after tolls and tolls, we could finally see the Statue of Liberty and the immense New York City skyline. We'd arrived. Gleaming with pride, we pulled into a hotel on Long Island. Steve was able to register the kids for school, so they'd start on the first day. We had done it!

There have been many times when I've wondered who I am now that I'm a mom. I've often felt like I'd lost sight of my bravery and the fierce independence that once flowed through my pre-mommy veins. But this trip reminded me that I am now, more than ever, a brave and independent woman. Capable of anything. Only this time, my bravery and confidence benefit me and, more importantly, my family.

Today, I desperately needed to do our laundry, so we attempted to drive to the laundry facilities. But I couldn't find my keys. The rain started coming down. I'm notorious for losing my keys, so my first thought was immense gratitude that this happened today and not when we were on our cross-country road trip.

I called roadside assistance, and we waited in the rain. Just then, an Indian wedding came outside, and everyone was dancing and celebrating. The groom's procession, complete with a decorated horse, made its way around the parking lot as we watched in amazement. The music blasted, and the DJ led everyone in dance. Afterward, Hennie and Tillie got to sit on the horse. It was the most spectacular event.

As soon as the wedding guests went inside, the car mechanic

arrived and jimmied the lock, but we still couldn't pop open the trunk. I'd locked my keys in the trunk before and had to do this exact same thing, but I couldn't remember how.

When Steve finished work, he figured out how to pull down the back seats and reached into the trunk to open it. But the keys weren't in there. Frantically, I searched the hotel room again and eventually found the keys. They were in my sweatshirt pocket, of course. No, I hadn't checked those pockets before calling for assistance. I'd checked the pockets of the fleece I thought I was wearing, but not the pockets of the sweatshirt I actually was wearing. And thus I ended my week of feeling like Supermom with a little dose of humility!

~Molly England

11

Roses Along the Executive Path

Believe in yourself! Have faith in your abilities!
Without a humble but reasonable confidence in
your own power you cannot be successful or happy.
~Norman Vincent Peale

The sudden blast of the telephone interrupted the quiet in the office on the Friday afternoon before Christmas in 1970. From anyone else, the call would not have roused further thought, but my mind rippled with curiosity at Bruno's request. Why did he want to see me? During the fifteen years I had worked at the small tool-distributing company, he had never shown the least inclination to socialize.

Bruno already rated as an important customer when I started typing invoices. If it had been up to him, I would have remained a billing clerk forever because he refused to recognize my move to the order desk. Back then, of course, the gender gap for job equality hadn't even begun to close. Even if progress had been made, however, Bruno probably would not have been affected. Along with an Old-World accent, he seemed to hold a medieval concept of women.

In spite of my best Dale Carnegie manner, Bruno always asked to speak with "one of the boys." Usually a man stayed in the office who could satisfy the requirement, so I didn't push to handle his calls.

As my inside sales coverage expanded, however, "the boys" devoted more time to outside calls. One day, all three men were out, so I asked Bruno if I could help. "Have one of the boys call me back," he said. My sense of personal pride went flat, but my professional sense said that a customer was entitled to a display of idiosyncrasy.

Eventually, though, it wasn't in the interest of good business to keep Bruno waiting. "I don't expect any of the boys back this afternoon, Bruno," I said. "If you want to give me the order, someone can look it over and get back with you if there's a problem."

That incident didn't revolutionize my relationship with Bruno, but it was a beginning. His preference definitely remained for man-to-man negotiations, but I was promoted to a second-rate order clerk. If he wanted information, though, it was essential that he speak with one of the boys.

Our business association might never have progressed beyond that point had it not been for the discrepancy in the order he gave me that allowed me to make points with Bruno. He grumbled when I said the part number and description didn't match, but offered a weak "thank you" after checking his records to find I was correct. An error in shipping can play havoc with the routine on an automobile assembly line.

Bruno gained confidence in me after that. Still, from force of habit, he announced one day that he needed some information and wished to talk to one of the boys. Before I could transfer the call, however, he amended his request. "Maybe you know," he said. "You seem to know a lot — for a woman."

Later on, business growth dictated some personnel changes in our company. I passed down the job of billing clerk to devote most of my time to customer relations. Also, the volume of incoming calls required a back-up person for the phone. Although a man was selected for the job, Bruno preferred speaking with me. "I'll wait," he'd say if I was on another line. Or, "Have her call me back."

In a few years, my duties as vice president forced me to minimize customer contact, but not with Bruno. For me, he represented achievement of my personal goals as a businesswoman.

The whole panorama of events flashed before my mind on that

Friday afternoon in 1970 when Bruno's telephone call turned social. At last, I was going to meet the man who played such an important role in my career, and I could hardly wait.

I was in the warehouse when Bruno arrived on Saturday morning. "Mrs. Bailey?" he asked.

We shook hands and then went into my office to talk. The exchange of words unrelated to business required great effort on his part, but a warmth flowed between us that needed no verbal expression.

After a while, acting more like a self-conscious fifth-grader than the tough businessman he was, Bruno pulled a little package from his pocket.

"A Christmas present," he said.

His choice of gift was affecting. He had come to regard me as a partner in business, but the little bottle of perfume said he also considered me female — that my womanhood was as significant as my executive ability. What more could a woman want? I'd already been earning a salary equal to that of the key men for quite a few years.

~Esther M. Bailey

Chapter 2

The Empowered Woman

I Found My Courage

The Big, Dead Rat

There is only one proof of ability — action.
~Marie von Ebner-Eschenbach

Last winter, we had rain for two straight weeks. It rained almost every single day. I would think, *Geez, if I wanted to live in Portland, I'd move to Portland. God knows I'd save money on rent.* It wasn't so bad; I caught up on writing and movies as the rain came down. Nothing could prepare me, though, for what I found one day in my back yard.

I went outside to put birdseed in the bird feeder. On my way back to the house, I noticed a tail. The tail did not look like one of my cats' tails. It was right behind my miniature tree, which I'd named Brooklyn. I took a deep breath, and then looked behind Brooklyn. It was a rat. A big, dead rat. Like many a woman before me, I yelled, "Eeek!" and ran back in the house. Why I did this, I don't know. The rat was dead. It would not harm me. I figured out the rat might've been killed by my cats, Ida B. or Opal. This was good; they were earning their keep. Or it died from the extreme weather. Either way, I had a big-assed, dead rat in my yard. I had to deal with it.

But I didn't want to. I had plenty to do around my house, work and life. I kept thinking about a Bailey White essay I had read years ago. Something had died under her house. Mrs. White (Bailey's mother) called an exterminator to get rid of the dead animal. He said, "Don't you have something like a husband to take care of that for you?" Bailey had to crawl under the house and get the dead animal herself.

Although I don't mind being alone, this was one of those times I wanted something like a husband.

> *I realized that maybe I didn't have something like a husband, but I had myself.*

The next day, I procrastinated. Got work done. Wrote a tribute to Elizabeth Taylor, who had died recently. I was hoping maybe the rat's family had carried him off for a Viking funeral. Finally, I went outside. He (or she) was still there. I sighed. He looked like Templeton the rat in *Charlotte's Web*. He definitely had Templeton's tummy when he ate too much at the fair.

I went back inside. I washed my hands and then grabbed some newspapers. Put on rubber gloves. Walked outside again. Did the sign of the cross. *Dear rat, I hope you had a good life.* I covered the rat's body with the newspaper, and then put it in a plastic bag. I ran outside and dumped it in the trashcan.

I went back inside, removed my gloves and washed my hands again. Afterward, I realized that maybe I didn't have something like a husband, but I had myself. And there are times when "yourself" is all we need — even when it comes to dead, big rats. Things have to get done, and if we wait around for someone else to do it, we'll be waiting for a long time.

~Jennifer Kathleen Gibbons

13

Would You Like to Dance?

This above all; to thine own self be true.
~William Shakespeare

I am waiting for the boy to ask me to dance. He is the best at doing the jitterbug. He doesn't ask.

My feelings are determined by junior high school boys, and I am not popular. I *will* be in high school, but not now. My pride is in the hands of these boys.

That dancer, the most popular boy in school, lives across the street. He is a basketball star, too, although he has not yet grown into a man's height. He tends to dance with the girls who will also kiss him. He knows how good-looking he is, even at twelve. Many of my classmates are competing to dance with him, to be his girlfriend for a night, a week, a month. He is a sassy charmer. He knows he is number one.

I am not one of the girls who want him, but I love to watch him dance. He is a great dancer who has impeccable rhythm and knows all the latest steps. He is dazzling on the dance floor.

One day, I am twelve, and the next I am sixty-three. The decades have brought me the marriage of my dreams, three incredible careers and a life in which I have been myself. One of my greatest passions is dancing.

My childhood girlfriend is coming into town to attend the fiftieth anniversary of our high school. She talks me into going. I am not sure why she has to talk me into attending because I loved high school. I was president of my junior class and spent four years being part of many activities.

I am not sure that this type of party, which is open to graduating classes spanning fifty years, will offer quality time to reminisce and visit. I receive some phone calls from old friends who have come to town. I decide to go.

A small group of my classmates attend, maybe fifteen or so. Most of these classmates were with me in junior high as well as high school. I am thrilled to see them. One man walks up to me and says my name. I struggle to recognize his face. He then says his name and smiles. It is the star dancer of my adolescence, my former neighbor, the jock my preteen girlfriends lusted after.

We catch up. As others arrive, I greet them and am greeted warmly. Everyone looks great. Sixty-three never looked better. These are the people of my youth. Their place in my life is special. The memories we share are our beginning years.

The band is getting ready to play the oldies. As the music begins, I walk toward the dance floor and turn. He catches my eye as I extend my hand toward him, motioning for him to join me on the dance floor. The best jitterbugger in sixth grade takes my hand, and we engage in a graceful and wild ride, singing the words to every song. He is still a great dancer.

When our dance ends, I motion to another childhood friend and then another. Each man joins me on the dance floor, one at a time. I had never danced with any of them back in our schooldays. Now I am enjoying their individual style and movements. On that dance floor, they are meeting me for the first time. And it is I who has asked them. I chose and picked the men with whom I wanted to dance.

One of my sisters is also there. When I talk to her at the end of the night, she tells me how wonderfully I danced, and how exciting it was that all the boys/men wanted to dance with me.

I smile to myself. I will always love the girl who was twelve and watched the dancers, but a woman of sixty-three never felt better on the dance floor.

~Elynne Chaplik-Aleskow

14

It's Not about Me

What we say is important... for in most cases the
mouth speaks what the heart is full of.
~Jim Beggs

I shifted my weight in the hard chair, picked at my cuticles, and berated myself. *What in the world have I gotten myself into? I'm clueless about interacting with reporters. How frumpy am I going to look?* I smoothed my navy-blue skirt. *Will my brain freeze in the middle of the interview? Even worse, am I going to disappoint everyone?*

Next to me in the television channel's green room, chewing her lip, sat another mom like me whose son also served in the military. As we waited to be called for the interview, she clenched her white-knuckled hands in her lap.

She's nervous, too, I thought.

As our chapter's Media Committee Chairwoman, I felt responsible for my fellow Blue Star Mother. *What can I say,* I wondered, *to give her courage?* I gently squeezed her hands. "We're going to do well."

She attempted a smile that didn't reach her eyes.

I waved toward the studio. "This will be easy compared to what our sons are asked to do."

She flexed her fingers. "That's true."

This interview isn't about me, I thought.

My nervousness disappeared, and I breathed easier as I focused on how to best articulate our message.

Thirty minutes later, I felt lighthearted as the other mom and I walked toward our cars. "We did it!" she said.

I punched the sky with both fists. "Yes!"

With big smiles, we hugged each other goodbye.

When I got home, I called my friend Georgia, a professional speaker. "I'm surprised I didn't get tongue-tied during the interview," I said. "As a teenager, I was painfully shy."

"Really?"

"Thankfully, raising an outgoing son made me less shy. Even so, whenever I do any public speaking, I feel like I trip over my words. But today, I did okay. In fact, I had fun!"

> *It's about something bigger. I'm like… an ambassador for the other moms.*

"So, what's changed?" she said.

"While I was encouraging the other Blue Star Mother right before our interview, it felt so freeing to realize it wasn't about me. It's about something bigger. I'm like… an ambassador for the other moms. It's important to us to get out our support-the-troops message."

I swallowed the lump in my throat. "And when I think about the sacrifices the troops have made on our behalf, I want to give something good back to them."

That revelation — "It's not about me" — served me well while working with the media and also when I volunteered, along with other moms, to share our message through public speaking. I put together a presentation I titled "The History, Happenings, and Hope of Blue Star Mothers." To help control my nervousness, I memorized my opening and closing, and practiced my speech. I collected props to help me remember my points.

I arrived early to meet people before my first speaking opportunity on behalf of our chapter. I chatted with a man whose back curved with age yet whose eyes twinkled under the brim of his WWII Veteran cap. Another man, with Vietnam Veteran patches on his motorcycle jacket, told me about the Patriot Guard Riders, who stand guard at a fallen hero's funeral. Tears pooled in a young woman's eyes when she told me her brother was deployed.

As the host introduced me, I took a deep breath to loosen the tightness in my chest. *It's not about me,* I thought. *Focus on others.*

I made eye contact with several individuals seated in different parts of the audience before I opened my speech with a snippet of John F. Kennedy's inaugural address. "Let every nation know, whether it wishes us well or ill, that we shall pay any price, bear any burden, meet any hardship, support any friend, oppose any foe to assure the survival and the success of liberty."

I held up the Blue Star Mothers banner and gave a brief overview of our organization's history. I felt my shoulders relax as I explained that we — the moms of active military and veterans — support our nation's troops and vets, along with their families and each other.

I then listed a few of our chapter's many activities. I pointed to a priority-mail box brimming with items like granola bars, toothbrushes, and DVDs. "With the help of a generous community, each year we ship thousands of care packages. We welcome home returning troops at the airport and armories." I ran my hand over a lap quilt and described the groups of women who sew them for the wounded service members who are recuperating stateside and at Landstuhl Regional Medical Center in Germany. I read snippets of thank-you notes we'd received from men and women in uniform, including one from a soldier who'd written:

> *Thank you for your continued support. Without the love and well wishes, we would be lost…*

I moved to my third point. "We hope you'll consider different activities we're involved in and join us, as you can, in support of our troops."

I wrapped up with JFK's more well-known quote: "President Kennedy said, 'Ask not what your country can do for you — ask what you can do for your country.' As a veteran himself, I believe he would be proud of our troops who have answered the echo of his call with their service to our country. Our troops give so much — and ask for so little," I paused. "And so, my fellow Americans, today ask not what our troops can do for you, but what you can do for our troops."

| **I Found My Courage**

A few days later, Georgia called and asked how I did with my new speech.

"I didn't feel like I stumbled. This time, I spoke with passion. I felt supercharged. What's interesting is that I never made an appeal for money, but people in the audience gave me some to help with care packages."

I gave the same presentation many times at schools, churches, corporations, nonprofit-group meetings, and community events.

Several years later, I spoke at an Independence Day event. *It's not about me,* I thought as I waited offstage for the mistress of ceremonies to introduce me. I pictured my son, Ty, and the other men and women in uniform I'd met who could not be present.

I also imagined a nameless young soldier serving in the Middle East. After returning from a mission, would she remove a heavy helmet and wipe sweat and dust from her face? Did she long to put in earphones and let music take her home, if only for the span of a song? Would she be surprised when she received one of our care packages at mail call? Would frown marks between her eyebrows smooth a little? Would the box, and the love it represented, bring a smile to an otherwise somber face?

I took a deep breath as I stepped up to the microphone. I felt the power of purpose, of a worthy cause, of something bigger than myself as I began speaking: "In his inaugural address, President Kennedy issued a challenge that still applies today…."

~Linda Jewell

15

My Brother's Keeper

A part of kindness consists in loving
people more than they deserve.
~Joseph Joubert

Breathing a sigh of relief, I looked in my rearview mirror, grateful for the distance I was putting between my car and that of the drunk driver as he weaved all over the road. At the same time, I felt guilty.

You can't just drive away. You have to get him off the road! My conscience nagged at me. Or it may have been one of my angels.

"There's nothing I can do. I can't be responsible for his actions," I countered. I was young and slim. A lightweight female does not take on a drunk male driver. And this was before cell phones, so I had no way of alerting the police to come and get this guy off the road.

You're going to look in this mirror and see some poor, unsuspecting family killed because you did nothing. Those thoughts hammered at me relentlessly. I had responsibilities as a human being.

"I'm not my brother's keeper," I said out loud, but without conviction. As the words reverberated, the meaning hit me, and I knew I was. There wasn't anyone else, so the job was mine. I eased up on the gas, realizing I needed to be back behind the drunk. Even then, as I wrestled with the dilemma of getting him off the road, I never paused to think about repercussions. I never thought he might be dangerous.

I had just wanted to get home. I'd been away in the mountains for a few days on an assignment and was excited about seeing my family.

When I'd first noticed the erratic driving of the car in front of me, I had become concerned. He was traveling under the speed limit, but wandering too much. I worried about whether the driver was falling asleep, suffering a heart attack, or drunk at the wheel. I stopped wondering. The driver had crossed the centre line into the oncoming traffic lane. As he swerved back, I saw him toss the brown beer bottle onto the highway.

Oh, balderdash, this guy's smashed, I thought as I watched the bottle explode. My only thought then was to get safely past him. That done, I thought things would be fine, except that inner conversation kicked in.

Now, as the drunk approached again and passed me, the beginning of a plan took root. If I pulled abreast of him, I could honk and motion for him to pull over. That was the theory, but when I put it into practice, he just looked confused and decelerated. After I repeated this two more times, he slowed to the legal speed on a city street, but I was still no closer to getting him to stop. Perplexed and worried that we'd soon have to contend with more traffic, I once again pulled alongside of him, with a silent prayer for this to work. Not comprehending what I wanted, the drunk responded by slowing more and pulling over onto the shoulder. Then I watched in horror as he lost control of his car. The ditches in the area were roomy with gentle slopes. A good driver could drive in and out without mishap. The drunk drove in and stopped, but made no move to get out.

Was he hurt? Sick with worry, I pulled over and ran down to his vehicle. Whether or not I would encounter a mean, enraged drunk had not crossed my mind. He sat slumped, looking as spent as the litter of bags and bottles throughout his car. I rapped on the window. "Are you all right?"

He nodded as he rolled down the window.

"Give me your car keys. I can't allow you to drive." My words, crisp and authoritative, hung in the air and surprised me.

He stared for the briefest of moments, and then reached for his keys and placed them in my outstretched hand.

"If I allowed you to drive in your condition, you could cause an accident." I spoke of how devastated he would be if his actions caused a death. "It would haunt you and walk with you throughout your life."

He seemed to feel an explanation was called for. "I've been up all night. I worked late, and then there was a farewell party. We never stopped. I never thought… I needed to get home… I didn't realize…" He groped for words and then stopped, wilting against the seat, realizing there was no defense.

I opened the door. "Come up to my car, and I'll drive yours out of the ditch."

Minutes later, after getting him settled, I started his car. The impact of the situation hit me. I had a very inebriated man on my hands, and my plan had not gone further than this point. *Okay, angels, what do I do with him?* If I took him with me, that would leave his car stranded an hour from the city. Ideas were examined and tossed.

While I was back up on the highway, listening for a second time to the man explain how he had ended up driving in an unsafe condition, phase two of a plan established itself in my mind. We were on a long, flat stretch of road. That it was not busy had been a blessing up until this point, but now to carry out my plan, I needed traffic. As if on schedule, a car appeared on the horizon. I told the stranger to stay with my car. He offered no arguments as he leaned, using my car to steady and support his body. Like an obedient child, he stood motionless (well, almost) and waited. Placing myself in the pathway of the oncoming car, I began waving my arms like a traffic controller on a runway. The car slowed to show four men looking at me open-mouthed.

"I need one of you to drive this man's car into the city. He is drunk, and I cannot allow him to drive," I explained. Even as I spoke, the passenger in the front was putting on his shoes and nodding.

A slight female, still in her thirties, I stood there in command with a voice that said, "No arguments!"

I gave the men an explanation of the situation and told them to drive the man home. There were no questions. Everyone nodded and said, "Okay."

Returning to my car, I told the drunk of the arrangements, assuring him that both he and his car would arrive home safely. That's when he reached out. He took my hand with one hand and placed his other hand on my arm. I felt no apprehension. He smiled at me and said, "I want to thank you for caring. No one has ever done something like this for me. I just… thank you. You are so… unbelievable."

I took my hand away and squeezed his shoulder. To this day, I have no recollection of what I said to him in response. I remember the wetness in the corners of his eyes. I remember walking him to the car of the Good Samaritans who would take him safely home. And I remember thinking, *Good, now I can go home.* I was relieved that my guardian angels and his were likely doing double time!

~Ellie Braun-Haley

Law School at Forty

*Courage is doing what you're afraid to do. There can
be no courage unless you're scared.*
~Eddie Rickenbacker

ay it please the court." Those words are
enough to strike terror into the hearts of
most attorneys I know. They are the first
words you speak when you address the
Wisconsin Supreme Court in an oral argument. The words are ritual,
as standardized and formulaic as Kabuki theatre. And I was about to
say them myself... if I didn't faint first.

I have a framed photo on my desk at work. It dates from perhaps
a year before I started law school at the age of forty, and only a few
months before I would break my back in a horse-jumping accident,
spend three painful months in a body cast, and have the world as I
knew it divide into "before" and "after."

In the photo, I'm standing in a winter woods, with my four children
gathered around me. They range, in that picture, from about three
years old to thirteen. We are surrounded by pristine snow and bare
trees, and framed in a pretty fieldstone archway. I am beaming, and my
entire universe revolves around keeping them warm and out of harm's
way. If someone had walked up to me then and told me that in a few
years I would not only be a criminal prosecutor but find myself arguing
cases before the state supreme court, I would have given them the same
look as if they'd told me I was really the Queen of England. I might

54 | **I Found My Courage**

have smiled pleasantly, rolled my eyes… and then called the police.

But fate had other plans. Barely a year after I was lifted off the sandy soil of a riding arena on a backboard and loaded into an ambulance, my youngest son started kindergarten — and I started as one of the first official part-time students enrolled at Marquette University Law School.

Only days later, an oppressive cloud of pessimism and self-doubt descended on me during orientation as I sat, surrounded by dozens of my fellow law students, who were young enough to be my children. What was I thinking? How could I possibly compete with kids who could close the law library every night and then go out for drinks and debate legal theory over pitchers of beer? I had four kids, a dog, two elderly horses, and a marriage that was on the verge of collapse.

But driving home, I reminded myself that I'd already borrowed the money for the first year… and I might as well show up for class the following week. I studied like crazy for four hours at school every Friday morning, ran the kids as usual to tennis and soccer and gymnastics and volleyball, and skipped class to go along on field trips and serve hot dogs at the grade school. And somehow, through it all, I managed to get on the Dean's List and stay there.

There was one serious barrier for me to conquer, though. All my life I'd suffered from a crippling fear of public speaking. The first time I was called on to "brief" a case in front of a law class, I was terrified. While I knew the subject well, I barely choked out the words in a gasping, trembling voice.

After that first disaster, I made myself confront my demons. In every single class after that, I read ahead and raised my hand, determined to say something on point. Little by little, with every attempt, my heart stopped pounding quite so hard, and my voice quit quavering so much. But it was still very much an uphill climb. When the rest of my classmates wore suits for our first oral arguments, I wore jeans and a T-shirt that read "Best Mom in the Whole World." It was there to remind me that if I fell flat on my face in school, I still had a life. If I had to do that day over, I'd still wear the same thing.

Three and a half years after I started, I graduated. I soon lucked out, landing a newly created part-time post as a state prosecutor. I truly felt that I had the best of both worlds — I could charge cases and make bail arguments, and still get home in time to drive to soccer practice.

As a former journalist, I naturally gravitated to writing projects — briefs, motions, research, appeals. I was in my element, putting things on paper. And then one day a co-worker turned up at my desk with several pounds of paper for me to review. He had won a TPR ("Termination of Parental Rights") case at trial before a jury, but the judge had later refused to terminate the parents' rights based on a technicality. What did I think?

I had been on the job for less than a year. I knew nothing about the Children's Code. But after reading the statutes and the judge's decision, I thought that the judge had gotten it wrong. My boss gave me the green light to file an appeal.

A few months later, the decision came down from the Court of Appeals. We lost. Once more, I was asked what I thought. We'd now lost the case twice in a row... but I still thought we were right. I got another green light, this time to go knocking on the door of the state supreme court. The court said, "Come on down." And I was absolutely terrified.

The stakes were high. On one level, the case was about whether a three-year-old child who had been placed in foster care for very good reasons could be freed up for adoption by a family who wanted him. On a deeper level, the court would decide just when the courts should stop favoring a parent's right to stay connected and start considering the "best interest of the child."

The mother tiger in me kicked in with a vengeance, and I spent weekends working on the case. I pulled over to the side of the road to jot down ideas on paper napkins. I sat cross-legged on the cold floor of the courthouse basement, poring over nineteenth-century law books, trying to trace the path in the law from when children were considered property to the realities of the present day.

And finally the day came to argue before the high court. I had brought my older son with me for company and moral support. I took him to lunch beforehand at an Italian restaurant. He offered to share his breadsticks, but I had some more Pepto-Bismol instead.

It was my turn to go first, as the person who had asked the high court to hear the case. As I began to speak, I could feel my chest tighten and my air supply go dangerously short. My voice shook for a bit, but it passed. I remembered that what was at stake was far more important than what I was afraid of, and my breathing finally returned to normal as the justices started to pepper me with questions about the case and the law.

> *I remembered that what was at stake was far more important than what I was afraid of.*

Gratitude and relief flooded through me when I finally got to sit down and turn the hot seat over to the attorney on the other side. When the court was done with our case, my son, my co-worker and I left the courthouse and stepped out into the sunlight. I looked at the sky and declared, "Thank God I'll never have to do that again!"

As fate would have it, I was called on to pitch another case to the high court just a month and a half later. And I went on to argue three more after that, winning four out of five. Who knew?

Even now, the thought of saying the words, "May it please the court," can make my heart race and my stomach lurch. As for that first case… the decision eventually came down months later — unanimously in our favor. I like to say that the good guys won that day.

But win or lose since then, every time I look at that picture from the snowy woods, I remember how far I've traveled.

~Mary T. Wagner

Flight to Safety

God provides the wind, but man must raise the sails.
~St. Augustine

I nearly fainted after the airline clerk looked at me and said, "I'm so sorry. There is a problem with your tickets."

My mother had arrived in Germany from the States for a visit, and now my children and I were flying home with her before my husband found out. I gathered my composure before the clerk apologized for giving me such a fright. She explained, "You and your children can fly as scheduled, but you cannot be on the same flight as your mother because it is already full." At last, thankful and relieved, I held our three tickets securely in my hands.

A friend who worked in the Army's Judge Advocate General's office had warned me, "Abusers get worse, not better, and I urge you to leave your husband as soon as possible." I began making plans that day to leave Germany, where we had lived for two years.

"Daddy does mean things to Mommy," my two youngsters told their visiting grandmother when they stayed in her room. After my husband left the house for work, Mother questioned me at breakfast. Relieved, finally, to tell the truth, I no longer covered up his cruel, abusive bullying.

She stayed with the children while I drove for one last appointment in the Army's dermatology clinic. During the nine months I sought relief for a strange skin condition, I never saw the same doctor twice. The skin on my hands sloughed off in sheets. The different doctors who saw me during those months prescribed steroid creams and bandages. However, this doctor looked back through all my records of treatments and noticed that my condition was worsening. He looked at me and said, "You must make a very hard emotional decision if you want to overcome this."

Without telling the doctor about my marriage situation, I resolved to follow through with my plan to start a new life. I felt sure that God had spoken through this doctor. The handwriting on the walls of my heart flashed in neon letters, YOU NEED TO LEAVE YOUR TORMENTOR.

If my husband suspected we would not return from the States, I feared he would keep the children with him. Finally, I told him this truth: "The children and I will visit with your parents and other family members while we're in the States." That satisfied him and he agreed that was a good idea. The following day, I taped a large cardboard box together and began filling it with the children's clothes. Underneath their duds, I put in my family silver, the only valuable thing I packed.

My husband drove us to the Frankfurt airport many miles from our house. After we arrived, hugs were exchanged, and then my children and I walked onto our plane. My legs trembled as we boarded and located our seats. My mother's plane left about thirty minutes later. The children were excited about the airplane trip, but soon went to sleep.

Nine hours later, we arrived in New York, connected with Mother, and then caught our plane to New Orleans. I rented a car and drove to her place in Baton Rouge. With the time change and hours of travel, I had been awake more than twenty-four hours. We all slept soundly. When we awoke, it was the Fourth of July, and the movie *Yankee Doodle Dandy* starring Jimmy Cagney was on television. Later, festivities celebrating America's birthday were televised on PBS. My daughter, six and a half, and my son, five, were the perfect ages to squeal with delight over the fireworks. Jet lag captured us again, and we enjoyed more restorative slumber the second night home.

Mother returned to work the following week. I made phone calls and learned that it takes a minimum of a year to obtain a divorce in Louisiana. After I telephoned my sister Bobbie, she urged me, "Come to Houston. Your kids will attend John's school. Think of the fun those three kids can have." She added, "A divorce in Texas doesn't take as long as in Louisiana."

Before we left Baton Rouge, the children and I went to see their paternal grandparents. The promised visit with my husband's parents was fulfilled. Everyone exhibited good spirits when we said goodbye with hugs and kisses.

I prayerfully considered our situation a couple of days before I bought three tickets for our Greyhound bus ride to Texas. The trip seemed like an exciting adventure to the children. Bobbie and her six-year-old son met us at the bus depot in downtown Houston. My kids jumped up and down when they saw their cousin John. I felt bolstered by Bobbie's practical nature as we drove back to their house in Houston.

My kids enjoyed a slumber party in the carpeted living room with John and his two older siblings. I fell into a restful sleep in the guest room. The following morning, my sister suggested that I talk to a friend of hers, an attorney. I agreed. She made the appointment and drove me to his office. She assured me, "This lawyer and his wife have been our friends for years. He will give you good legal advice."

He outlined the steps necessary to file for divorce in Texas. Before we left, he asked me, "Would you consider taking a job here as my secretary?"

I hesitated a little and then agreed. I thought, *Since I haven't worked in a while, the fast typing skills I learned in high school will be useful after all.*

Next, Bobbie and her husband contacted friends who had a car for sale. After I bought it, the kids and I named it Gray Goose. A day later, my dear sister contacted a woman who owned a house for rent, which we viewed. I paid the first month's rent when I signed the lease, delighted to hear the school bus stopped in front of the house.

Next, I composed a letter to my husband's commanding officer in Germany. I explained our situation. I asked him to order the release of our household furniture stored with the Army in San Antonio before we moved to Germany. A few days after we moved into the rented house, the furniture arrived. By the time school began in August, the children had three new playmates living across the street. Their mother kept my two after school to play with her children until I returned home from work.

The bravest thing I ever undertook was to move forward with the escape plan. Once I made up my mind, it was the most significant day of my life. A week after we arrived at my sister's house, I awoke one morning and noticed something I hadn't seen in a long time: my hands were miraculously cured, with new, smooth skin.

~B.B. Loyd

The Chosen One

Against the assault of laughter, nothing can stand.
~Mark Twain

I stumbled into the kitchen in a bit of a daze.

"They picked me," I mumbled.

My husband's eyebrows crinkled in confusion. "What's that?"

"They, uh, th-they picked me to, to, um, per-perform," I stuttered slowly, my mind still processing the news.

"They, who?" Eric asked. "What are you talking about?"

"You know that writer's workshop I'm attending in the spring?" Eric nodded.

"Well, last month I got an e-mail from the director of the workshop. She said that anyone who was interested in doing a stand-up comedy routine during the last night of the conference should send in their name," I explained.

"And you submitted yours?" Eric asked, befuddled. "That shocks me."

"You're not the only one," I replied, my voice quivering. "I did it on a whim, knowing that tons of people would throw their hat in the ring. I never figured I'd be one of the twelve chosen at random to do it. Turns out, I was wrong."

"And how do you feel about that?" Eric asked. "Excited? Anxious? Annoyed? Afraid?"

Yes. Yes. Yes. And yes. It was safe to say that my emotions were all over the map. When I first got the news, a surge of elation shot through me, immediately followed by a wave of terror. I wanted to celebrate by eating cookies, but I was pretty sure that I might toss said cookies.

There was a time when I wouldn't have been drowning in this much trepidation over making people laugh. I once readily found the funny in life and flourished in its beauty. But ever since my mom's tragic death three years earlier, I seemed to have lost my sense of humor. I longed to immerse myself in boisterous laughter, to relish joyful anticipation, and to throw myself into a scary adventure. In the past, on the occasions when I forced myself to engage in something that petrified me, I was always pleasantly surprised by the outcome. Auditioning for a lead role in the school play. Telling the cute guy in my college class that he smelled good. Asking a *New York Times* bestselling author if he would endorse my book. Every experience enriched my life in some way.

So, when I saw the opportunity to perform a stand-up comedy routine in front of a crowd of two hundred, I thought, *Wow! That sounds terrifying. I should totally do it!* And in a moment of blissful confidence, I wrote, "I'm interested," and hit the "Send" button.

Then, when I learned I'd been selected, I panicked.

What have I done? I fretted. *What if I throw up? Or fall down? What if I forget my material? Or pee my pants? What if I get a bad case of stage fright or a horrid case of the hiccups?*

After thoroughly exhausting every possible what-if scenario, I sat down at my laptop and began crafting my routine.

"Last week, I found myself taking time out of my busy morning to take a quiz that told me what my chicken name was," I wrote. "Now, why I felt compelled to find out this nugget of information is beyond me because I'm pretty sure I'm never going to be in the position of having to fill out medical paperwork or legal documents that will require me to divulge my official chicken name. But since I took the quiz, I can tell you all that you are looking at… Foxy Fluffybottom."

My strength wasn't in joke writing, but in storytelling. Therefore, I pulled from my life and hoped that the material would resonate with the crowd. I discussed everything from my preteen son's inability to apply deodorant to my husband's morning obsession with reading his iPhone while parked on the potty.

Over the next month, I wrote, revised, and finessed my three-minute routine, practicing it out loud any time I was in the shower, out for a run, or driving alone in my car. I worked on reflection, inflection, and projection, all while trying to push out of my frazzled mind the one thing I feared most: rejection.

> **Clearly, this was Mom welcoming me back to laughter, joy, and adventure.**

Maybe this was a mistake, I mused one day during a low self-esteem moment. *I rather like being comfortable.*

I was on the verge of forfeiting my spot when an e-mail came through from the workshop director.

"I just wanted to wish you luck on your upcoming stand-up show," she said. "Have fun! We will all be rooting for you on April 2nd."

When I saw the date in black and white, the little hairs on the back of my neck stood on end. It hadn't dawned on me until that very moment that I would be performing on the anniversary of my mom's death. Clearly, this was Mom welcoming me back to laughter, joy, and adventure. I could practically hear her voice urging me, "Go on, Christy! You can do it!"

I couldn't disappoint my mom. She had always been my biggest supporter.

When the night of the show arrived, Eric asked me if I was nervous.

"Yeah," I said. "But mostly I'm excited."

Finally, my name was called. I inhaled deeply and stepped up to the mic, straining to catch a glimpse of the audience as I squinted in the bright spotlight.

When I opened my mouth, my breath caught in my throat. But I continued.

As I began my set, I heard bursts of laughter as well as my husband's soothing, distinctive chuckle down front. I felt the reverberation of clapping in my chest and cheeks.

My three minutes flew by in a flash. When it was over, professional comedienne Wendy Liebman, who emceed the show, extended her arms for a hug and whispered in my ear, "Was that really your first time? You're a natural!"

As I exited the stage, members of the audience stood and applauded. Eric planted a kiss on my cheek.

"Congratulations! You did great!" he beamed. "I'm so glad you were the chosen one."

"*One* of the chosen," I corrected him.

"I don't know," Eric replied. "I think your mom would say otherwise."

~Christy Heitger-Ewing

19

The Plunge

It is courage, courage, courage, that raises the blood
of life to crimson splendor. Live bravely and
present a brave front to adversity.
~Horace

s my boyfriend Nathan and I rounded the last corner of the path, the sight of the bridge spanning the Cheakamus River pushed acid up in my throat. "Ready?" He gripped my hand while we approached, and then set out on, the bridge. The river raged 160 feet below us.

It wasn't just our planned bungee jump that terrified me — it was also the fear of losing my developing independence to the gamble of a second marriage. Nathan hadn't yet proposed, but we'd booked a trip to Las Vegas with our best friends, so I knew a proposal was coming during this weekend getaway in Whistler.

We signed the waivers, and then I faced the bungee operator who held up a red fabric harness. "For me?" I joked. "You shouldn't have." He helped me determine which appendage went through which space before cinching it tightly to my body.

"Don't grab here." My guide pointed to the harness clip that would attach to the flexible line. "It will pinch and rip your skin. Who's going first?"

Nathan tipped his head in my direction to give me the choice. If I was going to look foolish, I'd rather get it over with before he did something handsomely athletic.

"Me," I said. "I want to go first. He's done this before. I haven't."

When it came to marriage, the reverse was true. Nathan didn't realize it, but I did. There were no guarantees.

"Perfect safety record," I heard one of the operators tell the people ahead of us.

I tugged at my harness, trying to make the thick fabric sit flat. I balled my hands into fists to stop fidgeting. Over the past two years, I'd learned to hide my depression and anxiety. I never wanted anyone to notice I was different. Now, a few months into recovery, but standing on this bridge with Nathan, the tight throat, stiff shoulders and racing thoughts seemed rather appropriate, and not a symptom of what I was working to overcome. Perhaps throwing up would be even more suitable.

"How you doing?" Nathan whispered as we waited for another fool to jump and then be reeled back up. Fully harnessed, the idea of tossing myself into a gorge was oddly easy to accept. But I wasn't first in line yet.

"I think I'm fine," I choked out.

"I'm nervous, too," he confided.

Nathan's honesty reminded me of his acceptance and gentle pushing for me to be more than I'd previously allowed. He didn't dole out compliments, but instead pointed to things, like creating a really great dinner, to help me see the success in what I'd done. He saw my potential, even when I didn't, and he watched me create a more independent self than had existed before.

Nathan found ways to help me love myself and not rely on his (or anyone's) compliments or input to feel good. It was a new form of independence, but the potential of another botched marriage was more terrifying than a leap from a bridge.

"Ready?" the bungee guide asked.

I nodded, knowing I was anything but. Nathan grinned and gave me a thumbs-up, but tapped his foot rapidly. Seeing his nervousness softened my own a little.

Legs stilted, I approached the walkway. A pint-sized diving board extended over the river too far below. Trees lined the sides of the ravine.

The guide hooked me to the main cord and told me to let my body go limp during the drop and rebounds. Little of what he said made sense. I had no context.

I inched to the edge of the platform jutting out from the bridge, intending to jump while looking at the river and trees below. It was all right there before me, ready for my leap of faith.

It was too scary, too intense. I couldn't do it. I couldn't toss myself into the void in front of me.

I turned my back to the canyon, clutching the walkway handrails while my heels hovered above nothingness. I looked into Nathan's smiling face.

He mouthed, "You can do it. We can do this."

I found an increment of strength I hadn't felt before. I wasn't ready, but I would be. I convinced myself I'd jump in a second or two.

I hadn't intended for the handrails to slip from my grip. I lunged through the air, reaching out, wanting to hold that solid familiar comfort for a little longer, but it was too late. I was gone. Falling.

The desire to flap and flail came from the half of me screaming to move my body. The other half froze, recognizing the futility in motion.

Air whizzed. Trees blurred. The material world blended with emotion.

Calm. Anxiety. Love. Fear.

A slow, soft resistance gradually caught me, and then pulled me back up toward the bridge and sky.

A moment of inertia, then back down. Up. Down. Up. Down. I was uncertain how long each bounce would last or when I'd stop, but I knew I was safe and had done something brave.

My limbs hung like a rag doll as the operator cranked me back up to the bridge.

"Are you okay?" he asked. "You were so quiet and still, we thought you'd passed out."

I smiled, feeling a little proud of myself. "I'm fine. I'm recovering from anxiety and depression, so I just kind of went with it."

"You have anxiety, and you did this? Wow. Good one."

Nathan hugged me. He had the harness around his ankles, not

around his torso like mine. His swan dive was far more attractive than my stone-like drop, yet I knew he had much less to overcome.

As we walked off the bridge back to the parking lot, a pair of women watching the jumpers stopped us.

"You did that?" The older woman pointed at me.

"Yes, she did." Nathan smiled.

I did. I'd taken the leap. I wouldn't jump off that bridge again, but I knew I would marry again. I would marry Nathan.

There would be ups and downs, but I would be safe and brave. I could handle it.

~Ronda Payne

20

Do It Afraid

Think like a queen. A queen is not afraid to fail.
Failure is another steppingstone to greatness.
~Oprah Winfrey

I wiped my sweaty palms against my khakis and glanced at the dashboard clock: 7:58 a.m. Across the parking lot, a young woman carried an armful of books and headed toward the front doors. *Should I go in?* Registration began at 8:00, but the first speaker didn't start for a few more minutes. I'd wait. Conference attendees were probably mixing and mingling, sipping their lattes and discussing their latest novels.

I tapped my fingers against the steering wheel, trying to ignore the annoying voice inside my head. *Writing for the church newsletter doesn't make you a writer. Anyone can write for a church newsletter.*

I watched a couple more conference-goers weave their way through the parking lot and disappear through the front doors. My stomach flip-flopped. *How did I get myself into this?* Instantly, I knew. It began several months ago when my pastor preached a sermon I couldn't ignore.

It was a time of transition in my life. After ten years of full-time motherhood, my youngest had started kindergarten — and I felt lost.

"Now what?" I asked my husband. "Should I go back to my old job? Pursue a new career? Return to college?" Curt encouraged me to follow my dreams.

"You can do whatever you want," he said, putting an arm around me. "But don't just settle for any job. Do something you feel passionate about."

In my heart, I knew my passion: writing. But writing was a risky endeavor. What if I wasn't good enough?

It seemed silly, being afraid to write. It wasn't like some masked man was going to jump out of a dark corner of my office and shoot me if I typed a lousy sentence. I tried reassuring myself. What's the worst that could happen? An annoying voice inside my head answered.

You might look like a fool. Others will discover you have no idea what you're doing. You could fail.

So, I ignored the dream, tucking it away — until the next Sunday morning.

> **"How many times do we limit ourselves because of fear?"**

"How many times do we limit ourselves because of fear?" My pastor's eyes scanned the congregation. "How often do we miss what God has for us because we fear rejection and worry too much about what others might think?" I fidgeted in my chair. How did he know I'd been struggling with fear?

Over the next several minutes, I scribbled down notes and words of encouragement. But I'll never forget what he said as he concluded.

"If you have a desire in your heart, don't let feelings of fear stop you." I nodded in agreement.

"It's okay to be afraid," he said. "In fact, it's normal to feel fear. Just don't let fear control you. Trust God with that fear. God will walk with you through your fear."

I wrote down three simple words and underlined them as my pastor spoke.

Do it afraid.

Over the following months, those three words became my motto as I stepped out of my comfort zone and into the wonderful, yet overwhelming world of writing. I began reading every book I could find on improving my craft. In time, I worked up the courage to submit articles for publication — and had lots of practice coping with rejection.

Meanwhile, the relentless voice in my head worked hard to discourage me. But I didn't give up. "Do it afraid," I said as I pushed myself to write another article. *Do it afraid,* I thought as I e-mailed a magazine editor. "Do it afraid," I said as I signed up for a writers' conference.

And afraid I was.

My heart thumped in my chest as I walked into the first workshop of the conference. Like the new kid in a junior-high cafeteria, I searched for a seat in a room full of strangers. But those awkward feelings didn't last long. By the end of the workshop, I felt at home. The speakers shared valuable tools for improving my writing. They also challenged and inspired me to persevere.

Perhaps even better, I formed new friendships. Meeting other people with a heart for writing energized me. These were my people. As someone who does her best work secluded in her office, it was nice to know I was not alone — especially when I realized I wasn't the only one with a doubting inner voice.

In the months after the conference, I continued to follow my pastor's simple but powerful advice. I joined a critique group, entered a writing contest and signed up for another conference. Every time I pushed myself, my confidence grew. Eventually, doing it afraid led me down a path to publication.

Today, I am still pursuing my dream. When insecurities creep in, I remind myself that the only way I can truly fail is to quit. Being successful is more than hitting a bestseller list. Real success is doing what I love. I may have sweaty palms and butterflies in my stomach, but I will always succeed when I keep doing it afraid.

~Sheri Zeck

21

Gratitude Regained

*We gain strength, and courage, and confidence by each
experience in which we really stop to look fear in the
face... we must do that which we think we cannot.*
~Eleanor Roosevelt

The pale light of dawn seeped through the floral curtains as I lay quietly in my bed next to my young daughter. The snowfall from the evening before had made it the perfect morning to wait until the furnace kicked on. I lay there and thought about the past few months. "I just can't handle parenthood," John had said as he packed his belongings.

Unpaid mortgage bills were piling up on my desk for a house that would not sell. I couldn't see a way to turn my life around.

Then, despite the familiar sounds of rats in our walls, I drifted back to sleep until I was reawakened by a noise. It wasn't the rats this time. I figured it was our cat.

I pulled up the covers, loving the moments of being half asleep, half awake. I heard what sounded like scraping metal. I didn't want to get up to check on it. My daughter stayed sound asleep next to me.

For a moment, I allowed myself to be lulled back into a partial sleep. Then, a shot of icy cold shocked my body. The hair on my arms and neck stiffened. I sat up in bed. Full alertness came to me at lightning speed. I noted the cat was asleep on the bed. I turned toward the open doorway. A bobbing beam from a flashlight shone in the hallway. Someone was in my house.

I took a half-moment to question if I had the strength to handle this. Then my thoughts flashed forward to possible endings, and I made an inner declaration that enough was enough. I flung myself out of bed and charged for the door. "Who *dares* come in my house?" I said.

With full force, I met him at the threshold of my bedroom. I pounded on his chest and pushed him back. "Get out of my house!" I screamed over and over. He seemed stunned at first. Somehow, I had enough presence of mind to take mental notes of him. I would need that later to identify him to police. Dark-blue plaid wool coat. It was puffy. He must have layers underneath. That's right. It had snowed last night. Navy knitted cap. White male, stocky. Latex gloves over knitted gloves. I had a moment's recognition of the incredible danger my daughter and I were in, and somehow a new strength dawned within me.

Power surged through me — a power I had never known. I was aware of sparkling iridescent gold. I was a goddess, a vengeful goddess. I pounded on him and pushed him away. He took backward steps, moving away from me. I pushed on. He would normally be taller than me. But somehow I was towering above him. One foot, two feet, and then three. I was enormous. "Get out of my house!" I pushed him over the threshold of the front door. I slammed and locked the door, and then ran to my daughter.

In the moments that followed, I returned to my normal size. I phoned the police, who arrived in minutes with a canine unit. Although detectives worked on the case for several months, the man was never found.

What was found, however, was gratitude for my life. I made the best of a challenging situation and began to take steps toward greater joy. It took time and it wasn't easy, but I persisted. I can't explain the gold iridescence or how I grew so tall that I looked down on the man. I hadn't experienced anything like it before, and I haven't experienced it since. It doesn't matter. Now I wake up in the morning grateful to face each new day.

~Kelly Rae

22

Remember to Breathe

Nobody can go back and start a new beginning,
but anyone can start today and make a new ending.
~Maria Robinson

I stared into the barrel of that pistol, and my muscles froze. Lot's wife must have felt like this when she first looked back at Sodom. My eyes, not yet turned to salt, locked onto the would-be shooter's face. His tight-lipped grin sent my mind whirling into a "what's-wrong-with-this-picture" search. The strain of his grin reduced his eyes from spheres to almond slivers, full of nothing but black pupils. Seconds felt like hours as I remained focused on those pinpoints. How long would it be before I stopped breathing? Then I noticed I had already stopped.

I had come into the bedroom from the bathroom and found the lights on in the middle of the night. He was lying on the bed. He looked so comfortable, leaning on pillows propped up against the headboard, with his arms resting gently against his chest and his legs under the blanket. His hands were together as if in prayer, but pointing straight toward me, beneath cold steel, a pistol aimed slightly upward in a trajectory that would have pierced my sternum. He wasn't breathing either.

Would he shoot me? Would he really do it? I thought back to a day, four years earlier, when we had said to each other, "Till death do us part." Then I thought about the bruises that had come and gone over those four years, bruises that had gotten increasingly larger and

I Found My Courage | 75

more difficult to conceal with each succeeding incident, harbingers of today. And I remembered the marriage counselor who said, "If you go back to him, he will kill you some day."

I recalled one time when he had told me about hunting, how he loved the power and how he liked it when the deer looked at him just before he fired his rifle. How after he'd lock on, he'd make a noise to get the deer to look his way. What a rush he got seeing its fear. It was so much better than the actual kill that the execution was anticlimactic.

> *I couldn't get his weapon away from him, but I could take away his power.*

Then it struck me. He was savoring my fear, prolonging his enjoyment before the anticlimactic event. The more I let him see my fear, the more likely he would shoot me. I couldn't get his weapon away from him, but I could take away his power.

"What are you doing?" Air had moved up from my diaphragm into my larynx, tickled my vocal chords, spilled across my curling and undulating tongue, and exited between my lips. I used that exhaust to unfreeze my muscles. My feet moved from their set-apart, broken-stride position and came together. My bare heels and toes sank into the plush white carpet. My shoulders reset. I was firmly grounded and breathing again, and I wanted to keep it that way.

I saw his chest fall. He set the gun on the night table.

Whatever inkling of love that had lingered in me for my husband died in that moment. Three days later, after he left for work, I stuffed my clothes into large, black trash bags and squeezed them into my car. I tied a mattress from the daybed onto the roof and moved into an unfurnished apartment thirty miles away. I went back to work the next day as if nothing had happened. Then I went back to school, finished my undergraduate and graduate degrees, and advanced in my career. Eventually, I remarried, and I retired.

This happened to me almost a half-century ago. But if you read the news, you might think it happened only yesterday.

~Marilyn Haight

The Empowered Woman

Doing What's Right for Me

Gray

It is not by the gray of the hair that
one knows the age of the heart.
~Edward G. Bulwer-Lytton

was walking my dog when a friend pulled up and rolled down her car window. "Oh, my God!" she said. "I've wanted to do that for ages! You are so brave!"

It was the first time Elyse had seen me since I let my hair go gray.

I'd been thinking about taking the plunge for a couple of years. I was sick of coloring my hair. Sick of the outlay of time and money. Sick of the seaweed hue the chlorine in the pool turned it only weeks after coloring.

I was also weary of colluding with a culture that saw a sixty-year-old man's silver-gray crown as "distinguished" but expected women of the same age to have hair that was impossibly golden or brilliantly brunette. I was fed up with the cultural expectation that I look younger than my age.

About twelve weeks elapsed between the day I stopped coloring my short, afro-styled hair and the day I left the last vestiges of my chemically prolonged youth on the salon floor. During those awkward months when the top of my head looked like a vanilla cupcake with chocolate frosting, I felt like a walking Rorschach test. What did my friends see in this morphing design?

Many women, some good friends and some barely acquaintances, decided that my decision was sufficiently universal that they had to share their thoughts and feelings with me. They voiced many concerns: What would my kids think? Would my spouse like it? When I look in the mirror, would I see my mother? Or worse, my grandmother?

What happens when one defies cultural norms and brazenly courts ageism? I was struck by how many women ended their conversations about my hair with "It's so great that you're doing this. Good luck!" They vicariously wished to live the dream but also recognized that, for the granny who suits up to cross skydiving off her bucket list, a little luck couldn't hurt. Like the canary in the coalmine, they collectively waited to see if I would survive.

Most of them, like Elyse, applauded my courage for having traveled somewhere they were still too timid to go. Still, I was struck by the number of women who ended the conversation by reminding me, "You can always color it again if you don't like it." It was a sisterly gesture of unconditional acceptance should my silly experiment turn out to be a bust.

Brave is laudable but not safe. For so many of us, there is something dangerous about not looking young. The pressure to look young drives us to purchase youth-enhancing concoctions so implausible we would never consider buying into such hokum in any other realm of our lives. It drives some into misery, others to the dermatologist for injections, and others under the knife.

Even my older friends who color their hair admit that they've been thinking about going gray for years, but feel they just aren't ready. Ready for what?

As un-PC as it may sound, I think the most honest answer to this question is: not ready to look old. This is particularly true of my women friends who work in corporate settings. They have earned their high-level positions through years of study, sacrifice, and hard work. Still, they are afraid that to look their age would somehow jeopardize their... what? Their credibility? Their value? Their power? Or is it something deeper? Their sense of self-worth?

Although I was (mostly) comfortable with my decision from the start, there were some false starts.

"How old were your parents when they died?" This awkward question was posed to me by a young intake nurse when I changed physicians recently. Before I went gray, the question had always been: "Are your parents still alive?"

I had only been fully gray for a few days and wore my new identity like an aging Peter Pan, full of bravado and uneasy with the range of feelings that could pop up in new circumstances. Reactive and relentless, I shot back, "Did you ask that question like that because I have gray hair?" The poor woman was flustered and mortified, but I would take no prisoners. "Do you assume I'm too old to have living parents just because I have gray hair?" She apologized profusely. I thought she might cry. With my defensiveness on full display, it was my turn to feel mortified.

Empowerment is an inside job. Giving oneself permission and authority to challenge norms is not for the faint of heart, and this gray business is a complicated endeavor. From hour to hour, I am resolved but insecure, freed but self-conscious.

As time passes, I am increasingly comfortable with my decision. Being gray suits the way I live the rest of my life. Simple. Quiet. Counter-culture. With this decision not to take action against my body's natural course, I have given myself permission to look my age, trusting that my esprit de corps will compensate for whatever assumptions onlookers may associate with a silver crown.

Early in my pilgrimage, I was jolted when I passed a mirror and was confronted with my gray-haired reflection. I was caught off guard but was not unhappy. I felt eager to embrace this familiar stranger, knowing that by accepting her, I was one step closer to more fully accepting me.

~Audrey Ades

Following My Heart

*One of the most courageous things you can do is
identify yourself, know who you are, what you
believe in and where you want to go.*
~Sheila Murray Bethel

It was midnight, and I was on my knees, cradling my throbbing head in my tear-soaked hands. I struggled to stifle the sobs that threatened to wake my two tiny children.

The call had come just hours before: I had gotten the job. After five interviews, three presentations, and dozens of writing samples, I had received a generous offer. An offer I would have celebrated at a different time in my life, but now caused me gut-wrenching agony.

An offer that needed my answer by tomorrow.

Friends and family were elated. A few years earlier, when my children were born, I had stepped off a prestigious career track. My peers thought I was crazy. Then, when my daughter was three and my son just two months old, my husband left. As that first harrowing year careened by, my financial stability took a precarious turn. My former colleagues viewed the job as a second chance. "You're back in the saddle!" extolled one. "A perfect excuse to go back to work," said another.

I was dumbfounded. My carefully cultivated life was coming apart at the seams, and the unanimous advice was not to mend the rips of my mommy wardrobe but to change back into dress-for-success. The peer pressure to accept this high-powered position was palpable. But it didn't feel right.

In fact, it felt unbearably wrong.

My former career had demanded all my time, energy, creativity, and passion. I still had those in droves, but I was joyfully applying them to my family. While I'd kept one hand in the professional pot, I considered my media work a side dish and nurturing my children the main entrée. Now, faced with an all-or-nothing decision, I visualized putting my children on the back burner where they'd go from two parents to less than one.

That was less than acceptable.

A freedom lover with an independent streak, I had never been content following the crowd. As a result, I had frequently made unpopular decisions. I had defiantly graduated high school in three years, brazenly become a journalist in a family of scientists and, years later, homeschooled my children (the ultimate act of rebellion).

> *Each new day dawned as a glorious invitation to write my own script.*

Following my heart had worked in the past, but a wrong move now could seriously jeopardize my children's wellbeing. To others, the decision was simple: live the dream, with its security and prestige. But to me, the decision gnawed; taking the job would critically compromise my heart.

Exhausted, I rose to my feet, and looked with swollen eyes at two framed photos of my kids. The quiet house felt alive, expectant, like it, too, awaited my decision. And in that breathtaking silence, I heard a voice. It wasn't timid. It was not compromising.

It was bold and certain.

You already have a job to do.

The words echoed through the room and struck their target — coursing straight through my soul.

Shaken, I made my way upstairs to check on my children, finding each curled up in a blissful sleep. I heard their breathing, soft and even. I became one with the moment. The breathing.

The voice.

You already have a job to do.

It was the dead of night, yet I felt enveloped in light and clarity.

The decision, indeed, was simple. I would decline somebody else's dream job and joyfully keep my own.

I felt a great weight lift off my shoulders.

What had been a sleepless night from stress turned into a sleepless night from adrenaline. I had a lot to think about now. There were definitely issues to face: I had single-mom status, two small children, no solid income, and zero child support. But all that was secondary. I was ready for action. And ready to shield my resolve from the backlash I knew was coming.

I started to plan.

I wrote and wrote, amassing pages of notes. I pursued my options for working for myself, rekindling every creative goal I'd ever had. Then I strategized how to maximize my income while still being present for my children. By morning, I had compiled steps one to one hundred with plans A, B, and C on hand.

Once again, my peers thought I was crazy. Some wrote me off. *You'll never recover your career this time,* they said.

Still, I plowed on.

I decided to fly under the radar for a while to ground myself and build my inner strength. I took on freelance work that allowed me to produce results and parent at the same time. I wrote and edited. I consulted and tutored. I stretched myself and discovered that I could learn anything if I devoted some time to it. Accepting assignments from legal editing to career coaching, I delved into professional areas I never would have as an employee.

It started slowly — really slowly. But the slower pace wasn't a tragedy; it was a godsend, allowing me to fine-tune my strategy, make better decisions and, most of all, be available to embrace those simple moments with my children.

It would be a lie to imply that the shattered pieces of my life fell beautifully into place. In fact, new challenges arose in quick succession. My estranged husband completely disappeared, I had to sell my home, and my children's seizures and life-threatening asthma worsened. But I was undeterred. I was on a path, and my heart was leading the way.

The freedom that came from calling my own shots was well worth the effort. Each new day dawned as a glorious invitation to write my own script. I could choose the scene, the setting, and the cast, giving my kids the starring roles. On rainy days, we'd stay home to tackle the to-dos with plenty of time for play. When the sun was full tilt, we'd head to the zoo with my backpack of work projects along for the ride.

From Little League games to theater performances, I made it to every one of my kids' big moments. My professional projects were the sub-plots, woven into the scenes to support the story of my family — not the other way around. To be sure, I lost a number of business opportunities. But each night, when I tucked my kids into bed, my heart was full. Over time, as my kids grew, my business did, too. My small family thrived.

My former co-workers were right. I never "recovered" my original career. And I have no regrets. I am blessed beyond words and forever grateful for the life that I have, a cherished closeness with my now adult children and a variety of fulfilling, passion-filled work.

I'm glad I trusted my inner voice. I know I'll face many more tough decisions in the future. And when I do, I'll remember to muster up my courage and follow my heart.

~Judy O'Kelley

25

The Greatest Risk Is Not Taking a Risk

Women hold up half the sky.
~Mao Zedong

s I stood at the crossroads where the isolated African village kissed the base of the imposing mountain range, the male villagers all asked the same question for a third time: Was I certain I wanted to climb the mountain?

Sure it had been climbed by local and foreign men, and local women, but a Western female, who arrived unaccompanied and wanted to climb the mountain, was not the norm.

I explained that I had been preparing for some time — in research and in physical strength — and showed them the permit I had from their government authorizing my climb. I stressed that I would be very pleased to keep their local traditions and hire one of their villagers as a guide, but it seemed to do little to ease their concerns.

The male villagers told me of the "quick mud" I would encounter. They reported that it would grab hold of my legs and could swallow me whole, emphasizing this would certainly be my fate given my small size. While they couldn't recall anyone this had actually happened to, they seemed convinced it was a real possibility.

The village women, on the other hand, clicked their tongues at the men in what I could only assume was the equivalent of shaking one's head in disagreement. They smiled affectionately at me, and a few women simultaneously raised their arms with fists in the air and made joyful, loud sounds at the back of their throat, which I took to indicate their support for my cause.

The men then went on to relay stories of unpredictable miniature elephants that they claimed were a fierce cousin of the calmer species we all knew of, which could endanger me on the climb. The longer I stood speaking to them, the wilder the stories of danger became, and the bigger my smile.

* * *

My mind went back to being a ten-year-old girl waiting in line with my great-aunt Helena for a table at our local restaurant. As she spoke about her upcoming trip to China, the others in line listened with great interest.

While at the time she had come to know a young Chinese woman from Hong Kong, whom she would meet up with in China, she was also to travel on her own to remote areas where foreigners generally did not have the opportunity to explore.

While I enthusiastically probed her with an onslaught of questions, so too did the other customers in line. Even as a child, it was easy to sense their disapproval of her solo adventure.

They asked how she would deal with the impending danger they assumed awaited her in a foreign land, and how she would be able to move around the country not knowing the language. One man even drilled her about her sanity for thinking that traveling as a solo female to an isolated area was an option.

In keeping with her usual character, my aunt calmly responded to all their questions with wit and humor, and took it all in stride. As a former teacher, she was always pleased whenever she was afforded an opportunity to share knowledge with others, whether it be historic facts or interesting cultural differences. She always did so in a humble way, making everyone feel they were her intellectual equal — and that day was no different.

When we were finally seated, I asked her why complete strangers seemed angry about her travels. As for me, I couldn't imagine anything more exciting. Travel to China seemed so exotic at the time, and I couldn't wait to tell all my friends about it.

She calmly explained that a woman traveling alone, especially off the grid, was a new idea for some people. Perhaps people were just fearful of the unknown and that which is considered new. She reminded me that the greatest risk is not taking a risk, and we should always follow our dreams.

***

After witnessing the overwhelming support and active voices of the local village women, the men agreed to an arrangement that seemed to put them at ease with my climb. In addition to the local guide I would hire, they also wished me to enlist the support of at least one porter and three guards with guns, for protection.

The women added their own request to the list — that my guide be a local woman to ensure I would be afforded protection by a "sister" while on a climb with all men — a dynamic I had not given much thought to.

It seemed all parties were winners in the agreement. I could contribute a little to their village's income, while finally being allowed to begin my journey with support and well wishes from the locals — men and women alike.

As I bid farewell and made my way down the dirt path toward the mountain, I was joined not only by my new mountain support team, but also by every village woman. While two women walked hand-in-hand with me, the others danced in circles around us as if we were on parade, singing triumphant-sounding songs.

I knew I wasn't the first Western female to make the climb, and I certainly wouldn't be the last. But with the women villagers proudly accompanying me, I felt an overwhelming sense of collective accomplishment. And looking at their victorious smiles, I suspected my "sisters" felt the same.

~Melissa Valks

26

Winning On and Off the Court

*How wrong is it for a woman to expect the man
to build the world she wants, rather than
to create it herself?*
~Anaïs Nin

My rude awakening came a few months after my son was born. I sat in bed, alone in the dark, feeling confused, upset, and lost. As the crickets chirped an endless chorus outside my bedroom window, I wondered where I had gone wrong. My thoughts inevitably focused on my partner, the source of my present sorry state.

I first met my partner on a badminton court at the age of eighteen. Although we had now been together for nearly eight years, we were still very much children. Neither of us had the inclination to get a steady job. We saw ourselves as free spirits with no wish to be trapped in the nine-to-five grind. We got by as best we could, mostly from money earned through part-time work. Both being athletes, we spent most of our abundant free time either playing badminton or training to become stronger and better badminton players.

Then, out of the blue, I got pregnant. We knew our lifestyle would be affected, that things would need to change. Still, we were not willing to join the rat race, so we formulated plans to set up our own business instead. When those plans failed to materialize, our relationship went through a tremendously rough phase. Being a follower, I felt it was up to my partner to get us out of this predicament. After all, he was intelligent, outgoing — a born leader. I was just the shy one with no useful skills. As our finances took a nosedive, I began blaming him for everything that was going wrong. How could he do this to me, to us, to our child? The more I pushed for him to act, the more pressure I unwittingly put on his shoulders, while I waited stupidly on the sidelines for things to right themselves.

But things didn't change. They just kept getting worse.

That night, I went in search of a notebook and pen. I poured my heart out, page after page, until no more words came out. Then, a funny thing happened. When I read over what I wrote, I felt totally disgusted. If these had been someone else's words, I would have told this person to stop whining and do something already! And so, I decided to do just that.

The next day, inspired by my new resolution but unsure where to begin, I went to our tiny local library. After locating the half-filled self-help shelf, I came across

> **If these had been someone else's words, I would have told this person to stop whining.**

a book called *The Cinderella Complex* by Colette Dowling. Although it had been written years before, it seemed to have been penned specifically for me. In essence, it explained why women expect others to take care of them instead of taking charge of their own lives. It completely opened my eyes to my shortcomings and spurred me to make my own way in the world.

My situation didn't change overnight. But little by little, I started making progress. Instead of expecting my partner to fix all of our problems, I did what I could to help. I overcame my fears and insecurities and took my first faltering steps into the adult world. Eventually, I managed to get a "real" job. Since I had also discovered through my journaling that I had an affinity for writing, I took writing classes. To my great joy, it led to seeing my work published, which in turn served to further boost my self-esteem and put me in a position where I could truly become my own boss one day.

Twenty years later, my partner and I are still together. Thankfully, we have both learned from our mistakes. Although our shuttle doesn't always fly smoothly over the net, we have come to respect each other's strengths and weaknesses. But more importantly, we make sure to give the other space to grow. For me, that space keeps expanding, especially since my role shifted to become our family's sole breadwinner. Surprisingly, I wouldn't want it any other way.

~Pascale Duguay

27

Hometown Girl

He is happiest, be he king or peasant,
who finds peace in his home.
~Johann Wolfgang von Goethe

rms crossed over my chest, I lean against the door-frame of my lovely, two-bedroom apartment where I have lived happily for the last three years. I will miss the two luxurious bathrooms, the great-room's hard-wood floors, my balcony facing the lush green pines, and even the family sized dining area where I often ate alone. At my feet, my Shih Tzu, Chelsea, gives a half-hearted "woof" that echoes throughout the empty apartment.

It is time to leave, and yet a part of me wants to unload the waiting U-Haul, return all the furniture I worked so hard to buy and all of the hand-selected decorations to their carefully chosen places, and to continue with my single, independent life. Part of me wants to stay here because I love this haven that I created all by myself, and another part of me wants to stay because I fear the changes that remain in my future.

I was a small-town girl when I left the Midwest and moved to Houston, Texas, to make a life for myself. I knew I could never really be independent living anywhere near my old hometown, my family, or my childhood friends. To be truly free, I would have to rely on myself for survival. Houston offered grand experiences, the doorway to travel to many different places, and mostly, a chance to set myself apart from those "simple" kids I grew up with. I wanted not just more — I wanted something bigger and better — and Texas seemed like just the place to discover it.

Liberated life was exactly what I expected — most of the time. I did my student teaching in Rio de Janeiro, Brazil, and learned a great deal about Brazilian culture. I ate *feijoada* every chance I got; I sunbathed on Copacabana Beach; and I took overcrowded buses to remote villages for the weekend.

I went to graduate school and won a grant that allowed me to explore Ireland while I was studying to be a librarian; I thumbed through yellowed books in the Long Room, admired Ireland's literary history and cultural heritage. In the evenings, I tossed back a few Guinnesses with the locals in neighborhood pubs. I married another teacher, and we honeymooned in Mexico where we visited the ruins at Chichen Itza and snorkeled above the world's second-largest barrier reef. On a whim, I hopped a plane with co-workers to Beijing where I walked on the Great Wall of China, then took a night train across the country to see the ten thousand Terracotta Warriors of the first Emperor of China. Life outside of my tiny hometown was an adventure, and I had the whole world to myself.

Yet liberated life was often challenging and sometimes even heart-breaking. My husband loved my strong self-assuredness, my sense of responsibility, my obsession with adventure, and my naiveté. Unfortunately, that naiveté blinded me to my husband's serious problems, in business and with prescription drug addiction. I made ends meet for as long as I could, and made sure his doctors' bills were paid and that he had proper treatment. Eventually, when it was impossible for me to stay, I did the strong, responsible thing and moved on with my life alone.

I was always at my strongest alone.

I gaze at the living room wall where the couch used to sit and where I had my first post-marriage kiss. The dining room wall has a barely visible outline of a painting I had commissioned with my first solo income tax refund. Turning my head slightly, I imagine myself standing at the kitchen bar preparing hors d'oeuvres for my first-ever hostess gig — a book-club meeting. Then I look over at the guest bedroom where the carpeting reveals the indentations of a bed and dresser — the bed where my mother and a few other guests slept when they visited me.

My eyes sweep past the master bedroom door where I curled up so many nights to read myself to sleep and on to the balcony off the living room. My wind chimes are packed away now, and I will never again sit at my patio table here in Texas and watch the birds feed while the breeze plays with the ends of my hair. A sudden nostalgia and longing begin to weaken my resolve.

"You ready, baby?" says a husky voice behind me.

I take one last look at the apartment, turn, and close the door behind me. Looking up, I see the bright blue eyes of my fiancé, Terry, shining down at me. Those crisp blue eyes have been glinting with mischief at me since second grade when Terry would pull my braid and run, since middle school when he would tell off-color jokes and those piercing blue eyes would light up with amusement at my reaction, and in high school when he would invite me to go for a drive with him and then wink one baby blue before walking away. I smile up at the boy from my hometown who is now a man.

"I'm ready," I say. I scoop up Chelsea and scratch behind her ears.

It's hard to believe that I'm blissfully married and have been living in my hometown for nearly two years now. My old hometown is no different than it was twenty years ago when I left. Yet this little town is a different world compared to Texas. I stand at the window in the front room of the house where I live with Terry and my two stepchildren. Fat white flakes fall from the sky and coat the gentle rise and fall of the fields around our home. Birds peck at the feeder hanging in the flowerbed, and Chelsea lies curled up in an upholstered armchair. The wood floor creaks as I lean over and reach for a sweatshirt, then pull it on to fight against the winter chill. I haven't lost myself here as I had feared, haven't lost the independence I valued, or the feeling of being special that I fought so hard to discover during my travels.

Florence + the Machine blares from my stepdaughter Teresa's room, and I hear Thomas, my stepson, laughing at something funny on television. I smile when I picture those "simple" kids — small-town kids like me. Terry walks through the front room, talking on the phone, and stops to playfully swat my behind. I laugh. Later, I will go shopping with my mother and call my brothers to arrange a weekend movie with the nieces and nephews.

I have discovered something bigger and better, and it was here in my hometown all along—something more exciting than my solo life in Texas. I am a part of that something now. I am strong, I am independent, and I am complete.

~Erin E. Forson

28

Empowering Humiliation

Saying no can be the ultimate self-care.
~Claudia Black

he phone was ringing again. It was my neighbor, Sandy. "Hey, can Angie come over and play with Mary?"

"Just a sec. I'll ask her."

My six-year-old daughter had a worried look on her angelic face. "I don't want to go, Mom."

I spoke into the phone. "Thanks for inviting her, but right now isn't a good time."

Sandy persisted. "Mary is bored. Why don't you just send her down so the girls can play, just for a little while?"

"Well, I don't think…"

Sandy interrupted me. "The girls can help me make cookies. Ask her again, pleeeeez?"

"Okay."

I put my hand over the receiver and whispered to my daughter with urgency in my voice this time. "Sandy said you and Mary can help make cookies. Please, why don't you just go down there for a little bit?"

My daughter got big tears in her eyes. "But I don't want to, Mama!"

"Alright, *fine!*" I growled.

I got back on the phone and said something like, "I'm really sorry, but she just doesn't feel well right now." That fib sounded a little nicer than "She really doesn't want to come to your house!"

Sandy was not happy. That was clear in her abrupt reply. "Well, alright then. Bye."

As I hung up the phone, I felt tormented inside. But why?

I nagged my little one again, my voice tight and harsh. "I don't know why you couldn't just go play with Mary!"

Angie looked up at me, and her huge eyes reflected her own stress. I looked into her sweet, worried face, and something suddenly broke inside me.

> *It was so very difficult for me to say "no" to anyone.*

What are you doing to your child? She's only six! That voice of truth screamed from a very deep place within me. It jolted me to the core.

I held back my sobs long enough to say, "No, no, honey. I'm sorry. It's okay if you don't want to go over there. You don't have to."

I escaped to another room, and the dam broke. I'd known for a while that I had a serious people-pleasing problem. I had some sort of ridiculous fear of making anyone upset. It was so very difficult for me to say "no" to anyone. Yet in that moment of pressure, I'd put that same burden on my innocent child's shoulders.

I was overwhelmed with shame, confusion and despair.

It was one of the best, most life-changing moments of my life.

I remember another transformational time during that same year. My sister dropped by unannounced with her two young children. She asked if I could babysit them while she went to work that evening.

I said, "Umm, well, I really have a lot to do tonight." She said that she'd been called in to cover someone else's shift, and she really needed the money.

I could feel the conflict rising up inside me. I had two young children of my own. I gave in to short-notice babysitting for her on a regular basis. I was so very tired.

Reluctantly, I said, "Well, okay."

Sis stayed to visit for a while before leaving for work. I was trying to be pleasant, but I was wearing my resentment like a thick blanket around my shoulders.

My sister asked, "What's wrong?"

I hesitated, but then the truth blurted out. "You put me on the spot like this all the time! It sure would be nice if you'd ask me in advance."

She looked me in the eye. "This is your own fault. If you didn't want to do it, you should've said no. You can't agree to do something, and then blame me! Blame yourself!"

Ouch! I was furious at her for saying that, but it was the hard truth I had to hear. That happened many years ago, and I have reminded myself of it numerous times since then.

How could I have been so blind? Why did I almost always go into automatic "yes" and keep-the-peace-at-all-costs mode?

I had to find answers and get help to learn how to stop.

Yes, my empowerment had to start with my humiliation. What? Aren't humility and power opposites?

That's the ironic beauty of all this. I had to hit the floor, sobbing on my knees, to realize I needed help to change my life.

I bought a book and took a class about healthy boundaries. I sought out a good counselor and started going to therapy.

It's been a continuous eye-opening journey for the last twenty years.

There have been other books, mentors and counseling sessions since I started on my road to recovery. This long journey has empowered me in many ways. Mostly, I've learned how to have honest relationships with others and with myself.

My "yes" means yes, and my "no" means no — without inner turmoil, resentment or false guilt. Well, usually. But I'm still learning and open to receiving help. I know that's where my power and freedom are.

~Diana Bauder

29

The Power of Words

Whatever words we utter should be chosen with care
for people will hear them and be influenced
by them for good or ill.
~Buddha

I stood outside my professor's office in Parlin Hall, staring at the black flecks on the hallway floor and thinking about my final grade.

After three years as an English major, I had finally found the courage to take my first creative writing class. Words were my secret best friends, and although I hadn't told anyone, I wanted to make a career out of them someday. Surely, I thought, my grade would be an indicator of my future success.

The door creaked open, and Professor Mills invited me into her office. She pulled my story out of a file on her desk and shoved it into my hands. A large, red C glared back at me. My eyes fell to the floor. My first instinct was to drop the paper and run.

But Professor Mills wasn't finished. She raised her eyebrows, and with a tiny smirk, said, "I'm afraid you'll never be a published writer."

Heat rose to my cheeks. I managed to mumble goodbye as I turned and grabbed the doorknob. All the way down the hall, those words bounced around my head. All the way home, I wondered if they were true.

When I crashed onto my bed, the tears finally came. I wasn't just a bad writer; I'd never even get published. Right there, at the age of twenty-two, sprawled on my peach-colored quilt, I gave up my dream of having a writing career.

Life went on. I earned another degree and began teaching elementary school. I got married and had a family, but I never gave up words completely. I continued to read, but my writing consisted only of some secret scribbles in a handmade paper journal.

Something changed shortly after my thirty-ninth birthday. Perhaps I finally recognized the emptiness that had come with ignoring my own need to write. Perhaps it had something to do with an approaching milestone birthday and the realization that time was not infinite.

I was determined to squash Professor Mills' words, which had been ruling my life for too long. It was time to get reacquainted with my dream. It was time for me to get published.

I began writing after the kids went to school, in the car in the pickup line, and in the middle of the night when I had insomnia. I spent hours at the library and the bookstore, reading and researching magazines and publishers.

At first, I wrote everything — from recipes, crafts, essays and articles to short stories, activities, greeting-card verse and poetry. I wrote for both children and adults, and began submitting my work to magazines and newspapers. When the rejections arrived, Professor Mills' words buzzed in my head again. But I kept going.

Almost a year later, it finally happened. I quickly leafed through the magazine to find my work. There it was — a short paragraph about my mother's peanut butter cookies. The magazine paid me ten dollars, but those dollars felt like gold. I was a published writer!

I continued to submit my work — 118 pieces that year — but I also racked up eighty-nine rejections. Each one felt a bit like opening an old wound. I reminded myself that not every rejection had to do with writing quality. I focused instead on the twenty-nine acceptances.

The following year, I enrolled in my first writer's conference. The doubts began somewhere along the 200-mile journey to the hotel.

What if this is just a silly dream? I wondered.

But the next morning, I took a deep breath and walked into the conference room, laptop in hand. Professor Mills joined me. "You'll never be a published writer," she roared in my ears.

I ignored her, and scribbled down all the writing wisdom I heard that weekend. I came home from the conference inspired and ready to work even harder.

I soon joined a critique group, enrolled in online writing courses and met other writers who told rejection stories similar to mine. I learned the writer's mantra: never give up. There was comfort in the camaraderie.

So I wrote more and submitted more. Rejections and acceptances rolled in, although never at an equal rate.

It wasn't long before I made it to another conference. This time, I signed up for an editorial critique. I found myself standing outside the meeting room staring at the brown flecks in the hotel carpet. It felt like Parlin Hall all over again.

As I sat down across from the editor, I wiped my sweaty hands on my pants. She pulled my manuscript out of her folder and looked up at me. I held my breath.

Instead of a smirk, she smiled. "This is lovely, lyrical writing."

I smiled back and started to breathe again. I listened, nodding my head, as she gave me constructive comments to improve my work. I thanked her and turned to leave.

All the way down the hall, her words danced around my heart. All the way home, I told myself they were true.

Two years later, I was still in my pajamas when the phone rang early one morning.

"Your manuscript has won a grant," a woman said. "Five hundred dollars."

"Are you sure?" I asked. This had to be a dream.

I had been focusing on writing children's books by that time, and a national award from a children's writing organization was both a shock and an honor. I put the money back into my writing education and dared to think that my dream looked brighter than ever.

But things got tougher before they got better. Three of my book manuscripts went to acquisitions meetings, but they were ultimately rejected each time. I signed with an agent shortly afterward, but later left the agent when I realized we weren't a good fit. I rewrote my children's novel, only to discover the agent who requested it didn't like my new version. Rejections flooded my in-box.

Professor Mills' words grew louder with these new challenges. It didn't matter that I was already a published writer. I couldn't keep her toxic words out of my head — words that made me doubt myself.

I took a break from writing then, but I continued to think about the power of words — particularly those six words that controlled my life and my dream. Surely if words had such power, I could find equally persuasive words to counteract them. Positive words.

So I began looking for comments about my work from teachers, peers, editors, and agents.

"Your work is ready."

"You're a talented writer."

"Your language is engaging."

I compiled a list and posted it above my desk. Each time I found an encouraging or supportive word, I added it to the list. My positive list had a significant and productive effect. I jumped back into writing not long after.

Eventually, I stopped counting the rejections — I still get them. Eventually, I even stopped hearing Professor Mills' toxic words. Instead I focus on that twenty-two-year-old girl who had a dream to build a writing career. I focus on using my words to teach, inspire and connect with others. Every day, I sit down, read my positive list and start writing.

~Annette Gulati

A Dream Fulfilled

Follow your bliss and the universe will open doors
where there were only walls.
~Joseph Campbell

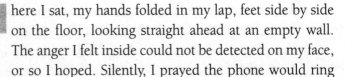here I sat, my hands folded in my lap, feet side by side on the floor, looking straight ahead at an empty wall. The anger I felt inside could not be detected on my face, or so I hoped. Silently, I prayed the phone would ring or that my boss, Jim Pearson, would hurry up and finish the report he was writing so I could type it into the computer.

I was bored out of my mind and had been sitting like a statue for over an hour, waiting — and seething. But that's what my boss had instructed me to do whenever there was no work left to be done. When I tried to show some initiative, Jim said, "You are to sit quietly at your desk like a lady and wait, or go find another job." He threatened to fire me so often that I expected it to happen on any given day.

Jim was a tyrant. He criticized and humiliated me in front of my peers every chance he got. It was 1984 — there was little I could do to change the situation. Until I found a new job, I was stuck.

While sitting there, I had plenty of time to ruminate about how I wound up in such a predicament. Never in my life did I want to be a secretary or work for such a despicable man. But as far back as I could remember, I was prepped, prodded and poked into the position, forced to take every secretarial course offered in school. My mother, a legal secretary, often talked about how exciting it was to work for an attorney. She loved her work. But when I told her I had no interest in doing that kind of work, she said, "There's nothing wrong with being a secretary. It's respectable work."

"I know that, Mom," I said. "It's just not what I want to do. I want to be a musician." But my plea fell on deaf ears. Eventually, I relented. And just before my nineteenth birthday, I got a secretarial job at a large corporation in New York.

Earning my own money and becoming self-supporting was empowering, but I was miserable. The work was monotonous. Sitting at the same desk, seeing the same people, and doing the same work day after day was unbearable. To suppress my boredom, I changed jobs frequently, which allowed me to learn many new skills and hone the old ones.

At one company, I worked in the finance department on my first IBM Personal Computer. Months into the job, there was a massive layoff, and I took on the responsibilities of the Financial Analyst. The manager — the only other person left in the department with me — trained me on

I was never so thrilled to be fired in my life.

all the software. I became fascinated with the PC and wanted to learn everything about it. When the computer broke down and remained unrepaired for weeks, I opened it, hoping to find out what made it tick. Somehow, I managed to fix it and put it back together in one piece. It was a risky move, but it paid off. When my boss refused to give me the title or salary for the analyst position, I decided to move on, taking some excellent computer skills along with me.

That's how I wound up working for Jim Pearson in the finance department at a chemical corporation in Connecticut. I had the computer skills he needed. And from day one, I hated my job. I hated Jim Pearson more. He was condescending and arrogant and took great pleasure in offending me. I felt dehumanized by him. And his boorish behavior, which was infamous throughout the company, was tolerated because Jim was Vice President of Finance. I was more expendable than he was.

Working for Jim made me physically ill. Within six months, I had used up my sick time for the year. My doctor advised me to quit. But with increasingly more bills to pay, job hopping wasn't as easy as it once was. And working late most nights made it difficult to schedule interviews. The opportunity to learn all the software programs used at the company helped me get through some difficult days. But the more adept I became at the computer, the more threatened Jim became.

He stopped allowing me to take the company's training classes, and before I could leave my desk, I had to get his permission. He insisted on knowing my whereabouts at all times. While I didn't like having to sit at my desk "like a lady" and stare at the wall when there was a lack of work, I did it without complaining. But when he demanded I call him "Sir," I wanted to throw something at him. I had dealt with harassment on the job before, but this was on a whole new level. My work environment had become too toxic. I had to move on.

But before I was able to secure a new job, Jim crossed the line. My car had died in the parking lot and was towed to a local repair shop that closed at the same time my workday ended. It wouldn't reopen until 8:00 the next morning. Knowing this, Jim refused to let me leave a few minutes early to get the car. And securing a ride or taking a train home wasn't possible. I was going to be stranded overnight.

Trying to reason with Jim was futile. He said, "You're not allowed to leave this office unless it's on your lunch hour or the end of the day. Get your car on your own time, not mine." It was the straw that broke the camel's back. Immediately, I went to Human Resources, filed a complaint, and walked out the door.

The next morning, Jim called me into his office. "Your employment here is terminated effective immediately," he said.

Like a wave rolling out to sea, the stress that had been bottled up inside me for so long washed away. "Oh, thank God!" I exclaimed. I was never so thrilled to be fired in my life, and it thrilled me all the more that he knew I was thrilled. It was the most empowering moment of my career.

That day, a new dream emerged. I vowed to never work as a secretary again, and I decided I would work for myself instead. I started a computer software company and developed a sizeable clientele. After discovering that I loved to build and fix computers and networks,

I opened a computer repair business, later integrating the two. My business flourished for the next twenty-four years.

Becoming an empowered woman didn't happen overnight. It took many years to lay the groundwork, and there were many missteps along the way. The journey was long and hard, but I emerged from it a new, independent woman who lived life on her own terms. I wouldn't change any of those bumps in the road even if I could!

~L.M. Lush

31

Finally in Control

Good things happen when you
get your priorities straight.
~Scott Caan

"I hate Sunday nights," my five-year-old son, Jordan, said. "It means the weekend is over, and I have to go to daycare for five whole days before I get more days off to play."

"I know, buddy, but it's how things are," I said. "It's that way for me, too."

"Do you hate your job?" he asked.

I shrugged. "It's not so much that I dislike my job. It's more that I miss you and your sister so much during the week."

"I miss you, too, Mommy. I wish we could spend more time together."

I pulled him close so he wouldn't see the tears in my eyes. I truly didn't hate my job, but I did hate being away from my children so much. Like most working mothers, my kids spent long hours in a childcare center, and our evenings together were filled with dinner preparations, homework, and bath time. Many nights felt like a race to get the kids fed, clean, and to bed at a decent hour.

The weekends were our only time to just play and enjoy one another's company. I loved that time, but it wasn't enough.

I longed to spend more time with them before they started school full-time, but our family needed me to have an income. I felt stuck.

I was unhappy with my situation, but I didn't see a way to change it.

And then a friend of mine told me about a part-time opportunity that sounded perfect for me. It was a job I would love, and it would allow me much more time with my kids.

There was just one problem. The part-time job would mean a significant pay decrease, one I wasn't sure our family could survive. But I needed to find a way to make it work.

I made a spreadsheet of my current income and the associated expenses, like childcare, work clothes, and travel costs. I subtracted my expenses from my income, and I was shocked to see that the number had gone down by half. I was losing half of my income just to pay someone else to take care of my kids — a job I wanted to do myself.

It seemed counterproductive, but the sad truth was that our family needed the other half of my income to survive. We couldn't afford for me not to work.

Which left me right where I'd started — trapped.

Unless I could find a way to make the part-time opportunity's paychecks match the half of my current income that I actually got to keep.

I started researching preschools in my area, and found that the part-time childcare they offered was far less expensive than the rates I was currently paying. I practically happy-danced when I thought about my children in someone else's care for just a few hours a day, instead of the full-time hours we were currently apart.

I spoke to my friend about the scheduling logistics with the new job. "Could I put my kids in morning preschool and make this work?" I asked.

When she nodded, I felt a glimmer of hope. "And what about clothes? Would I need to buy a new wardrobe?" I asked.

My friend shook her head. "You could wear what you have on right now."

My glimmer of hope sparkled brighter.

I started a new spreadsheet with the part-time job's income and the associated expenses. The income was far less than what I was currently making, but the expenses were too.

Tears filled my eyes as I realized this could actually work. I ran the numbers by my husband, who was skeptical at first.

"Think of how often we eat take-out food, simply because I worked all day and didn't have time to cook dinner," I said. "If I'm only working mornings, I'll have more time to cook at home, and that will save money."

Gradually, he saw my reasoning and agreed. I resigned from my full-time job and accepted the part-time position. I pulled my children out of full-time day care and placed them in the mornings-only preschool.

Each morning, I worked at a job I loved while my kids attended a preschool they loved. Each afternoon, we read books, baked cookies, and snuggled on the couch watching movies. Gone were the rushed evenings with no time to enjoy one another. Gone were my constant feelings of guilt and loneliness because I missed my children.

I stopped dreading Monday mornings and started enjoying life. I was actually happy.

Quitting my full-time job was a huge risk, but I did it with my eyes wide open. Through research and extensive planning, I was able to make the right decision for myself and my family.

I used to feel trapped in a situation I couldn't control, but now I'm in control of my own life.

~Diane Stark

32

I'll Try Anyway

"I can't" are two words that have never been in
my vocabulary. I believe in me more than
anything in this world.
~Wilma Rudolph

ince birth, the world has had expectations of me as a black woman. I was born into a big, bustling family that straddled the line between poverty and working class. I grew up in Bushwick, Brooklyn, a New York City neighborhood filled with the same kind of families, many of the adults and teens working low-wage jobs and on public assistance.

Our parents, some of them immigrants, and others long-time residents of the neighborhood, strove to provide us what we needed for our schooling. They would purchase supplies for dioramas and science-fair projects, with the little money left over from groceries and other necessities. They would leave work early to attend an assembly or meet with our teachers, and they'd stay up with us all night as we wrote yet another book report.

Despite our socio-economic status and appearance, many of us on the block that I grew up on managed to become successful adults. This motley crew of Puerto Ricans, African Americans, Irish, Dominicans, and Italians, attended our zoned public school—I would attend a private boarding school for high school—and then went on to college. We work in banks, in schools, in media, music, and art, in healthcare, in politics… some of us even own our own businesses.

Others have returned home to continue lifting up their families and the neighborhood.

We may have been financially poor, but we were emotionally and spiritually wealthy in our tight-knit community. We knew who we were and what we were capable of — but most of all, we had big dreams, and our families and communities helped to foment that desire. With that came a natural, easy confidence, and a vision to do big things and be great people who could eventually change the world.

My goal in life is to always learn, expand my knowledge, experience new things, and move along the continuum of human progress. I never set out to prove anything to anyone, but my life speaks for itself and I hope that what I do proves to people that you don't know a person or their capabilities, until you *know* a person. No one who meets me, for example, imagines that I, a large African American woman, am an ultramarathoner, even appearing on the cover of running magazines.

> **"No one ever passes this test."**

Back in my school days, people didn't expect me to be smart and well read. No one expected me to be a classically trained singer who spent her high school Saturdays studying music theory and solfège, and taking voice lessons from an internationally acclaimed teacher. In addition, no one expected me to be a good writer, and they were surprised that I had won awards for my poetry. Some couldn't see past my skin and gender, and they would try to dissuade me from trying things they just knew I wouldn't be able to do. But I did them anyway.

So when I went from prep school to college, I wasn't surprised to be underestimated. "No one ever passes this test, you know," said Maurice Porter, the self-assured senior voice major, as I tried to rush past him in the narrow hallway of Robertson, the building that housed most of the tiny, airless practice rooms at The Oberlin Conservatory of Music.

"Thanks. I'm going to take it anyway," I said, "just to see what the test is all about, because everyone's telling me not to take it. It must be really hard." He was still blocking my way and I was annoyed. I needed to get to Bibbins 206, where I would sit for an hour and rack my brain about dead European men, whose creations I seemed to have a special affinity for.

"Well, you're wasting your time. Why don't you just go and practice? C'mon you're a freshman, and you're a voice major. Voice majors never pass the music history exemption test. Hell, they never even take it. You need to be in the practice room," he said, shaking his head with a sympathetic smile and walking away. Continuing to warn me, he called back over his shoulder, "Only like, European violinists and pianists ever pass the test. It's their music anyway."

Maurice was a legend at Oberlin. Everyone listened to what he had to say, even though he was sort of a jerk. His incredible vocal talent — his melismatic gospel seemed to lend itself flawlessly to the demands of *fioriture* in bel canto opera — and his equally fluid keyboard skills in both styles were astonishing in such a way that one was overwhelmed simply by being in his presence. People listened to what he said and followed his advice. Even seasoned professors and professional musicians paid attention to this twenty-something.

The exemption exam tested one's knowledge of various periods in the western classical tradition, from early-medieval and renaissance idioms to modern serialism propagated by the likes of Arnold Schoenberg and Anton Webern. We were to identify each piece of music by period, composer, genre, historical context, and instrumentation. Monteverdi, Scarlatti, Bach, Handel, Mozart, Beethoven, Schubert, Brahms, Strauss — this was the test that I had been preparing to pass for four years… Stockhausen. Stockhausen? *Who the hell was Stockhausen?* That part I left blank.

Fortunately, Stockhausen's existence and contributions to contemporary classical music didn't have the disastrous effect on my exemption that I had feared. The list that was posted that same evening outside of Bibbins 206 contained my name and the names of two other freshmen, who turned out to be Hungarian and Russian pianists.

***

What was next?

"No one ever gets out of the writing requirement at Oberlin," said my good friend Jon Fitz, an editor at the *Oberlin Review*. "You shouldn't even try. I mean, your stuff is good and everything but don't like, waste your time."

"Okay, um, thanks," I said, rolling my eyes and walking away with the paper topic in hand.

You know what happened.

~Mirna Valerio

33

Changing More than Diapers

Follow your heart, listen to your inner voice,
stop caring about what others think.
~Roy T. Bennett, The Light in the Heart

The obituary in the alumni newsletter caught my eye. I was surprised to see one of my long-ago college instructors, Professor B., had passed away. I had neither seen nor thought about him for more than ten years. His photo brought back memories, none of them good.

My friend Nancy and I were in Professor B.'s engineering materials lab class in college back in the early 1980s. We were the only two young women in a class full of young men. I recalled the day when Professor B. was describing and showing new types of materials. As we passed around a new material that was designed to be highly absorbent for use in a disposable diaper, Nancy treated it like a hot potato, teasing that she didn't want anything to do with diapers! Professor B. let her have it. "Better get used to it, young lady," he'd proclaimed. "In ten years, you won't be working as an engineer. You'll be home raising children and changing diapers, as you should be."

The room fell silent. We were all stunned. Nancy had earned the respect of everyone in the class for her abilities, and none of us thought she should be spoken to that way. We all knew she would make a fine engineer, and if she chose to be a mother, she would make a fine mother, too. Although those harsh words were directed at Nancy, I knew they were meant for me as well. The young men in the class spoke up for Nancy with heartwarming support. Along with our fellow students, Nancy and I finished the semester, completing Professor B.'s class.

Just over ten years later, Professor B. was dead. At that time, Nancy was an engineering manager at a regional power company. I was working on my Ph.D. in biomedical engineering at a different university. Neither Nancy nor I had children, and we both had promising engineering careers. Professor B. had been wrong! His obituary said that he had two daughters; I wondered what kind of opportunities they'd had in life with him around to discourage them.

Twenty more years went by. I learned that Nancy had followed her passion, earning her master's degree and becoming a green/sustainable-energy consultant. I became a mathematics and engineering professor at a women's college. My job involved teaching and demonstrating engineering concepts to future teachers. The engineering class was hands-on, designed to enable future teachers to experience and master engineering concepts so they could, in turn, teach them to children.

I was hired midyear and worked hard to learn the material just ahead of the students. It didn't take long for me to realize that this was a required course for education majors, and many of them were only there because they had to be. Many were intimidated by math and engineering concepts. Some students even told me that they chose to teach kindergarten so they wouldn't have to learn math! But part of the goal of the course was to get future teachers excited about math and engineering, so they in turn could pass this excitement on to their students.

My weekend class included many women in their thirties who were raising families. Some were already teaching informally and had gone back to school to earn a teaching degree. At the beginning of the semester, they arrived with their course materials and serious looks of doubt. Part of my job was to help change their attitudes.

As the semester progressed, I watched my students discover, piece by piece, that they could master engineering concepts. They had each purchased a set of pink tools for the course. They learned about and built circuits, magnets, mechanisms (including levers and linkages, gears, and pulleys), trusses, and plumbing systems. During each unit, the students worked in teams to put together the concepts they'd learned to design and build functional engineering projects. At an open house to show off their work, they taught what they had learned to their fellow students and visitors. This classroom full of women — mothers who had changed many a diaper — wowed each other and their audience by demonstrating their engineering knowledge. Even Professor B. would have been impressed by their final projects!

As I watched these women discover their own power, I saw them take what they'd learned and apply it in real life. One woman began using her pink tools to fix things around the house, something she'd never done before. She confided that she was proud of her pink tools — and glad her husband didn't borrow them! While I'd initially thought to myself that the pink tools were kind of silly, I now understood their appeal.

A woman in my math class, after learning about compound interest and how to use the mortgage calculator on a credit-union website, refinanced her house and used the money she saved to run for the state senate. That's empowering!

When I look back over the past thirty years, I'm proud of how far we've come since Professor B.'s class. Perhaps Professor B. was a product of his generation. As products of our generation, Nancy and I followed our dreams. In turn, I was excited to pass on my math and engineering knowledge to my students, who followed their dreams to become teachers of another new generation.

My students taught me something, too. When they researched women inventors, they discovered that a mother named Marion Donovan had invented the disposable diaper to reduce her laundry load! By necessity, she became the "mother" of several related inventions, and she held several patents. In an aha moment, I thought, *We should have known that disposable diapers were invented by a woman. The joke has been on Professor B. all along!*

~Jenny Pavlovic

34

Broad Comedy

The thing women have yet to learn is nobody
gives you power. You just take it.
~Roseanne Barr

We huddled in the library, arguing in hushed voices. "You just can't. That's why," my boyfriend countered.

"Am I not funny? Is that it? I should at least be allowed to audition. Is that against the regulations, too?"

"Look. It's an all-male comedy group. You're a girl. They're not going to change the rules for you. It's been around for more than fifty years, and there's only one requirement besides humor. You can't audition because you don't have a…"

"Chance? The funny bone is not a gender-specific part of the anatomy. I'm as funny as any of those guys. They should let me in!" I gathered my books in a huff and left for my audition.

I was turned away immediately at the door.

My boyfriend Howie was a member of The Mask and Wig Club, the University of Pennsylvania's guys-only comedy group. I was jealous as all get-out. Steam escaped from my ears when I met him later that night.

"Why don't you join the all-girl comedy group instead?"

"They don't pull in the big audiences."

"Well, that's 'cause women just aren't as funny as men."

Okay, that was it! I joined the all-girl comedy group, determined to let my funny shine. But as our spring show came and went, the frustrating truth dawned on me. A guy playing an old granny is hilarious: voice pitched in a high, wavering falsetto as "she" waggles her sandbag breasts around her waist and chucks her false teeth at her son-in-law. A girl playing an old grandpa is just, well, not that interesting. Was it possible that Howie was right? If I wanted to get the big laughs, I'd have to play with the big boys.

The next September, I pulled my hair into a high ponytail and tucked it under a military beret (very Ferris Bueller — this was the 1980s, after all). I threw on a flannel shirt, jeans and a canvas jacket, and polished it off with a pair of black high-tops. I practiced my walk in the dorm room mirror. I looked like the real thing. Now I just had to be funny.

Howie had been promoted to Chief Wigger (no joke!), but he wouldn't be able to make the preliminary auditions, so I had that on my side. I breathed a sigh of amazed

> *I was a girl playing a guy playing a girl!*

relief when they let me in the door in my slacker-boy costume. I read from the script, ironically playing the role of "the girlfriend" on a bad first date. I was a girl playing a guy playing a girl! I figured I was in good company. Shakespeare created all kinds of characters who disguised themselves as a different gender, not to mention Joan of Arc and Yentl.

I killed it! The three guys on the panel laughed and laughed. I had written my name on the casting application as Dennis. "That Dennis guy is hysterical," one guy said to another as I was leaving. I was out of the room by the time I realized they were talking about me!

I made it to callbacks! Now I was really nervous because Howie would be there, and I thought he might be mad if he recognized me. Or worse, he might think that I was trying to undermine a sacred system, which I was.

Beneath my baseball cap, my bunched-up ponytail was dripping with sweat, and the jacket I'd borrowed was hanging off my thin shoulders. I was mid-scene when Howie stood up from the table. "Hey!" he said. "Take off your hat!"

I'm still not sure if he recognized me, or if he just hated actors in hats. But either way, the jig was up. When I took off the cap and shook out my hair, Howie's jaw dropped. The other Wiggers fell sideways laughing, a couple of guys applauded, and somebody shouted, "That's the funniest thing I've seen all day!"

I didn't get in.

But I didn't give up, either. I loved comedy. So, I petitioned the school to fund a co-ed improvisational comedy group called Without a Net. We held auditions, and by that spring we performed our first show to a modest house. Word got around, and we sold out the next night. We added an extra weekend.

My relationship with Howie didn't last long after that, but Without a Net did. They still perform on campus today, thirty years later! If you are in Philadelphia and have a hankering for a belly laugh, check out one of their shows!

It's not that men are funnier than women, or that women are funnier than men. But we lift each other up and, together, we're hilarious.

~Ilana Long

Chapter 4

The Empowered Woman

Going It Alone

35

Going for More, Again

Fear less, hope more; eat less, chew more;
whine less, breathe more; talk less, say more;
love more, and all good things will be yours.
~Swedish Proverb

I slowly raise the lid of the computer. A pop-up reminds me I have a message from Six, my developers in England. I click the e-mail. "Hooray," it says. "We're happy to tell you we're finally ready to go live!"

I've waited two years for this moment. But instead of excitement, I feel woozy. The Oxycontin is kicking in, muffling the burning pain in my abdomen; an IV hisses softly near my shoulder. A halo is beginning to form around my husband's head as he sits and reads in the chair at the foot of my bed.

This is déjà vu. Nearly twenty-seven years earlier to the day I'd been sitting in a similar hospital bed in New York City, experiencing a similar searing abdominal pain from a C-section. (I'd asked the nurse if someone had left a pack of burning matches on my belly.) Same type of lovely, narcotic blur — except the earlier version came from morphine, the painkiller of choice back in 1991. The other difference today is that no nurse is walking up to me and handing me a delicious-smelling baby who is going to take over the next twenty years of my life!

Except that, wait, yes, isn't "the business" — my new Internet site called CoveyClub.com — my new baby? And hasn't it arrived just in time to kill the heartbreak of my empty nest? JJ, twenty-seven, is settled and working in New York and Lake, twenty-two, is ensconced in Boston. Both are happy and prospering. And as we know, every mother is only as happy as her most miserable child. So I am happy. Really happy.

I hit return and type: "Sorry guys. Launch will have to wait. Just had an emergency appendectomy at 3 a.m. Going to sleep."

Oh wait. Another parallel. Twenty-seven years ago, after twenty-eight hours of labor, the doctor was stitching me up when the nurse came around the partition to hand me JJ; gazing upon that gorgeous little square head that refused to come down the birth canal made me start crying with such uncontrollable force that the doctor knocked me out so he could finish sewing. The last thing I said that day: "Give him to Jeff. I'm going to sleep."

And so go the parallels in the life of an entrepreneur. At age sixty-one.

It's a life I embarked upon two years ago when the company I worked for decided to close the magazine I'd run for eight years (yes, that was my business baby) called *More*. *More* was the only magazine dedicated to upscale educated forty-plus women. It had a passionate readership of 1.5 million but not enough advertisers to support its mission. Even though all the facts and figures prove that women over the age of forty control 40 billion dollars-worth of household spending — and have the freedom to decide where to spend it — upscale advertisers are so terrified that older women will stigmatize their brands that they refuse to lay down the bucks for any vehicle that is not Millennial-oriented.

The saddest, and in retrospect most prescient, day for me occurred a few months after I'd begun as Editor-in-Chief at *More*. It was 2008, smack in the middle of the Great Recession when I had lunch with a very famous designer who had, twenty years earlier, sketched my wedding dress on a napkin during a similar lunch. "Lesley," he said leaning in over his spicy tuna roll, "the only people who are keeping my stores open right now are women over forty. But I just can't advertise to them."

Yet he had no problem advertising to fifty-year-old men in the *Esquires* and *GQs* of the world. It was age prejudice: up close and personal. And I battled that stigma — in both advertising and Hollywood for nearly a decade. Just imagine trying to convince an obviously forty-plus actress to admit she is more than thirty-five so she would do *More's* cover! It's insta-death because, as one of my agent friends revealed to me confidentially, the male actors write their contracts requiring any love interest to be at least fifteen years younger than they are!

I adopted a countervailing mantra: "Aging is not a disease," I would say politely. "It's not something you can outrun or outsmart. It happens to everyone. It will happen to you." But I gave up mentioning it to the twenty-five-year-old media planner who was glancing at his watch every five minutes while obviously thinking, "Geez, can't wait to get to basketball practice. Wish I could get my mom's friend here to hurry up."

And I'd lost jobs before. Back in the 1980s I'd been hired by the famous *New York* magazine editor Clay Felker to help create an evening paper competitive to the *New York Post*; I was honored to be given one of the most coveted writing spots in the city. But, due to poor advertising sales Felker's paper closed after only one year and I was out on the street. Two decades later I was running *Marie Claire* to killer newsstand sales and dozens of awards. That lasted all of five years, because even great success is no guarantee of longevity in the world of magazine publishing.

Luckily, losing *More* magazine in 2016 was different. When I'd been forced out of *Marie Claire* it was 2006, pre-social media boom. None of my readers — many of whom had been following me since my days as editor-in-chief of *YM* and *Redbook* magazines—could locate me. When *More* came to a crashing halt, however, I was able to snap a last photo of the staff and post it to my personal social media. Hundreds of friends, competitors, and readers jumped in to say how sad and angry they were that a magazine of such intelligence and quality was being shuttered. Readers posted photos of the final April issue with their coffee mugs, mourning the fact that their favorite read was going away. Hundreds of them encouraged me to "reach higher," "not give up," and strike out on my own. One even offered seed funding for my next project!

Even though I was hard at work on my masters in Sustainability Management at Columbia — and ready to stop shaving the hair on my legs, don Birkenstocks and let the hair on my head go gray while I saved the world from climate change — my readers convinced me that I should create something radically new in media. Six-hundred-twenty-seven of them took a fifty-four-question survey that allowed me to create a map of what CoveyClub should look like. (FYI: The word "covey" means "a small group of birds"). My supporters were clear: though they wanted great reads, they also wanted live and virtual events that would challenge and connect them, group escapes and travel. I set aside my severance pay from *More* to fund the business, found a fabulous web developer and began writing down every idea that popped into my head.

> *Being my own boss after forty years is a delight that takes some getting used to.*

While CoveyClub can't be *More* magazine (I don't have a staff of thirty-four fabulous editors and a multi-million dollar budget), it can be inspired by the incredible energy and enthusiasm of a readership that refuses to be invisible no matter what advertisers say or do. That is why it is a club and there are dues. Members are helping to fund this project themselves.

Being my own boss after forty years is a delight that takes some getting used to. I'm still learning that I don't have to build consensus or ask anyone's permission before I try something new. And every day is a learning experience.

Have I walked into technical walls? Missed deadlines because I don't have enough help? Been mortified when a new Covey member called the technology I'd chosen for sharing and connecting women "a mess"? Yes. Yes. And yes. But I can tell you this. Every morning my eyes fly open at 5 a.m. and I'm as excited about going to work as I was at twenty.

I am learning and growing and making a whole new slew of friends with whom I have richer, more meaningful interactions than I ever did in the corporate world. Am I terrified of failure? Sure. Do I think sometimes that I'm risking my sterling reputation on something that may go bust? Absolutely. But I don't care. I'm in it for the journey — wherever that may lead. CoveyClub.com launched on Valentine's Day 2018, two days after my emergency appendectomy. I'm still going for more!

~Lesley Jane Seymour

36

Lighting Fires

You simply have to put one foot in front of the other
and keep going. Put blinders on and plow right ahead.
~George Lucas

"It's getting cold in here. Let's have a fire," I suggested. The late-afternoon gloom accentuated the penetrating dampness that is winter in Lima, Peru. My visitor, like me an expat American married to a Peruvian, had been my friend since the day we met as teachers at the American School. As young mothers, we shared beach towels, recipes, kitchens, and the disquieting news of simultaneous unplanned pregnancies. She dropped by often to comfort me with her friendship, to listen and offer moral support. A year had passed since the evening my husband doubled over with pain after dinner, and I rushed him to the clinic with acute pancreatitis. Even though enough time had passed to dull the ache of his passing, I cherished the constancy of her presence.

She settled into the low chair near the open fireplace, stretching her long legs and tucking her hands into her sleeves.

"All by yourself?" she said.

"Of course. Why do you even ask?"

"Well, I couldn't. I'd have no idea how to start. Carlos takes care of things like that. I have other talents." Her smile said it all. Secure. Protected. Safe.

I felt the familiar tightening in my chest. I was thirty-five, the mother of four children under thirteen, and a widow. Even though I felt proud of the way I was coping with my new life of Total Responsibility, there were these conversations with my women friends — so ordinary, so natural, so guileless — that brought the contrast in our lives into focus like a blast of cold air when I least expected it.

There was the pain of absence, too. We were sitting in the living room of the spacious home my husband and I had built — every tile, every window, every plumbing fixture the result of our mutual decisions, before all the decisions became mine alone.

This small fireplace we had designed was open on three sides. If the logs were not placed exactly in the center, the house filled with smoke — as we found out the first time we lit it, moments before our guests were to arrive. Over time, we worked out how to lay the fire so the chimney would draw properly — the tight newspaper balls, just the right kind of kindling, just the right length of logs.

"Really? If you want a fire, you wait for him?"

She nodded, without a trace of guilt.

"Is this an ideological stance? You think there is something primal about men and fire?" I couldn't keep the edge out of my voice.

I knelt to the basket of newspapers so she wouldn't see my face.

"I guess I could if I had to. I've just never bothered to learn." She snuggled farther down in the chair and stretched her arms out wide.

I know. He's always there to do it for you. I heard her unspoken reality, so different from mine.

"I see."

Suddenly serious, she inspected her fingernails (with some embarrassment?) as I turned and fiercely began to make balls of newspaper, then selected the pieces of kindling. My hands trembled as I arranged the newspaper balls, the kindling and the short logs just so on the wrought iron grate. I lit the match.

All the things I wanted to say to her formed in my mind and stayed there. It wasn't her fault. Her husband was still alive. But…

Some day, it will happen to you! We don't get a warning! Don't take your time together for granted. Learn, learn everything you'll need to know now! Ask him! Light your fires together while you can!

"You're really good at that," she commented as the flames caught, and the welcome warmth reached us.

"Well, yes," I murmured, dusting off my hands on the back of my skirt. I sat next to her and smiled. "I've learned to light my own fires."

~Nancy G. Villalobos

37

The Empty Room

Even on the weakest days I get a little bit stronger.
~Sara Evans

I peeked through the front window, saw his familiar face and wondered when he'd become a stranger. He continued up the walk, past the river birch trees, and knocked on the door.

"I'm here for the furniture," he said, with defeat in his soft brown eyes. I glanced toward the pickup truck in the driveway. His buddy Richard gave an awkward half wave.

"Yeah. Uh... hi." I stroked my half-combed hair and pushed it behind my ear. I wondered if he missed me.

He stepped inside our former dream house — a refuge we'd designed and built shortly after the birth of our youngest, now in kindergarten.

"I'd like to take this stuff... this room of stuff." He motioned straight ahead toward the living room. "I think it'll fit into my new place."

"Yeah... Okay." I looked around slowly. "All of it?"

"Well, I need something to sit on. I need stuff. I have to live too, you know."

"Yeah, of course. That's fine."

As always with him, it happened fast. Out went the leather couch, the two chairs and the unusual coffee table shaped like a painter's palette that I had picked out a few years ago. He took the lamps, the books, the plants and the art off the wall. The last piece to go was a small Shona sculpture with a family of figures carved out of serpentine. It had been a Mother's Day gift.

After a few trips, the room was bare, except for a large area rug that stretched from one end to the other.

"I guess that's it for now," he said, wiping sweat from his forehead. "We can figure out the rest later."

I nodded and shut the door behind him. The unexpected echo sounded like ten doors closing.

With the kids at Grandma's, the house was strangely quiet. I stared at the empty room for a long while, thinking I should vacuum and maybe move a few things from other rooms in there. I thought about the decorating magazines lined up neatly in rows at the store. It was only two o'clock. I could pick up a magazine and maybe stop at a furniture outlet on the way home. Instead, I walked upstairs and slipped into my bed, pulling the covers over my head.

> *I realized that sometimes emptiness is just a wide, open space.*

The next morning, the sun streamed through the window and woke me. I still wore my yellow sweatshirt and ragged jeans with the hole in the knee.

I went downstairs and looked into the belly of my house. It was empty.

I needed to escape the emptiness for a while, so I started searching for distractions. First came the older guy, with the boyish grin, looking for a wife. At least that's what he implied on the way to the restaurant. By dessert, I learned his youngest would be heading to college soon, leaving an empty nest behind. Then came the busy investor, who dated to fill the space between days with his kids. And then the young divorcé, who still parked on the far left of his garage as if she'd be home soon.

I learned fairly quickly that dating wasn't going to do the trick. My focus shifted to other things, like my fledgling communications business.

One Saturday, I stumbled into the self-help aisle at Barnes & Noble; I would be a frequent visitor for the next six months. I dug out my old running shoes and took myself to the gym a few times a week. I started to hit tennis balls against my garage, began writing again and signed up for sailing lessons. Eventually, I learned how to go solo to the neighbors' cookouts.

One Sunday, my kids and I volunteered to serve dinner to the homeless across town. Later that spring, we planted a garden in front of a women's shelter.

During all this time, the empty room remained untouched.

One summer evening when my kids were with their dad, I turned on some music, thinking I would hear it in the kitchen. Instead, the song called to me from the empty room's built-in speakers.

I tiptoed in and sat on the edge of the rug. Soon, I drifted toward the middle of the room. I lay down, closed my eyes and spread my arms open. I surrendered to the song, "The Prayer" by Andrea Bocelli. He sang, *When we lose our way, Lead us to a place, Guide us with your grace, To a place where we'll be safe.*

The next day, I put my dinner on a wicker tray and met Bocelli in the empty room for a picnic.

The rug was surprisingly comfortable. I settled in and looked around. With everything stripped away, I was able to see the simple lines of the room, the high ceiling and tall windows. I glanced westward and noticed something in the far distance. I blinked and shook my head.

Is that a view of the lake? How did I miss that?

I couldn't help but giggle.

The sun inched toward the horizon, painting bright orange and pink streaks across the sky that seemed to dance across the top of the water. I felt myself drawn toward the sun like the day lilies in my garden.

There on the floor in the empty room, I ate and watched the stunning show of color. It was a brilliant celebration. Soon, the last speck of orange gave way to nightfall.

As the moon gently lit the room, I realized that sometimes emptiness is just a wide, open space. Space to breathe. And maybe a little space is exactly what I needed… to find myself.

About a year later, we moved from that house. I never did furnish the empty room. I had grown to appreciate it exactly as it was.

~Mindi Susman Ellis

38

Stepping Out

Dance for yourself. If someone understands, good.
If not, no matter. Go right on doing what interests you,
and do it until it stops interesting you.
~Louis Horst

Though it was only 6:30 a.m., Charles, the health club's informal early-morning deejay, was already working the CD player. As I dragged in, readying myself for my workout, "I Heard It Through the Grapevine" filled the room. Instantly, I perked up.

"Great music, Charles," I said, and swiveled my hips. Charles bopped over and took me in his arms for a quick spin. He was a great dancer, smooth and easy to follow, with just the right mixture of sassy rhythm and classy style. I could have danced all morning with him.

"You're good," he said when the song ended.

I grinned at the compliment and floated to the nearest treadmill. I love music and felt I could be an excellent dancer if only I had the right partner. But I had always fallen for the kind of intellectual guy who would rather make a move on the chessboard than the dance floor. Even my beloved partner Ron got an uncomfortable look when I mentioned any musical movement other than folk dancing. While I was happy to occasionally fit into a square or circle with seven other people and bounce around to Celtic music, I still fantasized about gliding onto the floor wearing an elegant black gown and being swept away by a suave man with a Fred Astaire style. In my fantasy, I followed him effortlessly, myself a vision of grace and glamour, gazing into his eyes, one with him and with the music.

And although this morning I was in a health club instead of in a ballroom, and I was wearing a T-shirt and sweats rather than a gown, I felt a portion of my fantasy had just been realized.

All day that dance stayed with me, and I wondered how I could bring more such moments into my life.

"Want to take dancing lessons?" I asked Ron that night at dinner.

"There's a Scandinavian folk dance class starting next month," he said.

"No, I mean swing or waltzing."

He paused and stared at his uneaten broccoli. "Well, if it's really important to you, I guess I could take a lesson."

Throughout the next week, I analyzed how important it was. I realized Ron was in an impossible situation: It would take him years of lessons to capture the élan, mastery and style of my imaginary dance partner.

Days later at the health club, I heard a different kind of music and noticed two women practicing line dancing steps. I stopped to watch, wondering if I could match the moves. They looked complicated but fun.

"Come practice with us next Tuesday," one of the women said, smiling warmly. "I'll teach you."

So, four days later, instead of dutifully walking two miles on the treadmill, I stood behind Pat and tried to learn the Funky Chicken and the Wobble. I stumbled and stepped on my own feet, missing the turns, unable to follow the constant "right" and "left" directions. At the end of the hour, my face was red with embarrassment and exertion.

But Pat reassured me. "You're doing great. Come again next Tuesday."

I felt as though I'd been given a blue ribbon. The dancing was exhilarating, and I returned the next week. Slowly, I caught on as Pat patiently repeated the Grapevine, Booty Shake, Cha Cha Cha, Right-Hand Turn, and Two-Step.

As we practiced the Cajun Bounce, people dropped by to watch, and Pat invited them to join us. But everyone demurred, saying, "It's too hard" or "I can't dance." As I practiced the song yet again, I felt proud I'd been willing to try something new. The steps were getting easier, and I thought I'd found a form Ron and I could do together. Since he loved circles and squares, perhaps he could happily move straight into lines.

After my sixth lesson, I told Ron, "You should come to the gym and join us. It's so much fun."

"Well, I will if it's important to you," he answered.

I pressed my lips together so I wouldn't blurt out my frustration. Why did I have to spell out again and again what I wanted? Why couldn't Ron just smile, take me in his arms and dance me across the living room?

During the next week, I asked myself, *How important is this?* But I couldn't come up with a concrete answer.

At my next lesson, we started on the movements for the Twist, and soon it was just me and the music. That's when I finally understood: I needed to take responsibility for my dance fantasies. Pat had shown me the way. As we swiveled around, counting our steps, I visualized myself on a dance floor, wearing my usual jeans, T-shirt and tennis shoes, happily Grapevining and Two-Stepping, part of a glowing group of strangers, all moving in sync. No longer did I yearn to be guided around an elegant dance floor; I was becoming my own perfect partner.

~Deborah Shouse

39

I Chose My Way

*Grief is like the ocean; it comes on waves ebbing and
flowing. Sometimes the water is calm, and sometimes it
is overwhelming. All we can do is learn to swim.*
~Vicki Harrison

When my husband died in a car accident—just
a few short months after my father's death from
cancer—my boss was very kind and told me to
take as much time as needed. There was no rush;
the position would be waiting for me when I was ready. But after a
month off, I headed back to the routine and for a reason to get out of
the house and back into society.

The chiropractic clinic where I worked was small. We knew our
patients well, and they knew us. They knew my dad had died and
expressed their condolences. They also knew about this latest loss,
and I braced myself, gathering every last ounce of courage I had to go
in and face the looks of pity, the averted eyes, the offer of hugs and
condolences. I mentally prepared myself for all of it so I could keep
my composure throughout the shift while keeping my sanity.

And so I sat at the reception desk, with a smile plastered on my
face, accepting the kind words and the hugs, and ignoring the averted
eyes.

But nothing could have prepared me for what happened halfway
through my shift. A patient came in and broke down in tears upon
seeing me. As she bent over, she choked out the words, "It's horrible.

My husband died sixteen years ago. It doesn't get any easier. It just gets worse."

My welcoming smile faded. The tears I'd been holding back were seconds away from breaking through the dam I had created. "Excuse me for a moment," I managed to say. I somehow made it the ten feet to the bathroom before the dam broke. I fell to the floor, sobbing uncontrollably.

A brave colleague followed me into the bathroom and held me while I sobbed. I will never forget her kindness and the courage it must have taken to follow me into the depths of my darkness. I will also never forget the intention I set at that very moment: *I will never make someone moving through grief feel even worse. In fact, I will be proof that life does get better.*

> **I've felt like a great success and an epic failure—all in the same day.**

Of course, I had no idea what I had signed up for with that intention, or how hard it would be. But, oddly enough, every time I really did want to quit, someone would say to me, "You know, I don't know how you do it. If I were you, I'd just lie down and die." or "Whenever I think my life is bad, I just think of you and realize it could be worse." My outward response was always a hint of a smile or a faint head nod. My inner response was, "I'll show you. One day, you will want to be me."

And so I kept going. I started doing things I told myself for years I couldn't do. Some were baby steps. Others were big leaps. Like run a marathon. And go to raw vegan culinary school, which everyone thought was really weird. I detoxed, meditated, journaled, and moved when staying in the home I had bought with my late husband felt too haunted.

"Are you over it? You must be over it by now," people would comment after a year out, two years, three. No, I wasn't "over it." I never would be. But I would not use my pain as a crutch. I was determined to transform it into something beautiful that would shine bright.

The tears continued to come, less frequently, more frequently, and then less again. When I thought I was safely out of the tight grip of grief, it would tap me on the shoulder. "Hey, don't forget about me.

I'm still here."

Mistakes were made along the way. Lots of them. Decisions were made out of fear or trying to fit myself into a formula for living the best life, doing what others thought was right.

Then I started heeding the call of my heart. Trusting in my own inner voice — that little voice that had piped up on the bathroom floor, telling me it would get better. Urging me to trust, have faith and believe.

Sometimes, I got sidetracked, thinking success was in numbers or money, never feeling enough. Later, I realized true success was feeling good and doing the things that brought me joy. Success was having real heart connections with the beautiful souls who walk this planet with me. Souls who were navigating their own path of pain through devastating deaths, divorces, loss of health or sense of self and were determined to create a new path.

I've felt like a great success and an epic failure — all in the same day. I learned that's the undulating path of life, and to roll with it with more ease.

It's been ten years now, and I'm still working on it. When I lose my way, I step back and look through the lens of gratitude to see true success. Every little step (like getting out of the house and gathering courage to face the world while holding my grief) is really a big win.

I'm grateful for every breath.

And every smile.

And every hug.

And every soul.

I made my choice. I stand before you today as proof that it can, and does, get better.

~Aimee DuFresne

40

Doing It for Bill

Travel and change of place impart
new vigor to the mind.
~Seneca

I decided something extraordinary for myself after my friend — who waited for me outside a posh restaurant on a busy Saturday night during a cold, winter spell — yelled at me through her tears that she had been freezing. I asked her why she didn't wait inside.

"I'm not going to go inside... *all by myself!*" Tammy said.

And that said it all. Being alone was motivation enough to freeze. Was I to be blamed for that? Nope! But I wondered what my own freezing point was.

I was determined to not "freeze" myself out from a concert, or a café, a dance club or bar, just because I was a party of one. I made a list of all the things I wanted to do but could not find anyone to do them with. It was longer than I had expected. Even accepting a house party invitation depended on who was going and what exact time a friend would arrive so we could enter together.

I wrote out that list, but I didn't do anything about it until I met Bill. He was the senior I was to visit one day as a volunteer at the senior center. I never volunteered for anything, but when this workplace initiative came up and many opted not to do it, I felt it was time. After all, how could one day out of 365 be scary when it was just visiting some old folks?

Bill had outlived his twin brother, parents and friends. He never married and had no children. Mentally astute, with a soft voice and dry humor, he was eighty-two years old. He was physically incapable of moving around unless he was in his wheelchair, which he called his convertible.

"I got to take her out," he would say. I thought he meant the same outdoors that everyone living outside the facility would experience, but he chuckled and said, "We aren't allowed to go outside unless all of us are going. That doesn't happen too often."

There were many like him, wheeling from one long corridor to another in their convertibles, and then pivoting to return and do it all over again. This was the only freedom Bill had now.

So, after he talked about his life, his youth, what life was like "behind bars," and music, movie and television legends like John Wayne and Clint Eastwood, he turned the light off himself and pointed it directly at me.

"What do you want to do that you always wanted to do but were too afraid?" he asked.

It was like he knew I had put that list together! Amazed, but willing to see where this conversation would go, I gave him my list. I never thought of it as a bucket list, although Bill said we were never too young or too old to make one. The "tiny stuff," he called it — like going to a movie alone on a weekend or drinking coffee in a café without having any cellphone, magazine, or book to read — seemed lame to him. But when I told him about the really big item on my list, he said something so profound and meaningful.

I told him that I had racked up four weeks of overtime from work, and there was no way I wanted to waste them cleaning house or doing errands. I could, though, book a trip to the "land of the rising sun" — a place I knew nothing about, including the culture, language, people, or places to go or stay. I just wanted to go to see how resourceful I was without a safety net and perhaps even to see if I enjoyed my own company.

"What's holding you back?" Bill asked.

I explained all the risks and dangers, and just when I tried to verbalize more reasons, Bill stopped me in a roar of excitement. He said, "If you can't do it for yourself, do it for me!"

Understand this: Bill was a stranger to me. I owed him nothing when I first met him, but maybe I did after a few hours together. He exchanged my time for his wisdom.

He spoke about how life at the home was spent doing the same thing every day. There were the same faces, the same rooms, the same noises, the same smells, and those same convertibles lined up to be driven down the same hallways that were his world's boundaries. Although he had accepted his fate, he assured me that if he had my legs, he would make a beeline to the front door and never look back to say goodbye. He would keep walking, and walking, and walking.

I gave him a kiss on my way out. I promised him that I would book that trip. In his parting words to me, he said that he would imagine Japan in March with the cherry blossom trees blooming, and me there. And that would be new scenery for him as he drove his convertible down the hallway.

Less than one month after meeting Bill, I booked my solo trip. I left for Japan during their cherry blossom season, and I found myself good company for a whole month's worth of memories. I took Bill with me in spirit and just kept walking.

~Wendy Ann Rich

41

Finding My Way Home

Home is a shelter from storms — all sorts of storms.
~William J. Bennett

My palms felt sweaty and cold, and I could not stop my legs from bouncing up and down. Clearly, I was nervous, but I was also excited as I sat across from my real estate agent in the title office, going over paperwork. After a few more signatures, I was going to be a home-owner. At twenty-five. It was one of the best days of my life, second only to becoming a CPA a few months prior. I always had a plan, and this house was definitely a part of that. I had wanted my own piece of the American Dream for as long as I could remember, and I was about to get it — in all its brick, seven-room, ranch-style glory.

The purchase was major in more ways than one. My birth mother had given me up for adoption when I was born. I was homeless and alone until I was adopted by a sweetheart of a woman who ran a successful business but couldn't have children of her own. Six years later, she was on her way to a work meeting when her car slid on some ice, hit a retaining wall, and went airborne before landing off the side of a steep embankment. She lingered for about a week in intensive care before she passed away. I didn't even get to say goodbye. And just like that, I was orphaned. I was alone. And homeless. Again.

A couple of weeks later, I went to live in Mississippi. The courts appointed my adoptive mother's sister as my legal guardian. She made it clear that she was only providing somewhere for me to stay until I graduated high school as dictated by the courts. The next ten years were miserable. A few months before my high school graduation, she told me that I should stop applying to colleges because I needed a job so I could afford a place to live. She couldn't (or wouldn't) take care of me on her fixed income after my Social Security checks stopped. A week before my graduation, she reminded me again that I had to leave her house after I graduated since her guardianship would be terminated. I graduated and found myself alone. And homeless. Again.

I knew that day was coming, and I had planned for it by joining the Army Reserve in the fall of 1987 before my high school graduation. After what happened with my adoptive mother and the tragic, impoverished life I had been forced to live in a town that was economically segregated, I was never going to be caught out there again without a plan. The day after my graduation, I left for basic training at Fort Dix, New Jersey. I am not sure I truly understood the oath I took to give my life for my country, but I certainly understood that I would have room and board. I had also received a full academic scholarship to my college of choice, and they'd agreed to hold it for me until I arrived in the spring.

> *I had a home. No one was going to put me up for adoption and make me leave it.*

I ended up meeting my biological family that summer. But, more importantly, I met a cousin who lived in the same city as my college. She and her family welcomed me with open arms. She let me live with them when school was out during the year and every summer until I graduated. While my college classmates were partying and having a good time, I was working multiple part-time jobs and preparing myself for life after college in the real world. I knew I didn't have a safety net, so I couldn't fail. I decided on a career as a CPA because I could make enough money to support myself.

After I signed the last of the paperwork, the title officer happily gave me the keys to my beautiful new home. Luckily, there were no speed traps between the title office and my new place because I don't even think I stopped at any traffic lights getting to Lacewood Cove. I even loved my new street name. I pulled into the driveway and quickly hopped out of my car. I sprinted to the door and could barely turn the key because my hands were shaking so badly. I ran inside just in case it was a dream, and I woke up. I collapsed right there on the freshly carpeted floor of the bare living room and cried. I bawled my eyes out for what seemed like thirty minutes.

I stopped crying long enough to look at the four walls of the room I was in, and it all finally sank in. I had a home. No one was going to put me up for adoption and make me leave it. No one was going to die and force me out of it. No one was going to treat me badly and tell me to leave it. In that moment, I had never felt so empowered. I had felt so lost when my adoptive mother died. Suffering through years of physical violence, I had worked hard to become the person I was meant to be. And as I looked around that bare room that day, I knew I had finally found my way. Home.

~Sheila Taylor-Clark

Mr. 99.89%

*I wanted to be an independent woman, a woman who
could pay for her bills, a woman who could run her
own life — and I became that woman.*
~Diane von Furstenberg

There it was in black and white: "Subject A is NOT ruled out as the father of subject B, with 99.89% certainty." It was all so clinical yet the undeniable validation I had been seeking for more than three years. The man I had been married to and shared the promise of a future with was proven to be the biological father of our son. As I held that single sheet of paper, I was consumed with vindication and anger, but mostly a profound sense of sadness for a dream deferred.

When I first received the e-mail from my husband informing me he was "staying in the U.K.," my son Christian had just turned nine months old, and his father had seen him a total of four weeks since his birth. Essentially, he was a stranger to him, so Christian wouldn't feel the void. On the other hand, this news floored me and completely turned my world upside-down. It was not so much an emotional blow — I have always been very handy at compartmentalizing the practical aspects from the more cerebral ones. It was more about coming to grips with the fact that all my expectations of our life as a family together, coupled with the many sacrifices I had made professionally and personally during the past decade, had been shattered by two short sentences emanating from a twelve-inch computer screen.

My husband and I met while I was living in London, employed as the marketing director for his father's company. For the first few years, we had nothing more than a cordial professional relationship. In fact, we probably had two non-work-related interactions during that initial period. Gradually, we developed a friendship, followed by a romance and marriage. We were able to keep it hidden from our colleagues. Our family members were aware of our relationship, but we were able to keep our colleagues out of the loop — that is, until that damn stick turned blue. It was not the first time a blue stick would impact my life.

We had already been married for almost two years before I became pregnant. It was unplanned and unexpected. Nonetheless, after the shock wore off, I became extremely excited at the prospect of impending motherhood and the new journey my husband and I would take.

The choice to relocate and raise our child in the States was mutual. The better quality of life, access to my family and the fact that my husband's company wanted to expand to the U.S. market were all factors in our final decision. Therefore, when I moved back to Philadelphia in order to prepare for Christian's birth, there was no hint that life would be less than idyllic. I was seven months pregnant at that point, and my husband would spend the next year dividing his time between countries until we were settled.

After our son was born, my husband was present for about a week and then felt compelled to "get back to work." To be honest, it was fine with me. He was reacting to what I assumed were typical first-time father fears, so I attributed his indifference to that. He showed no real interest in feedings, diapering or even holding our son. I spent the next few months living with my mother. I looked at houses to buy, researched commercial properties and offices for the business, and reveled in being a mommy, sleepless nights and all. Soon after I gave birth, I became ill. No one could conclusively come up with a diagnosis, so I was in and out of doctors' appointments on a regular basis. Later, we would discover I had multiple sclerosis.

My husband eventually travelled to the U.S. for an extended period to sort out his residency visa. Rather than the logical decision to live with Christian and me at my mom's, he opted to rent a place in the city. He argued it was easier for him as he had access to the train to New York for business. Again, it all seemed rational, and with everything else going on, I did not have time to be more introspective about his snub.

My daily existence remained the same, filled with hospital visits and taking care of my infant son. Understandably, my focus was not entirely on my husband, and he made it perfectly clear he was not happy. He would make the occasional visit out to my mom's house, but never stay the night. He argued he did not want to impose — *on his wife and son?* The cracks were starting to show, but I still had no clue as to his real intentions.

A few months shy of our son's first birthday, my husband had to return to London for personal reasons. He was advised against it for fear of compromising his visa status. He went anyway.

Precisely a week later, I opened that e-mail from him. It said simply, "Lucy, I have decided to stay in the U.K. This just isn't what I expected it to be." I remember turning my computer on and off about five times, expecting the words to change. The lack of sleep was causing my mind to play tricks on me, but each time the result was the same. My husband had cowardly informed me he wanted out. We had been abandoned. All couples go through hiccups in a relationship, particularly during moments of great change, but mature individuals push through it together.

Before people become parents, they tend to think more viscerally. They can be vulnerable and disappointed by others, but it is a manageable discomfort. When they add a child into the equation, that pain becomes profoundly overwhelming. I once was told that having a child means allowing our hearts to exist outside our bodies. Before I had Christian, it was merely a cliché. But now every breath he takes is my own. Every tear he sheds, every laugh and every thought is an extension of who I am. Therefore, he is my ultimate priority.

After a year of trying fruitlessly to get my husband to communicate, I realized I had to go through the courts. He offered no support nor showed any interest in Christian or me. He feigned sudden poverty despite living in his parents' $5 million Kensington home. Then, when that tactic failed, he said he doubted he was the father and demanded a DNA test.

At first, I refused. I was not going to subject Christian to that to satisfy his father's newfound neurosis. It was ironic that during the entire marriage, the nine-month pregnancy and the first year of Christian's life, there was never a question of my fidelity. Conveniently, it was only when asked for child support that I suddenly became "get-lucky-with-Lucy" in his eyes. Seriously, we had worked together and lived together. When was this supposed clandestine moment to have taken place? During those five minutes we were apart at the grocery store? While he was in the organic-food aisle, and I was choosing between Oreos and Chips Ahoy? Finally, against legal advice — apparently, by law, the husband in a married relationship is automatically recognized as being responsible — I relented.

When the results came back, all I could think of was that old Ivory Soap slogan: "99 44/100% Pure." In our scenario, however, the subject was far from pure: My husband was 99 and 89/100% dishonorable.

So, I have essentially had to start over, and despite a court order, we still receive no support. But I am more than okay. I run a consulting business now that helps people reinvent themselves after life has thrown them a curveball. It turns out that Christian and I are 100% better off without Mr. 99.89% in our lives.

~Lucy Alexander

Adventure for One, Please

You have to leave the city of your comfort and go into
the wilderness of your intuition. What you'll discover
will be wonderful. What you'll discover is yourself.
~Alan Alda

I was ready to embark on a new adventure. Italy and Greece had been haunting my travel dreams for several years. I'd gasped at pictures, listened enviously to other people's personal stories and become mesmerized by countless videos. I was ready to make this lifelong dream a reality.

As I began to map out this amazing trip, I thought about who could accompany me. My good friend? No, she had vacations planned already. My sisters? No, they weren't as passionate about traveling as I was. As I continued to cross people off my list, I found that I was left with just one option: I'd go by myself.

Solo travel wasn't a foreign concept to me, but I had never experienced it on this scale. I had never taken an international flight before, and although I was quickly becoming excited about everything I had been planning, I didn't know if I could pull off such an itinerary by myself. But as I continued to plan the trip, I realized that this would provide a great opportunity for me to step out of my shell. My quiet and introverted personality could do with a little social experiment. The plans were non-stop — hotel bookings in Rome, Venice and Milan, train adventures throughout Italy, tours that included stops at all the key monuments and restaurant reservations for this party of one. As daunting as the logistics were, they kept me excited as the countdown went from months to weeks and then days.

When the sun finally rose on the day my adventure was to start, I suddenly became a little scared. I'd been counting down for weeks to get to this day and now that it was here, I was wondering if I had made a mistake. Could I really do this on my own? Despite my reservations, I made my way to the airport. Once I settled into my overnight flight, I gave myself a much-needed pep talk.

"Deon, what are you nervous about? So you've never taken an international flight before — so what? So you've never been to this part of the world before — so what? So you didn't think you'd be doing your bucket list trip alone — so what? You wanted this, and you made it happen.

My quiet and introverted personality could do with a little social experiment.

Be proud of that and understand you are doing something that a lot of women would never do. Smile and know that you've got this, and you'll be okay."

I gave myself a little grin, buckled in and landed in Rome with a completely different feeling.

It's hard to describe what I felt as I drove through the streets. I was in a partial state of shock that I had finally made it. I sat in silence with other passengers as we gazed out the window and took in how Rome does morning rush hour. Check-in at my hotel was a breeze, and I spent the next two days traveling from site to site. The Colosseum, Trevi Fountain, the Vatican and the Sistine Chapel were wonders to behold.

My day spent in Venice was special. After a torrential downpour caused people to find dry surroundings, I made my way to a pizzeria in Piazza San Marco. As I patiently waited for my order to arrive, I made light conversation with a woman who was sitting nearby. Once I confirmed I was traveling alone, she gave me the biggest smile and commended me for being brave enough to take on such an ambitious trip on my own. She then courageously shared her painful story about becoming a widow two years earlier and how she and her husband had dreamed of visiting Italy. She said although she was traveling alone, his spirit was the best company, and the location was providing the ideal comfort. Hearing her story confirmed to me that women travel solo for a variety of different reasons, and I had made the best decision to take this adventure on my own.

The remainder of my trip was truly outstanding. Along with visiting Milan, Florence and Lake Como, I also had the pleasure of exploring Greece. I walked through the white-washed buildings in Santorini, took in the magnitude of the Parthenon in Athens, visited the beautiful beaches in Mykonos and admired the amazing views in Corfu. But I wasn't done there. I also fell in love with Montenegro, spent quality time in Croatia and made a stop in Switzerland.

The freedom of being on my own was amazing. There was no better feeling than making a spur-of-the-moment decision knowing it would only affect me. I didn't have to worry about pleasing anybody because I was in control of what I did each and every step of the way. I recount the experience of sipping a glass of wine while staring high up at the Duomo in Florence, thinking that I had truly outdone myself.

I flew home realizing that this was an experience that every woman should have — whether it be a staycation in her local city, a road trip to a nearby destination, or a backpacking adventure across the world. Every woman should know what it feels like to explore all this amazing earth has to offer on her own.

To this day, when people ask me about that magical trip, an indescribable presence still comes over me. The adventure was so joyous that a second trip is in the works, and I'll be going with the best company of all — me, myself and I.

~Deon Toban

She Flies with Her Own Wings

Keep up your faith to go high and fly, even after
so many pains and sorrow. You can turn from a
caterpillar to a butterfly. Life gives you a
second change: a call to grow.
~Ana Claudia Antunes

For many years, he held her back
He told her not to dream
He was like a river wild
She like a gentle stream
She craved love and happiness
But kept it all inside
Spent her days in quiet fear
Tethered by his side
She watched the sky with wishful eyes
And dreamed of when she'd fly
Cried herself to sleep at night
As life just passed her by
Caged by life's own cruelty
She was captured in his grasp
While he raised his hands in anger
Hers in prayer she clasped
One day her prayers were answered

For she left him far behind
Released the chains of hurt and hate
And all the ties that bind
Now she flies with her own wings
In skies pearlescent white
Loosed from the bounds of all her fears
She soars in graceful flight
Where she lands will still be seen
The world's an open slate
She'll write a story all her own
For now she holds her fate
At last she's free, no longer caged
And no matter where she'll roam
Those injured wings, now greatly healed
Will guide her safely home

~Ruth Kephart

The Empowered Woman

I Stepped Outside My Comfort Zone

45

Light My Way

*One of the most important things we adults can do for
young children is to model the kind of person
we would like them to be.*
~Carol B. Hillman

I was sitting at the kitchen table squinting to see the small print. The overhead fluorescent light was broken, and I was awaiting the return of my husband from church to fix its tubular bulb.

My daughter, Hope, came into the kitchen and asked what I was doing. She was sick, and we had stayed home from church for her to rest. I explained I was having a hard time reading because the light was out. Hope asked me why I didn't just go ahead and change it. I explained it was a tubular bulb, and I was just going to let Dad fix it later.

She put her hands on her ten-year-old hips and said, "I am so disappointed in you. You are setting such a bad example for me. Do you want me to grow up to be a helpless woman, waiting around for a man to come and rescue me? I'm just so disappointed."

Sounding just like her mother, Hope shook her head and coughed her way back down the hall to her room.

She was right. I was setting a poor example, a precedent for dependency, a road map for my daughter to not try to take responsibility for her life and just wait for a man to come and fix up everything. There

I sat in a dark room because I was unwilling to learn a new skill and give myself light. Why in the world was I choosing darkness?

I went to the garage, found the replacement bulb, read the directions, stood on the kitchen table and changed the light bulb.

Voilà! Let there be light!

I called Hope back into the kitchen where I sat reading the newspaper without squinting, right there under a bright new light.

She was so proud of me and could hardly wait until her dad came home to show him.

For years, I had been telling my daughters to be strong and independent, that girls could do everything boys could. But my words were pale in comparison to my actions… until the light finally shone down on me!

~Malinda Dunlap Fillingim

46

Red Lipstick

When in doubt wear red.
~Bill Blass

olling around in the bottom of my make-up drawer is a tube of red lipstick. I bought it on a whim — hiding it between some mascara and a bottle of concealer like it was something dirty. Shame pinkened my cheeks. The clerk smiled politely when she swiped it across the scanner. I know she was thinking I would never wear it, so why was I buying it?

I looked away and grabbed a tube of lotion. "Do you like this brand? I'm never sure which kind to buy. I have super sensitive skin, and scented lotions sometimes set it off," I said.

Distract.

Distract.

Distract.

She looked at me with a measuring gaze. "Sure, I think that one's nice. I haven't heard much about its sensitivity to skin, but that one there," she pointed to another tube, "that one is gingerbread, and those holiday scents are to die for."

"Fantastic," I lied. "I'll take one." I gave it to my cousin as a Christmas gift. She always liked that kind of stuff. After paying for my items, I escaped to the safety of my car. I opened the bag, and sitting there was the fresh tube of red lipstick. Cellophane protected it from the rest of the world.

Protected me from it. From the repercussions of wearing something so scandalous.

Red always feels dangerous.

Beautiful.

Sexy.

Red always feels like the things I am not.

Things I'll never be.

Like I don't deserve to wear it.

I needed new glasses. Buying them online made avoiding salesclerk judgment that much easier. I still couldn't shuck my own judgments, so I bought two pair. The first was black rimmed.

Simple.

Normal.

Me.

The second, red.

Adventurous.

Whimsical.

Everything I want to be.

The day they came in the mail was both exhilarating and terrifying. I hid them away from the world. Away from judgment. Alone, I slipped on the red pair. I let the strange new image in the mirror wash over me. *Who is this girl, the one with the red glasses?*

I don't know her.

But I want to.

The first person who saw me laughed—a deep belly laugh, the kind that brings tears to the eyes and makes the face hurt. "What are you wearing? Oh, my god, please tell me that's a joke."

"What? These?" I said, pulling the red glasses off my face.

More laughter. "Oh, that's too funny. Oh god, you're making me smear my mascara. Is that like a gag pair? You're not going to wear them, are you?"

I walked away, my insides pushing me to run instead—to hide and never show my face again. I slipped off the red pair and put on the black ones. I blotted my eyes.

I will not cry.

I will not cry.

I will not cry.

"Oh, that's better. Those are cute. Those are you."

I touched my black glasses and tried not to cringe. When she was gone, I took off the black ones and slipped on the red pair.

They're bold. They're beautiful.

They make me feel bold and beautiful.

Before I could change my mind, I grabbed my car keys and drove into town, where I was forced to wear them until I'd finished my shopping.

"Those are cute. I love them!"

"Have you always worn glasses? I never noticed."

"I've been wanting a pair just like them. Where did you buy them?"

Bombarded for the next several days, I continued to wear them until they became part of my face. Part my personality. Part of me.

I am the girl in the red glasses.

Rolling around in the bottom of my make-up drawer is a tube of red lipstick. I think about it from time to time — like an old friend I haven't seen or heard from in a while. The only times we've talked were in secret. I paint my lips the color of whimsy and stare at the girl in the mirror. She's someone I dream of being.

She's strong.

She walks with her shoulders back, unafraid of the world at her feet.

She doesn't feel like me yet.

I grab my car keys and drive into town. Before anyone can stop me. I force myself to wear it all day. Maybe then, she will become a part of me, too. I am the girl with the red lipstick.

~Miranda Boyer

47

The Question

When you realize you want to spend the rest
of your life with somebody, you want the rest
of your life to start as soon as possible.
~ From the movie When Harry Met Sally

The year was 1988. My boyfriend and I had known each other more than two years. We'd even met each other's parents. It was the summer after we finished grad school. Chris and I had mentioned marriage a few times, but I had said honestly I wasn't ready. His friends advised him that if I didn't want to marry him that he should move on. But still he waited.

It is odd to realize that a misdialed (or perhaps crank) phone call set our lives down their current path. On a crowded Friday afternoon, I struggled through rush hour to dinner at my parents' house. Before leaving, I had called my parents to tell them I was on my way. This was something I never did. I tried to avoid road rage as traffic crawled along.

Everything turned upside-down when I arrived at the house. Hesitantly, my parents gave me the news. Chris's mother had called them shortly after I had. She had received a call informing her that her son and his girlfriend had been killed in a car crash.

I sat, stunned. Chris was at work, which was why he hadn't come with me. Maybe he'd had to drive somewhere. Maybe a co-worker was with him. It made no sense. I sobbed as I realized that this was the man I wanted to spend the rest of my life with.

Before I could get my own thinking together enough to call him at work just to check, his mother called us. She had finally been in touch with him. It was a false alarm. Relief flooded through me. It didn't matter how upset Chris was that his mother had yelled at him as if it were his fault she'd believed the story of an unknown caller. I was just glad that he was still around.

And then it occurred to me that Chris had tested the waters several times to see if I would accept if he proposed. My answers had not been encouraging, but it meant that he wanted to marry me and was willing to wait around.

I tried bringing it up again to let him know I was ready to say "yes," but I just couldn't figure out how. Tact had never been one of my fortes. He was completely unhelpful in all of this. He didn't understand because all through that fateful afternoon, he'd been hard at work at his office. Nothing earthshattering had happened.

The only way we were ever going to get engaged was if I turned the tables and proposed to him. To make sure he knew I was serious, I decided to get a ring. Trying to figure out what kind of ring to give a guy while I proposed was nearly impossible. There were no guidelines, no tradition. I remembered he liked onyx and ordered a custom ring.

Finally, ring in hand, I had to decide the how and when. Chris was not a romantic. I didn't want to set something up and have him think I was expecting a proposal. Once I had that ring, I was the one who was going to do the proposing. I envisioned returning to the restaurant of our first date, but realized that I didn't want to ask him in public.

Unable to stand the stress and suspense any longer, I nervously pulled out the box with the ring one evening while I was at his place, still unsure of exactly what I was going to say.

"Yes," he said, seeing the box.

"I didn't even ask you anything."

He put on the ring. "Yes, I'll marry you." It was as if he'd been waiting all this time for me to pop the question.

A short time later, he got me an engagement ring — I actually got to pick it out. We set a date, and everything else followed all of those typical wedding traditions. Just because we found our way to the path of engagement and married life a little differently didn't mean that we couldn't hope for a happily ever after, just like everyone else.

~D.B. Zane

48

Have Fun. Be Silly. Dance Crazy.

*What the new year brings to you will depend a great
deal on what you bring to the new year.*
~Vern McLellan

I was a serial New Year's resoluter. I'd show up at the gym each year on January 1st with a newfound enthusiasm to tone up and shed the pounds. And then I would quit. Every year. It was an endless cycle that lasted most of my adult life — post-undergrad through my late twenties — until the year of my thirtieth trip around the sun.

After an impromptu move to a new city on my thirtieth birthday, I joined a nearby gym. It was July, not even New Year's, but this time I meant it!

I'd always wanted to join the Zumba classes at my previous gyms. I would hear the music from the main floor and dream about sneaking into the back of the class to let loose. I'd press "Play" at home and, in my twenties, I even participated in filming a dance fitness DVD. All of this led to obtaining a Zumba teaching certification. But there was no way I was going to walk into a dance class. Everyone in the classes always looked like professional background dancers — smooth, fluid, and on the beat. Certainly, most were nowhere near my own size — well over 200 pounds and 5'9". And if they were, they stood awkwardly in the back of the room as if they wanted to remain invisible.

Just a few weeks after joining the gym, I thought long and hard about my reticence. The fate of my commitment to this new gym relied on mustering up the courage to take the Zumba class — and that courage really paid off. Not only did I find the strength to take the class, but I knocked down an existing no-new-friends wall in order to connect with four other amazing women (resolutioners who found love in dancing, too). We were front-row Zumba fanatics.

The four of us were regulars. Accountability partners. Friends. Each week, we texted each other and made sure we were en route to our favorite weeknight dance party. All of us, unique in our own rights, let down our hair and danced like there was no tomorrow. Personally, I was really proud of myself for finally having a regular routine. Almost a year later, I was still holding strong.

> *I'd never seen (in the flesh) an instructor who was a size 16.*

After seven months, our Zumba instructor quit without notice. Apparently, she left to open a dance studio in her hometown. The fitness manager alerted our class that Zumba would be cancelled indefinitely until she could find a replacement, which could take a few months. A few months with no classes?

Knowing that I had a certification collecting dust, I told my dance crew in jest that I'd be willing to teach the class so we could continue our weeknight parties. "We can't wait a few months!" I joked, but the ladies were serious in their support for me teaching the class. *Me? Teach the class?* Yes, I had the certification, but was I ready to actually teach an entire class? *I don't look like a fitness instructor. Will anyone even come to class?*

Reluctantly, and with convincing from my tribe, I submitted an application to the manager. She'll probably never admit it, but in response to my application, her eyes said, "Are you sure you're applying to be the instructor?" But the words that came from her mouth were, "Great, Tonya. I've scheduled an audition for you next Tuesday. By the way, you'll be auditioning in front of a live class."

I walked into my audition with confidence in the routine, but I still wasn't confident about my physical appearance. I'd never seen (in the flesh) an instructor who was a size 16. I loved to move my body to music, but I had a loose tummy and thighs that jiggled. Against my better judgment, I wore Spanx underneath and all-black compression leggings—an attempt to appear a smaller size. I was slightly discouraged when I heard a woman whisper from the back of the class, "Is she teaching the class today?"

The manager handed me a headset and turned on the music, but no one was prepared for what happened next. I froze. Not because I was nervous, but because I couldn't breathe from all the shapewear I had on. "Can I have a minute?" I ran into the bathroom where I stripped off all the uncomfortable clothes. The little voice—the same one that consistently popped up during resolution time—whispered again, "Be the exception to the rule this year. Just have fun, be silly, and dance like crazy."

Jiggly thighs and all, I went back into that room and showed the manager (and the class) why she couldn't pass up the opportunity to hire me as a Zumba instructor. I knew there were other women who felt like I once did—too afraid to walk into a fitness class because of insecurities or feeling too shy to dance their pain away. By teaching the class, I could show women how to have fun during the process of getting fit, and I'd be able to give an hour of hope to someone who needed it. I'd not only empower other women, but I'd be able to fuel my own confidence.

Needless to say, I got the Zumba instructor job on the spot. The same woman who was hesitant about attending class would now be teaching others. Strong, influential, and leaving it all on the dance floor. Now that's a resolution to be proud of.

~Tonya Abari

49

More than Coincidence

A friend may be waiting behind a stranger's face.
~Maya Angelou, Letter to My Daughter

bjectively, it was a beautiful Saturday morning in Colorado. The sun was shining, the air was crisp — a perfect day for an adventure. My mood, however, was dismal as I was limping down the side of the highway holding out my hitchhiker thumb. I whimpered in pain every time I put weight on my left foot, and I was choking back tears, trying not to look pitiful. I was carrying a thirty-pound backpack with three liters of water, a week's worth of ramen and oatmeal, and two months of camping supplies. I was 1500 miles from home, and I had never felt more alone. Twenty-five miles and two days into my attempted through-hike of the Colorado Trail, I was injured and panicking.

A few cars passed carrying mountain bikes while their drivers sheepishly avoided eye contact. Eventually, a red Jeep stopped beside me. I noticed a firefighter license plate and reasoned that axe murderers probably don't fight fires in their spare time… right? I put on my brave face as the driver, a middle-aged man with a goatee, rolled down his window and asked what I needed. My voice cracked slightly as I asked if he knew where the nearest urgent care was.

"Not that way," he said, pointing in the direction I had been heading. My heart sank. "But Woodland Park is about twenty miles that way," he nodded in the opposite direction. I briefly explained my circumstances and my injury. He paused for a moment, contemplating. "Get in."

Almost immediately upon throwing my pack into the trunk and plopping my body into the passenger seat, my intuition told me I had nothing to fear from this man. He told me his name was Chris, offered me a phone charger, and wasted very little time with small talk.

"Forgive me if I'm intruding, but I have to ask: Aren't you scared? I mean, you're alone, you're a woman, you're small, and you're injured!" I took a deep breath and tried to explain my theory on female-alone-in-the-woods anxiety.

"Yes, I was a little nervous when you pulled up, but I live my life choosing to see the best in people. Maybe I'm naïve, but I believe if you treat people as if they are good and expect them to treat you with kindness, that's usually how they will respond."

He looked surprised. "That's not naïve; that's brave." He explained his worldview from his background of firefighting and law enforcement. "I've seen a lot of bad things happen, and because of that I never leave the house without a gun. I don't want to scare you, but there's a gun underneath your backpack right now. I was on my way to the shooting range when I picked you up."

Forty minutes later, we arrived in town and pulled up to the health clinic just as it was opening. In the parking lot, Chris hesitated. He explained he didn't want to just drive away and leave me stranded, but he also didn't want to make me uncomfortable by waiting for me.

"To be honest, it scares me to think about who might pick you up if I don't take you back to the trailhead." I shoved my ego aside and accepted his kindness.

Much to my relief, X-rays determined I was merely experiencing plantar fasciitis — an inflammation of the tissue connecting my muscles and bones that could be easily alleviated with a shoe insert. Hallelujah! All that panicking for nothing!

After a quick trip to Walgreens and a brief "Hi, Mom, I'm fine" phone call, Chris and I were on the road again. The time passed quickly; our conversation was effortless and interesting. In addition to being grateful for his help, I enjoyed his company, and I think he felt the same. As we neared the trail, I was feeling energized and much more optimistic than I had been when Chris had found me a few hours earlier. I offered him gas money, feeling guilty for occupying his entire morning. He refused, saying the only thing he wanted in return was for me to let him know when I had finished the trail. I agreed, but still felt indebted.

"Well, I don't know if you believe in karma, but I hope the next time you need help, someone is there for you," I said. I thanked him for the 547th time, and we parted ways.

Fast-forward exactly a week later. I was hiking up the ski slopes of Breckenridge, uttering curse words and appreciating the invention of chair lifts. As I reached the summit, I noticed a man on a mountain bike approaching. I waved hello politely, and he stopped abruptly.

"Oh, my god, I cannot believe I found you." My heart rate increased as I tried to recognize his voice... his goatee...

"Chris?" I was unsure whether to feel excited or fearful. He stuttered, and his eyes filled with tears.

"I have never been a religious man, but I've been thanking God for you every day since I met you." I felt goose bumps creep across my skin as Chris described the day after he had helped me. He had been riding his bike when he crashed face-first into a tree. He pulled his lips apart to show me that his gums were still bloody, and most of his teeth were missing. Apparently, a random through-hiker had stopped to splash water on Chris's face and then walked three miles out of his way to drag Chris and his bike back to the highway to help him call an ambulance.

"I've been remembering the last words you said to me when you got out of my car," Chris said. "I truly believe it's because of you that man was there to help me."

Chris asked if he could descend the mountain with me, and I happily agreed, grateful for some company. I asked why he was so shocked by the help he received after his accident. Yes, it seemed more than coincidental that a hiker had gone out of his way so dramatically, but surely someone would've helped him, right?

| **I Stepped Outside My Comfort Zone**

"Yes, or someone could've robbed me blind and left me for dead!" I was fascinated by this fundamental difference in our worldviews. We became engrossed in conversation for several hours until we reached his car. Before we parted ways, Chris turned to me and said, "Sarah, I feel like I'm the one indebted to you now. You're at least twenty years younger than me, but I feel like I've been talking to someone twice my age. I've never met anyone who has impacted me so strongly in such a short amount of time. You've truly inspired me to be a better person."

The weight of this interaction didn't sink in until we parted ways, and I continued hiking. I realized if a total stranger could think I was awesome, there was absolutely no reason for me to continue doubting myself — no reason to shrink and downplay my strengths. In a society that encourages and profits from our fear, bravery is an act of rebellion. An empowered woman isn't fearless; she chooses authenticity and connection *in spite* of her fear.

~Sarah James

50

No More Standing on the Sidelines

Live life with no excuses, travel with no regret.
~Oscar Wilde

"How about Alaska?" my husband asked as he filled our mugs. Oh wonderful! They'd want to climb every mountain and search out brown bears in their natural habitat. Another vacation where I would get to watch everyone else have fun.

It was a long overdue trip we had promised to take with his father and sister. Saying "yes, one day we will" was easy when we first said it so long ago. Secretly, I'd hoped the day would never come. I loved them to bits, but I just didn't share their passion for the rugged outdoors. Bruce's family had camped in every state park between California and New York. They were adventurous travelers, hiking and sleeping in tents on the cold, dirty, bug-infested ground. I shuddered at the thought.

I took a sip of coffee as Bruce slid a glossy brochure across the table. Reluctantly, I picked it up. A cruise to Alaska? The ship was elegant with wide, marble staircases, glass elevators, luxurious staterooms, and plenty of amenities. I could just imagine the wonderful spa treatments, fine dining, and moonlit strolls around the deck. At last, a vacation I could enjoy! But I found it hard to believe his family was willing to spend seven days aboard this floating paradise.

I waited for him to throw his head back, laugh and say, "Just kidding." He probably wanted to rent a motorhome and travel hours to some awful campground, miles from any form of civilization where they could forage and fish and cook over a campfire. But he remained silent as I turned the pages, marveling at majestic snow-capped mountains, dazzling blue waters, and the regal glaciers Alaska is famous for.

"Okay," my eyes narrowed as I folded my arms across my chest, "what's the catch?"

"There is no catch," he said, hesitantly. "Except…"

"I knew it!" I slapped the table. "Except what?" My lips drew together in a thin line as I waited for him to explain.

"Except for the excursions." He turned to the computer where his fingers tapped across the keyboard. "Look at this."

ZIPLINE THE RAINFOREST OF ALASKA! flashed across the monitor. I watched in horror as throngs of tourists made their way high up into the canopy of trees. People below looked like ants, and the river like a strand of spaghetti. My stomach grew queasy. I could barely handle a Ferris wheel. One by one, each person was strapped into a harness where they hung suspended over a great chasm, and then hurtled across at lightning speed.

> *I was tired of standing on the sidelines as Bruce and the kids rode every roller coaster.*

"You've got to be kidding me!" I snapped. "I'll wait back on the ship! I can find plenty to do that's safer than that."

"C'mon, Sue. I want you to zipline with me. Just this one excursion, that's all. I won't ask you to do anything else. Please, honey?" He fixed me with his sad, puppy-dog eyes.

"Bruce, don't look at me that way. You know I can't do that! It looks dangerous! What if the cable snaps?" I couldn't watch another minute. I went to rinse my cup, put on a fresh pot, and start breakfast.

"It's not dangerous at all! I researched it. I can't find even one accident." He got up and put his arms around me. "Come on, honey. Please. Dad and Christine said they would go, but it won't be the same without you."

I wriggled out of his bear hug and started cracking eggs like crazy, whisking them into a froth. I hated saying no to him, and even more I hated the fear that held me back. I was tired of standing on the sidelines as Bruce and the kids rode every roller coaster in the amusement park. I felt left behind as I shot video from the safety of the beach as the family jetted by on water skis, a huge wake trailing foam behind them. And forget about parachuting from an airplane. I was so scared, I could barely hold the camera. My stomach rolled just remembering the bunch of them somersaulting in the blue sky, with puffy white clouds behind them.

Bruce, his family, and the kids always had a blast while I watched. I was tired of being a tag-along, the one too frightened to do anything. Maybe it was time for that to change. My heart clanged in my chest just to consider the possibility of ziplining, but at the same time, there was a tiny seed of hope that maybe, just maybe, I could do this thing. If only…

And that is how I found myself shivering on a crude wooden platform in the middle of an Alaskan rainforest higher than I had ever been. An eagle flew by. That's how high up I was.

I trembled as the tour guide clamped a helmet on my head and tightened the strap. "Okay, let's get you settled in the harness," he said. My body felt leaden as he strapped me in. My eyebrows drew together in fierce concentration as he told us how to use the hand brake.

"Relax," he encouraged. "No worries." Then he gave me a shove that sent me zooming across the broad expanse.

As I hurtled through the air, the wind whistled. I opened my scrunched-up eyes and was captivated by the breathtaking view of mountain, sky and river. I let go of a scream that rang out and resounded in my clunky helmet. I relaxed my grip on the line and threw my arms over my head in wild abandon, like I'd seen my kids do on the roller coaster, laughing wildly just like them. Next thing I knew, I was on the other side. I barely had time to squeeze the brakes, but I made a perfect landing on the platform. It was pure exhilaration. I pumped my fist in the air. I did it!

The rest of the day, everywhere we went, I smiled at everyone, basking in my triumph. I'd finally conquered my fear! I felt like a different person, one who was ready to face new challenges and even look forward to them.

The next morning, I was up bright and early. Bruce tracked me down at the excursion desk. "What are you doing?" he asked, looking totally bewildered.

"Signing up for activities," I beamed. "If I don't get our names on the list, we'll miss out. There's whale watching, salmon fishing, dog sledding. Oh, my gosh, there's so much to do." I piled the stack of brochures into his hands. From then on, I planned on being an active part of the family. No more standing on the sidelines! Never again.

~Susan A. Karas

51

These Are My Friends

There are no strangers here; only friends
you haven't yet met.
~Author Unknown

I was away when the landline rang. My husband took the call and answered confidently, "I'm sure she would be happy to."

I would have said, "No, I've never done that. I'm not qualified." But he said "yes," and the next day they contacted me with the details.

A women's conference was being planned for our church district. It was to be their first. The draw would be an outside speaker, one whose name everyone would recognize, which would be sure to increase the size of the crowd. However, several speakers from within the state were also being invited to speak. I was asked to be one of them.

Me! A pastor's wife in a small but growing mission church. The most public speaking I had done was in front of the students in my high school classes or when I taught leadership classes to small groups within the church. But to speak to women whom I had never met, I couldn't even imagine it.

The topic they wanted me to address was one I was passionate about, and before the conversation ended, I had consented.

During the next several months, I studied. I wrote. I prayed. I practiced. Somewhere during those weeks, I remembered that the two greatest fears people had were death and public speaking. I began to understand those fears.

The week before the conference was to begin we were notified that because so many women had preregistered there was a change of venue — to the largest church in the town. If only I could back out! But it was too late. My name was already listed on the program.

The architecture of the building was traditional — long and narrow with two sections of pews, a center aisle, and a balcony across the back. From my vantage point on the platform, the rows seemed to stretch forever, and it was packed — standing room only.

When I was introduced to speak, I rose and reached for the microphone. Suddenly, my legs felt like rubber. I thought my knees were going to buckle and I was going to fall if I kept standing there. I needed to move around to get the blood circulating once again. While this was happening, I said something to distract the situation. That's when I heard them break into a friendly laugh. They thought I was funny!

In that moment, everything changed. These people were my friends! Peace replaced fear, and confidence flooded over me. That's when I realized I was made for this.

Another invitation came from them the following year. For me, everything had changed, and I looked forward to the opportunity.

A few months after the second conference, my phone rang with another invitation. This time, it was to be to a much larger crowd. The "outside" speaker was inviting me to speak at their conference in a state over 800 miles away.

The event would last three-and-a-half days. Instead of several hundred attending, now there were several thousand. It was a plus that I was unknown to most of them because they had no expectations. I noticed that I was to be the eighteenth presenter and was not scheduled to speak until the last day. Plenty of time for my old fears to return.

But the moment I rose to speak, peace and confidence replaced fear.

During the next several years, my calendar began filling up with speaking invitations across the United States and abroad. And it all happened because of one phone call answered by my husband that forced me out of my comfort zone and into a whole new zone of empowering women just like me.

~Phyllis Bird Nordstrom

52

Learning to Stand

The way to develop self-confidence is to do the
thing you fear and get a record of successful
experiences behind you.
~William Jennings Bryan

When my well-meaning friend e-mailed me an article about a guy in Australia who teaches women to surf, I grimaced when I read that awful phrase "of a certain age." I wished that I a) had enough guts to try, b) had enough money to get myself to Australia, and c) had a body I would dare put into a bathing suit — an intimidating yet often overlooked aspect of this death-defying sport. In one efficient movement, my index finger hit "Delete." *Poof!* The thought of learning to surf at this point in my life was buried. Temporarily.

I was born in California, so everyone assumes that I grew up surfing. I can... surf the net, channel surf, and couch surf. So what if I can't get up on a board?

Plenty of looks come my way when people learn of my inadequacy. Over time, I have learned to ignore them. What I never learned to ignore was wishing that I could surf.

Last year, on the sandy beaches of Máncora, Peru, I watched the surfers with awe. A teensy, dark-haired girl, probably about six years old, carried a heavy board by herself, then jumped into the water and paddled off effortlessly. How I admired her confidence! A few moments later, she easily caught a wave and the attention of the older surfers around her. She was fabulous! The anguish of never even trying washed over me. I decided to take matters into my own hands — and go get lunch.

Before I could reach the restaurant, I stumbled across a "Learn to Surf" bungalow. *No harm in asking,* I thought. The man's tongue hung out of his mouth as he watched the gorgeous thong-clad girls nearby. I scurried away, my ego bruised. *You're too old to surf,* my doubting self chided. Another uneasy truth resurfaced: I don't have medical insurance. That nagging inner voice, even after having been squelched for decades, would not give up and coached, *You know no one here. Try!*

I focused on the more important issue: my growling stomach. I spied a fish stand and headed that way. There stood another stand, filled with the "real deal": three Latino surfers. Having spent much time around surfers, I can distinguish "real" ones from wannabes. These dudes' authenticity bounced off them! Like a gentle, invisible lasso pulling me in, one whispered, "Wouldn't you love to surf?"

> *Why, oh why, did I wait so long to learn?*

My older self's face said in Spanish, "Sure, but that boat sailed about thirty years ago."

He looked utterly surprised, assuring me, "You can do it. You're in great shape." Latinos know how to flatter! My ego deeply massaged, I actually began to contemplate this life-long obsession. Would today be the day?

"I don't know, I mean…" I started, sounding like a scared bimbette.

"*Mi amor,* if you don't get up, you don't pay."

What? I looked for the hidden camera. Instead, he threw a wet suit my way and introduced me to Melo, whose job it would be to make sure I stood up on the board. Before I had time to back out, Melo encouraged me, making me feel like the *reina de las olas* (queen of the waves) that he said I was.

After practicing a while in the sand, where I easily stood up, it was time to move the show to the ocean. I followed his broad shoulders and was thankful he carried the board for me. I was liking this surfing thing! Reading my thoughts, he flashed me a reassuring smile. Maybe because I had to concentrate so hard to understand (the entire lesson was in South American Spanish), I didn't have time to be terrified — until I looked at the first wave. I swear it grew as I stared at it. Transfixed, I could not move. The soundtrack from *Jaws* played in my ears. I was going to drown!

Undaunted, Melo coached me. "Do exactly what you did on land. Don't overthink it."

My brain froze; there were so many things to remember. *This is my dumbest idea ever! I will never be able to...*

"*Arriba!*" he yelled, our code for "Get up right now!"

Boom! A miracle occurred. Squatting, I dragged my other foot like he had instructed me. I was up on the board. Standing and everything! Oh... my... God! After a lifetime spent wishing but being too scared, I had finally done it! Earlier, Melo had cautioned that the second our minds wander and we start to think about something else, a beginner topples. Were I able to focus on anything but being in the moment, I would have jumped up and down.

I was surfing.

What had I been so frightened of? Splash! As I hit the water, I loved what I had done. I grinned as I had never grinned. I couldn't help myself and screamed, "Yesssss!"

Ah, shoot. Now I'd have to pay the owner.

Melo looked at me and beamed. He high-fived me, bursting with pride. "*Mi reina!*"

What an utterly amazing emotion, unlike anything I had ever experienced. How I wanted to feel that high of accomplishment again. And again. My old pal, self-doubt, snuck back in. Was that just a fluke?

"Ready to try another one?" Melo wanted to know, and my ecstatic self could only nod. I could barely think, *Let's give it a go,* when... Boom! Up I went again. What did people find so hard about this? Who knew? I was a natural. Me! I wasn't a natural at anything.

Why, oh why, did I wait so long to learn? I was kicking myself. I almost hit Melo. *Hold on! Wait a second...* He was on the back of my board, stabilizing it for me! No wonder I had gotten up easily.

He grinned. I grinned. The secret was out. "So, would you like to try one all by yourself?"

That next wave was the enemy! I couldn't even get to the crouching position, never mind standing. Perhaps, like having learned to Rollerblade in my thirties, it would take longer.

As we waited for the next wave, the discussion turned to my boyfriend and why he wasn't here. My sexy, younger teacher was asking me to go dancing later that night. Ah, surfing lessons — Latino-style!

Safely back on land, I was thrilled that the shrewd owner had asked for my camera earlier and had snapped a shot of me on top of the board. Now I wanted one of my fabulous instructor and me. Winking at me, Melo gave me his e-mail address. "Promise me you'll come back tomorrow, *mi reina*. I did.

Although I grapple with self-doubt, I want to become a good surfer, loving the sense of victory every time I manage to get up, whether I stay up for a second or for longer. After my best run yet, I wisely got off the board... beaming... until the next time.

~JC Sullivan

53

The Reluctant Scuba Diver

Life shrinks or expands in proportion to one's courage.
~Anaïs Nin

I have a fear of drowning. I think it must be the worst way to die: kicking and clawing to get to the surface, only to fail and start choking on water while still fighting to get one more breath. Despite this fear, I love swimming, but I tend to stick to the surface.

So when my dad told me that to be a marine biologist, which was my dream, I needed to be a scuba diver, I was very reluctant. Scuba diving had never crossed my mind. The idea of going deep under the water with weights dragging me down and a nonrenewable air source on my back was very scary. However, my dad would not take "no" for an answer. He found a Discover Scuba class through a local dive shop and signed us up.

The first time I went scuba diving was in a community pool. I wasn't scared because we were only eight feet deep, and I knew I could easily get to the surface if necessary. It was fun being able to swim around the bottom without having to come up for air. It was not as much fun seeing all the things that gather at the bottom of a public pool.

Since I enjoyed the overall experience, my dad signed us up for classes to get our certification. He pushed me to go to every class, whether it was in the classroom or the pool. I didn't like having extra homework on top of my college coursework, but I got through it.

I really struggled with removing my mask and regulator. I performed the removing and clearing of the mask perfectly, both in the pool and in the ocean, but the sting of salt water made me want to never do it again. Removing and then retrieving my regulator did not go as well. I was forced to remove my regulator from my mouth, watch it float away, and then grab it. The best way to do this is to lean to the side the regulator is on (typically the right), sweep your arm across your body, and capture the regulator in the process.

When it came time to do this skill in the pool, I was dreading the moment the dive master signaled me to perform. As my connection to my air tank disappeared beyond my line of sight, the panic began to set in. It grew stronger when I swept my arm and came up with nothing. I tried again, but to no avail. My body was screaming for air, and I scrambled to find something. I looked for my backup, but I couldn't find that either.

I gave up and bolted to the surface, which is exactly what I was *not* supposed to do. The dive master followed me, somehow convinced me to go back down, and had me do the skill again. The second time and during the certification, I did not push it as hard so it never fully left my sight. It was enough to pass. I got my Open Water Diver certification in May 2010.

Even after certification, my dad had to push me to go on dives to keep my skills up to date. I really didn't like to spend my weekends getting up early to jump into cold water and see practically nothing but underwater plants. I was so bored during a dive at Shadow Cliffs, which is the local pond, that I mentally wrote a story about a friendly swamp monster that lived in that lake.

However, one trip would change how I felt about diving. It was a safety stop on a dive in Catalina. I was resting at fifteen feet to prevent any potential decompression sickness while my dad looked on from above because the air in his BCD vest (buoyancy control device) had pulled him to the surface. A school of fish circled me, and then quickly disappeared. A sea lion passed by. The fish returned and vanished a minute later. The sea lion swam by a little closer. The fish came back again, but this time, they stayed behind me. Another minute passed. The sea lion swam straight for me. I thought, *Please don't attack me! I'm not trying to come between you and your food.* A foot from my face, the sea lion turned and swam away. My three minutes were up, and it was time to exit the water. To this day, this has been my best and most favorite safety stop. Shortly after this experience, I bought underwater cameras, both video and still.

Since then, I have had many scuba adventures. I earned a few more certifications, including Deep Diver, Rescue Diver, Nitrox Diver, and Zombie Apocalypse Diver. I have navigated through kelp, bumped into sharks, and seen all kinds of fish and underwater life. It has not always been easy. I know what it's like to have an anxiety attack at eighty feet below, to look at a blank screen on my computer while still going down, and to feed the fish after.

Out of all my trips, one experience outshines the rest. For incredible adventure and lots of marine life on every dive, there's only one place to go: the Galápagos Islands. The park fees make it a bit expensive, but it is worth every penny. We dove four times a day for most of our weeklong trip. We saw hammerheads, Galápagos sharks, and black- and white-tipped sharks, but nothing dangerous like a Great White. Moray eels poked their heads out of their hiding places in the rocks. Schools of fish migrated between feeding areas while schools of rays swam past and over us. We snorkeled with penguins and dolphins, and we witnessed marine iguanas feeding off the algae at twenty feet. There is nothing like diving in the Galápagos.

If my dad hadn't pushed me at the beginning and forced me to face my fears, I wouldn't have these amazing experiences and stories to tell. I had to learn how to calm myself when I did panic so I could handle the problem in front of me, which was usually that I was just freaking out, had momentarily misplaced my dive buddy, or was struggling with my equipment. I learned how to breathe, to quell the panic, and to see new worlds without ever leaving the planet.

~Sarah Reece

54

How *Jeopardy!* Changed My Life

Never did the world make a queen of a girl who hides
in houses and dreams without traveling.
~Roman Payne

The last time my (now ex) husband boarded a plane was when he flew back to the States from the Vietnam War. As he says, if they'd had a bus, he would've taken that instead. When I married him, I knew he'd never fly again, but figured car trips in our home state of Colorado could keep us busy for years — which they did. And, truth be told, I wasn't that crazy about flying, either. I was more than happy to ride shotgun or play with our son in the back seat while postcard scenery streamed past our windows.

A few years ago, however, I made the cut in an on-line *Jeopardy!* quiz and was invited to San Francisco to participate in a mock game and audition. If I wanted a shot at being on my favorite TV game show, I'd have to get to San Francisco. Driving was out; I don't like driving across town, let alone across the Continental Divide. So I'd have to fly. Thus began the process of learning to travel solo.

I know, I know. In this day and age, it's routine — if not *de rigueur* — for a woman to travel on her own. In fact, before my marriage, I'd flown alone several times. But there was always someone to meet me at the airport, help me with my luggage and drive me to my aunt's house or wherever I might be staying. I'd never flown to a city where I'd be completely on my own. Besides, after two decades of car travel, I was rusty and intimidated by the complications of flying post-9/11.

Before I could fly anywhere, though, I needed a reservation, and to make a reservation, I needed a credit card — which I did not have. I know, I know! But I'd heard so many cautionary tales about the evils of plastic that I was leery of them, too.

Pay it off every month, I warned myself. *Don't go overboard. It's only for emergencies.* If *Jeopardy!* wasn't an emergency, though, I didn't know what was. I took the plunge and was given a $15,000 line of credit — an exhilarating whiff of freedom.

> *I'd never flown to a city where I'd be completely on my own.*

After making the plane reservations, I had to figure out where to stay, how to get to and from the Denver airport as well as the airport in San Francisco, and how to get from my lodgings to the hotel where the *Jeopardy!* try-outs would be held. I considered staying at that hotel, but it was downtown and expensive. Besides, I wanted to be near Ocean Beach so I could walk along the shore, gaze out at the Pacific Ocean and treat myself to dinner at the Cliff House, where I'd been eons ago as a college student.

Online, I found a bed-and-breakfast within easy walking distance of Ocean Beach, and calculated the expense and logistics of shuttles and cabs. And, despite Henry David Thoreau's admonition to "Beware of all enterprises that require new clothes," I bought a cute game show outfit.

The awaited June morning finally arrived, and I was almost as nervous as a bride. But everything went like clockwork:

My house to airport parking, check.

Airport parking to Denver airport, check.

Denver airport to San Francisco airport, check.

San Francisco airport to bed-and-breakfast, check.

B&B to hotel, check.

Hotel back to B&B, check.

B&B to San Francisco airport, check.

San Francisco airport to Denver airport, check.

Denver airport to airport parking, check.

Airport parking to my house, check.

Phew!

Of course, many small adventures and encounters — not to mention the audition itself — were woven around my checklist. The people, the places, the sights of that magical city seemed to conspire to make my trip to San Francisco as delightful as possible. And I did not embarrass myself at the audition, which had been my main worry. Leaving the hotel after the try-out, I felt strong and capable.

I can do this, I thought. *I am doing this!* An attractive young couple even asked me for directions — and I was able to help them! I celebrated the day — and my burgeoning independence — with a wonderful dinner at the Cliff House, where I could watch the ocean out the window, feeling as if San Francisco had wrapped its arms around me.

Soon after my trip to San Francisco, the short plays I was writing began to get produced in places like Palm Springs, California; Kansas City, Missouri; and even New York City. If I wanted to see my plays, which I certainly did, I'd have to get to the theater myself.

I found myself traveling more and more, letting the roulette wheel of a play's production determine where I went. In one of the smaller cities — Grand Junction, Colorado — I even rented a car! Usually, though, I prefer to take cabs and shuttles, and I walk whenever and wherever possible. Most of the encounters that make a trip special seem to occur when one is on foot.

I never heard back from *Jeopardy!*. At the time, I didn't have a cell phone (no surprise), and they had warned they wouldn't leave a message. I console myself by thinking that they tried and failed to reach me. Whether they did or didn't is immaterial. *Jeopardy!* was the beginning of a process that now allows me to visit cities where the only people I know are characters on a stage. The ability to travel alone — to arrange the details with confidence and handle the unexpected with aplomb — turned out to be the best prize of all.

~Kristine McGovern

55

You Are Not Too Old

Just try new things. Don't be afraid. Step out of
your comfort zones and soar, all right?
~Michelle Obama

I worked at a local university and our office was staffed with a few student workers. One of the students was the quarterback of an intramural football team that needed a center. She overheard me talking to another student about how I had always wanted to play powder puff football, but never got the chance. The quarterback offered to let me come and try out for the position.

I was excited and scared. Excited at the thought of doing something I had always wanted to do, but scared I was too out of shape and too old to keep up with athletic twenty-year-olds. There was no harm trying out, though. I agreed to be on the field for practice.

My husband and children thought I was crazy but I didn't care. It was something I had to do for myself. It was a now or never moment.

My job at the university was sedentary and I had just taken up running to turn back the clock a little. Having just finished my bachelor's degree, doing homework all evening after sitting all day had taken a toll. My son was playing high school football, my daughter took some dance classes and I had all the mom responsibilities too. Between going to games, dance recitals, and house work, finding time for me seemed impossible, but I knew playing football with kids would motivate me to keep up with my running.

I showed up with butterflies in my stomach and low expectations. I just knew once they saw how out of shape I was, they would let me snap a few hikes and then go with a younger, peppier girl. During drills I was slow and I got winded very easily, but my desire to do this made me drive forward. Once the coaches and the players sized up my abilities, center was where I would play. No one else showed up to compete for that position, so by default, it was mine.

I couldn't have been happier! They took my shirt size, jersey number and my team name. I chose "Mama Platt" because it is what a couple of the students called me, and I chose my dad's football number from high school: 74. I still remember the moment I stood in a sporting goods store picking out cleats. Was this really happening? I couldn't believe it. These girls were actually going to let me be a part of the team!

When I was not practicing on Mondays and Wednesdays at the school, I was running as much as I could around my neighborhood. I wanted to get in better shape and improve my speed. Hiking the ball was the most nerve wracking part because I had to make sure I threw the ball backward and high enough from an almost squatting position. This part quickly became a muscle memory movement, though, and was not as problematic as getting so easily winded. Going from hiking the ball, to aggressive blocking and then bolting to the end zone was challenging. A few times I thought I would pass out, but the excitement of seeing those girls make touchdowns kept me upright. I even made a touchdown myself once! I remember driving home after that game and realizing I really can do anything I put my mind to.

My husband was incredibly supportive and my parents promised to come to some games; more out of curiosity I think. We won our first game, and our second and our third. Some nights we played two games back to back. It was invigorating, tiring and the most fun I have ever had in my life! We only lost once the entire season and ended up winning the championship.

Yes, it was the experience of a lifetime. I turned thirty-nine while playing flag football with college kids. I felt like Wonder Woman. I worked full-time, was an amateur runner, ran my first 5K, raised a family *and* played football. I still cannot believe I get to tell this story.

I learned so much about myself. I learned that taking chances can open doors to opportunities you never thought possible. I learned that accomplishing physical feats requires mental toughness. I learned that being open to doing the far-out and ridiculous is incredibly exciting!

I graduated with a master's degree at age forty-one, but I still think my season of football was the best part of my return to university!

~Rebecca J. Platt

Chapter 6

The Empowered Woman

Walk the Talk

56

Walking on Air

*By leaving your comfort zone behind and taking a leap
of faith into something new, you find out who you are
truly capable of becoming.*
~Author Unknown

I look down from where I sit on the low wall around the flat roof. I can see my textbooks waiting for me on the grass under the oak tree just across the sidewalk. That tree was so big and shady when I sat under it, but now it seems so insignificant from up here. I am petrified. Why had I ever thought that I could handle this?

On my walk home to family housing after my last class on this beautiful autumn afternoon, I noted unusual activity at the Military Science Building. To attract attention to the university's ROTC program, every afternoon this week they were offering the opportunity to learn to rappel down the daunting "cliff" of that stone structure, which is several stories high. My twenty-five-year marriage recently ended, so I hoped it would be diverting to spend a few minutes watching something new.

I sat cross-legged under the big oak and watched the experts on the ground rig a harness on one volunteer after another. They explained the technique before sending the tyros inside to climb the stairs and then reappear behind the parapet surrounding the flat roof. I watched for more than an hour. One after another, the learners on the roof were clipped to the lines, given another word or two of advice, and then helped over that low wall. And one after another, those novices came down that wall on those ropes, only a few "walking" carefully down, and only some landing in the bushes that by now showed evidence of a lot of traffic that week. Invariably, they wore big smiles as they stood to be un-rigged.

Despite my lifelong fear of heights, I was drawn to risk it, too. Everyone who tried it seemed to enjoy it. And if those young people could do it, so could this middle-aged student. I got in line.

There was no time to think about nerves while the instructor repeated to me what I had already heard him reciting over and over. The ropes and clips were strung around me to make a harness, which became almost a seat to suspend me from the belaying ropes. I went inside and found the flights of stairs and then the rungs on the wall to climb through the trapdoor to the roof. It almost seemed unreal that this unanticipated adventure was happening.

Before I knew it, I was first in line. And that is why I now sit here on the parapet. The view might be worth it, but my focus is strictly on regaining the ground — and that first step is a whopper!

"On rappel!" shouts the instructor beside me to the man holding the ends of the line on the ground below. "On belay!" shouts the anchor man in response, and my time has come. With my gloved left hand holding the rope in front of my face and the other gripping a rope held at the small of my back, I hesitate, inhaling another deep breath. That first move — to turn and face the solid stone with only wide-open space behind me and airy emptiness waiting beneath my feet — is almost more than I can force myself to take. *Don't pay attention to your primitive side. Use your head. This fear is not rational. You have seen all of those young people do this safely. Observe the evidence. It will work. Just do it.* So, with one more big breath, I step against the wall in front of me, inching one foot and then the other, and then try a little hop and then a big hop, pushing away from the building. There's time for one little swoop before my feet just miss a bush, and I am successfully back on the ground, smiling in elation.

Where are those stairs? I'll go again!

Another time up the steps, the remembered thrill carries me over the wall more easily, and I make another successful return to good old terra firma. This time, in big swooping bounds, I spring away from the wall and move down the rope, to swing back against the wall much farther down, touch with my feet and push off smoothly again. Is it graceful? I can't tell, but it feels elegant. It lasts only seconds. Those who rappel down real cliffs must be euphoric.

I am delighted that I have tackled this challenge and earned such a treat for myself. I retrieve my books from beside the tree and take them and my grin home. Both of my daughters have come in from school before me, and I am eager to tell them about the thrill of rappelling, but without mention of the courage I have verified is waiting in me when I need to tap it. I hold that knowledge to myself. While walking on air, I have spread my wings.

The next autumn, when the ROTC program again sets up to teach rappelling, I try it again, and it is still a thrill. I hurry home that late afternoon and convince one of my daughters, Karin, to come and watch, and maybe try it. Both she and I go over that parapet and come down, and the instructor takes her picture, beaming a proud, happy grin. She is thirteen years old, maybe the youngest volunteer they have found on campus. Am I the oldest? Certainly one of the older women, anyway. I say to the man who is rigging harness, "I'll be back soon. I want to go ask someone else to try this."

He replies, "Is it a red-headed daughter?"

In amazement, I say, "Yes! How did you know?"

Apparently, my nineteen-year-old daughter, Laurie, had come by earlier in the day and watched a little, and then took her turn, mentioning that she had to keep up with her mom. That must be a real nuisance — trying to follow after a mother who imagines she can walk on air, and then goes out and proves it!

~Jeneva Ford

57

Ask Me about My Bikini

*A mother who radiates self-love and self-acceptance
actually vaccinates her daughter
against low self-esteem.*
~Naomi Wolf

This summer, I will be wearing a bikini. Not because I lost a lot of weight. I haven't. Not because I have a burning desire to wear a bikini again. I don't.

The reason is because I have two daughters, and I want to show them that bikinis are okay, no matter who wears them. Short, tall, skinny, fat, no matter the skin tone or the cellulite.

Let me tell you how hard this is for me. I haven't worn a bikini since I was in high school. I'm not a small woman. I don't especially like to be looked at, especially when I'm in a bathing suit. I couldn't find a single picture of myself in a bathing suit, even though I lived across the street from the ocean for all of my childhood and went to the beach almost every single day.

Like most women, I am very conscious of my weight, and the product of a lifetime assault by the media about what my body should be. I was on my first diet when I was in the third grade. I read all those teen magazines trying to determine my shape and size. I'm a pear, by the way. I went through the low-fat phase, and I've joined Weight Watchers and LA Weight Loss. Until this last house purchase, I didn't own a full-length mirror because I never especially liked what I saw, so I chose not to look. I graded myself with letters. I was an A-B-C: A intellect, B face, C body.

My parents have been on a perpetual diet, trying to lose weight for the next event: reunions or cruises or the next beach season. They went through the SlimFast phase, the cabbage-soup diet, the grape-fruit diet, and the magical-drops diet. They were especially helpful in monitoring my diet as a kid, limiting my portions, especially sweets.

Since having daughters, I have tried mightily not to transfer my weight issues to my girls. Our goal as a family is to eat healthy foods, make good choices, and stay active. I've been in road races and triath-lons. I swim at least once a week. The girls are active in team sports and individual competitions. We don't have women's magazines in the house. We don't even have a scale in the house because I didn't want the girls to see me worry about my weight.

So it came as a surprise to me when my daughter, Wendy, didn't want to wear a bikini. She's thirteen, very active, and pretty self-assured. She also swims competitively. The thing is, a bikini would be so much easier for her since she has two medical devices on her body because of her diabetes: an insulin pump and a continuous glucose monitor. A one-piece bathing suit is harder to get on and off and has a much better chance of knocking off the devices. (Our insurance only covers so many applications per month.)

Because she's thirteen, I thought maybe it was a body image thing. She's got all these new curves now, so maybe she's not exactly sure what to do about them. So I talked to her about it, saying I really wanted her to try a bikini, that I was sure we could find one she was comfortable in.

Over and over again, she refused. It turns out, she doesn't want people to see her scars.

Wendy has a constellation of scars on her abdomen. The right side is from some intestinal surgeries. The left side is from her kidney transplant, and the star-shaped scar on the top is from a peritoneal dialysis catheter. The truth is, nobody really notices them, at least I don't. They're not ugly or red or jagged. When she's examined by surgical residents at the hospital, they look at them in wonder, like they're kids looking at the window of a candy store. Those scars, to me, show me that she is a warrior, and they're something to be proud of.

But she was afraid that people would see them and ask her about them, and she would be forced to give her whole medical history at the pool or the beach. I get it: That's a lot for a thirteen-year-old.

So we made a deal. If she was willing to try on some bikinis and find one she liked, I would wear a bikini, too. I told her, "Don't worry, kid. If I'm wearing a bikini next to you, nobody is going to be looking at your scars."

Well, guess what? She didn't just find one bikini she liked; she found two. So, I'm not going to lie… I panicked a little.

I am ashamed to admit that my first instinct was to go on some radical diet, but what exactly would that showcase to my daughters? That only perfect bodies wear bikinis? Wrong.

I told some of my best friends, who had a variety of reactions. Some sent me suggestions that were over-the-top ridiculous: *Star Wars* themed, gold mesh, or string bikinis that were smaller than a tissue. I wouldn't be able to blow my nose on a triangle that small. Some friends asked me if I could take it back, go back on my word, or wear a tankini. That would reduce Wendy's trust in me, so I couldn't do that. Some friends shared their own insecurities or their negative body image. Some friends applauded me.

Buying a bikini wasn't the easiest thing in the world, but I found a lovely size 12 black bikini with white polka dots. I bought a lovely cover-up to go with it. I've got a hat.

One thing is certain: I'm going to need a lot more sunblock.

I'm not going to say that I'm going to love every minute of wearing this bikini in public, but I am going to "fake it until I make it" with confidence. That is the very least I can do for my daughters.

I want them to know that their bodies are beautiful and powerful and theirs alone to love.

So this summer, if you see me in my bikini, please ask me about it.

~Darcy Daniels

58

No Room for Fear on the Stage

He has not learned the lesson of life who does
not every day surmount a fear.
~Ralph Waldo Emerson

I knew the content of the e-mail before I opened it. The subject line had given it away: "CONGRATULATIONS!" And the sender's name was one I recognized from the essay contest I had entered. I did a little happy dance in my chair, and with my heart racing, I clicked on the button to reveal the details.

My hands tingled as I read the salutation: "Dear Winner." Then I got to the part about reading at a literary festival, and my mouth fell open and the tingling stopped. I blinked at the screen as if that would change what I was seeing, but the words remained the same.

Certain there was a mistake, I toggled over to the contest website. I knew I never would have entered anything that required public speaking; it was something I'd avoided my entire life. Yet there it was — the disregarded detail — midway down the page. I slumped in my chair, switched back to the e-mail, and watched as the word "winner" became "loser" in my head.

With trembling hands, I called my husband, Roger. After sixteen years of marriage, he knew my shortcomings and the importance of agreeing with one's spouse. Surely, he would be my enabler. But the conversation didn't go as I had expected. Once we got past all the gushing, Roger said, "Don't be silly. Of course, you're going. What an honor!"

Honor? He didn't get it. Honor stood no chance in the ring when fear was its contender.

"How long is the essay?" he asked.

"Five-hundred words," I said, barely audible, knowing how ridiculous it sounded.

"Over in three minutes. No problem," he said.

No problem for Roger — the amazing speaker — who sought out opportunities like this. And with that comment, he was dismissed, and I hung up the phone.

Next, I called my best friend, Lisa. Despite being a music teacher, she had similar fears; she wouldn't lack compassion. But all thirty years of friendship got me was two minutes of comforting words, followed by a kick in the pants. I ended the conversation as soon as I saw it switching gears.

It was time to tackle this problem on my own, I decided. Maybe all I needed to do was reply to the e-mail and point out the three obvious, yet overlooked factors:

1. Writers and public speakers have drastically different skill sets.
2. My personal essay was quite personal.
3. I was a newbie to the writing scene, thus not smart enough to be speaking in front of a literary crowd.

I don't remember the exact wording of the draft, only that I sent it to Lisa to pre-read, and a text came through from her seconds later.

DO NOT SEND THAT E-MAIL! You sound like a woman hiding in a closet with her ten cats, afraid of the world!

I let out a sigh. It wasn't the image I was going for, although kudos to me for capturing exactly how I felt. The world did scare me from a stage. I did want to hide. But I hit the "Delete" button instead and started over.

Fiction would be the base of my next attempted reply. I said I had a previously scheduled engagement that might not be changeable, leaving my response ambiguous. I was hoping this way I could test out the water — see what the consequences would be if I chose to be a coward — before committing to the course.

An immediate response followed; it was the kind of answer my mother-in-law would give to a question about showing up for a family dinner.

"Attendance not required but HIGHLY recommended."

I spent the following days weighing the pros and cons. It was hard to look at myself in the mirror without recoiling. I felt pathetic. And worse, I was a fraud — a mother who had coached her middle-schooler through his public-speaking fears, but couldn't coach herself through her own.

With self-loathing fueling my fingertips, I composed a new and final e-mail that included the words "honored to attend." I bit my lip, closed my eyes, and clicked "Send."

Now it was time to open that closet door — and, of course, get rid of those cats.

The next day, I thought about the advice I always gave to my son about practicing and not worrying about those people in the room he deemed to be smarter. Then I got started by reading my essay out loud to my empty living room. The first time, I felt nauseous immediately. And dismissing the negative thoughts that popped up in my head became as exhausting as playing a game of Whac-A-Mole at the county fair. But I knew one thing: I wanted to conquer my fear more than I wanted to be comfortable.

I read the essay every day until my voice was hoarse and I could recite every word in my sleep. I continued to whack those moles every time they reared their negative little heads. And then it was time. The dreaded day had arrived.

Roger sat next to me that evening as I arranged and rearranged myself on my chair. It was standing room only in the hotel ballroom, and the festival was about to get underway. The sponsors thought an element of surprise would be "fun" for the finalists, so the order in which we were reading hadn't been disclosed. All we knew was that the emcee would start with honorable mention and work her way up to first place. There were two age groups, two categories and sixteen readers in all.

We were thirteen readers in when the waiting started to feel unbearable, and the nudging from my husband began. I turned my eyes in his direction and mouthed sternly, "Stop it!" Then the emcee called the third-place winner, and Roger nudged me again. He could hardly contain himself by the time he heard the words "first-place winner," followed by my name.

> *I made my way to the stage feeling dizzy.*

I made my way to the stage feeling dizzy. Standing at the podium with a pasted-on smile, I confronted the silence of the crowd. Then I adjusted the microphone, cleared my throat, and started. I was on autopilot when I heard the first gasp and realized someone was listening. Occasionally, as I looked up, I noticed people in the audience nodding their heads in agreement as if what I was saying made sense. And then the three minutes were over, and I was back in my chair reveling in what I had just learned: When we speak the truth and allow ourselves to be vulnerable, courage shows up, leaving no room for fear on the stage. It wasn't about being smart; it was about being human. I only needed to be someone who wanted to share an experience, hoping to help others overcome similar obstacles of their own.

I didn't tell many people that I had won prior to going, but that night I saw how courage could build confidence and words could inspire. So the next day, I posted a picture of the certificate on Facebook with a status update: "This is what getting out of your comfort zone looks like!"

And I'd do it all over again.

~Amy Mermelstein

59

Off the Ropes

The unending paradox is that
we do learn through pain.
~Madeleine L'Engle

I imagined a teaching campaign in China or an afternoon at a soup kitchen in my hometown. I never dreamed God would call me to a boxing club.

About nine months had passed since I'd filed for divorce. My college sweetheart, the father of our then one-year-old daughter, disclosed the news of his affair shortly after our five-year anniversary.

From stay-at-home mom to single mom, my life began changing faster than I wanted it to. My husband moved out ten days after his reveal, and I was on my own, trying to raise a soon-to-be toddler and turn my erratic career as a freelancer into something stable.

I had everything to fear, it seemed. How would I pay the bills? Could I keep my daughter home? How would I help her cope with our suddenly un-normal life? But when I began looking at my world through eyes of faith, I realized how much I stood to gain.

I had lived up to that point crippled by self-esteem that completely depended on what others thought. If someone said I was pretty, I could believe it — for the moment. And I would try to recreate that moment over and over with the same hairstyle or make-up or outfit, or all three. If a man showed me affection, I could believe I was worth it — until he decided to write me off because he was too busy or tired, and I was left to agonize over what I did, or didn't do, to make him suddenly turn away.

I had no sense of who I was or what I was worth outside of other people's opinions.

My self-esteem hit rock bottom when I found out about my husband's affair. As we sat in his truck in the front drive of our house — the house we had purchased together four years earlier, the house we had made plans to fill with different flooring and new furniture and more children one day — my stomach ached, and my body shook with fear when he said the words no spouse should ever hear. And as much as I hate to admit it, the first and only thought that ran through my head that night was, "I don't deserve any better than this."

> *He answered my prayer for self-esteem by sending me to a boxing club.*

How did I get there? I asked myself this over and over in the months that followed. But the more important question I began to ask was, *How do I get out?*

The old saying is true — God answers prayer in mysterious ways — and for me, He answered my prayer for self-esteem by sending me to a boxing club. I'm the kind of girl who does yoga and Pilates, not boxing. I watch *Chopped* on Food Network, not *Fight Night*. I hate conflict and cringe at violence. But on a Tuesday night in November, I found myself learning about wrist wraps and strapping on red gloves.

I hit the bag as hard as I could. I kicked until my shins bruised. I landed jabs and uppercuts and hooks until my knuckles began to bleed. When I left that night, my whole body hurt — in the best kind of way. I had pushed myself to do something hard, something completely new, something I never thought myself capable of.

There's a saying in boxing that a fighter's "on the ropes." That means he's (or she's) trapped, pushed against the ropes by his opponent and dangerously close to defeat. I think that's where I was in the final months of my marriage. *I'm not a fighter. I'm not strong.* Those are things I had said to myself over and over. Those are things I would have kept saying had I stayed home that Tuesday night, like I wanted to, and done yoga and watched *Chopped*.

God called me to a strange place so I could hit and hurt and learn something about myself that He knew all along: I am worth it. I am beautiful, inside and out. I can fight when I need to. I am strong. I now believe these are the best gifts I can ever hope to give my daughter. She'll never have a perfect life or the ideal family, but I hope, when she looks back on her childhood one day, she'll be able to say she had a mom who showed her what she's worth and how to fight to protect it.

~Rachel E. Ryan

Following My Own Advice

*Go within every day and find the inner strength so that
the world will not blow your candle out.*
~Katherine Dunham

"Be strong for him," they told me a thousand times.
But I didn't feel strong. I sat by my husband's
bedside as he struggled for air. He had a mask
on his face, wires on his chest, and not a single
hair on his head. The doctors reported that the surgery went well,
but the concern in their eyes reminded me of his critical condition.

I wondered how cancer could change a healthy, twenty-eight-year-
old man into the weak, frail patient who lay beside me. He coughed,
and I reached for a bucket and tissues — a conditioned response from
months of taking care of him. He told me he was okay, and I reposi-
tioned his mask so that it was centered on the bridge of his nose and
the strings hit an inch below the scars still fresh from his operation.
He smiled and mumbled that I was the only one who did that right. I
was glad to help him, but the circumstances were difficult to process.

I felt as broken on the inside as he looked on the outside.

My emotions rushed to the surface as I choked back tears. *Be
strong for him,* I reminded myself. I always considered myself a strong
woman, and I usually chose strength for myself rather than anyone
else. But this felt different. He was the patient, and I was the caregiver.

Since the day of his diagnosis, our lives had been completely engulfed by efforts to keep him alive. Occasionally, someone told me to take care of myself, but I thought I couldn't afford that luxury. There was no time for massages or spa days with his life in danger.

I loved him dearly, but I hated how my identity was slipping away along with his health. I dreamed of escaping the hospital, but the last time I left, the nurses forgot to bring his medications, and his recovery regressed dramatically. I was scared to leave him because I knew my presence calmed him. I squeezed his hand and assured him I would be in the bathroom down the hall.

I stood in the tiny hospital bathroom that I started to consider my only personal space. Barely larger than an airplane lavatory, I had to lean against the wall to put on a clean pair of pants and tie my shoes. I looked at my greasy hair and wondered if I should wash it in the sink. I settled on tying it back, washed my face, and looked in the mirror as cold water dripped from my chin.

> *I felt as broken on the inside as he looked on the outside.*

I didn't recognize myself. I tried to keep it together, but the tears wouldn't stop coming. I was overwhelmed and tired. I was scared and sad. But, above all, I felt lost.

My phone buzzed, and I tried to recompose myself. I opened a message from a friend I met in a cancer support group. Her husband had cancer, too, so many of her experiences were the same.

"Everyone says to be strong, but I don't know how to be," it read.

My heart broke, and the tears flowed even more.

I typed back a response. "Being strong is not the same as being stoic. It's okay to cry. It's okay to feel broken. Sometimes, strength comes from the brokenness. As much as you want to be strong for him, you should above all be strong for yourself. Don't forget that your life matters, too."

I looked at that message and realized it was exactly what I wanted someone to tell me in this moment. I looked in the mirror and read out loud to myself.

"Being strong is not the same as being stoic."

I needed those words. I was so busy labeling myself weak at the first sign of emotion that I wasn't recognizing the deep strength in my heart and soul.

"It's okay to cry."

I told my husband this many times but I needed to remind myself, too. An empowered woman doesn't have to be stiff and emotionless. Tears can bring power, courage, and determination.

"It's okay to feel broken. Sometimes strength comes from the brokenness."

We all go through hardships in life, and no one is spared from pain. We all have days when we feel like we cannot go on. But in those days, we often find our greatest strength. It is within ourselves, and sometimes we have to dig deep to find it. Sometimes, the brokenness allows it to shine through.

"As much as you want to be strong for him, you should above all be strong for yourself. Don't forget that your life matters, too."

I had no doubts about my love for my husband or the value that I placed on his life. But I was short-changing myself. I was so focused on saving his life that I was figuratively losing my own.

I wanted to recognize the woman in the mirror. I decided to start by acknowledging her strength and beauty. I resolved to believe in her. I declared that no matter what curve balls life threw, she would get through it.

I took a deep breath and stood a little taller. I walked down the hallway with newfound confidence. I sat by my husband's side and told him, "I know this is hard. I won't pretend that it's not. But I also know that we can do hard things because we are strong."

He pulled himself up to sit on the edge of the bed, something he hadn't done by himself since surgery.

With tears on his face and a smile in his eyes, he reached for my hand and said, "I think you are right. We are stronger than we think."

~Julieann Selden

61

Marching for Science

Passion is energy. Feel the power that comes from
focusing on what excites you.
~Oprah Winfrey

y hands were shaking uncontrollably and it felt like my legs were going to give out from under me. Would I fall backward in front of all these people who were staring at me and listening to me? Could they see my paper fluttering around as I tried so incredibly hard to focus on the words that I spent hours putting down on paper? Would I be able to get through all those words, or would one of the doctors in line behind me need to rescue me after I smacked my head on the stage?

Public speaking had been my nemesis for as long as I could remember. I tried to conquer my fear of speaking in public on numerous occasions throughout my life. In high school, I took a public speaking class that forced me to give weekly speeches in front of my peers. Back then my face would burn and sweat would drip from my palms.

During college and at my first few jobs, I would get ridiculously nervous just asking questions in a group setting, and especially when I had to give a presentation or lead a meeting. I usually relied on reading my notes.

Then in my mid-thirties, I decided to join the world-renowned public speaking group Toastmasters. There was no escaping my fear, as I needed to speak in some capacity at every meeting. It became utter torture to prepare speeches and try to recite them from memory. To make it even more stressful, we were rated and forced to compete with other speakers to win an award. You would think that I would walk away from these experiences as a polished speaker. Nope. Nothing seemed to work.

It was not until recently, when science and scientific institutions were being attacked, that I decided I must speak out for what I believe in, even if that meant standing in front of a large group of people. I would rather hide under my bed than be caught giving a speech, but something was different now. It was as if the world had shifted on its axis.

I was concerned, and frankly furious, about how scientific facts were being brushed aside by the powers that be. I believe so deeply in the value of science. Science gave me my children. Science keeps us safe every day as we eat, breathe, and travel. Science has made this country a place where dreams come true — this is why we all need to protect science.

In addition, science is part of what I do. I am a science writer focusing on parenting, wellness, and environmental issues. My previous work experience includes jobs at incredible science organizations like the National Academy of Sciences, the United States Environmental Protection Agency, and an environmental consulting firm. Everything that I write somehow links to science, and I try to get readers to understand how science is intertwined in their daily lives. I even write a blog called "Happy Science Mom," so clearly science is a huge part of what I live and breathe every single day.

That's how I ended up on that gigantic, frightening stage on that sunny Saturday in April — Earth Day. I mustered up all my courageous energy and volunteered to speak at the March for Science in my local community. It was a historic day around the globe for those of us who want to protect science. Hundreds of thousands of people participated in about 400 marches and rallies in thirty-seven countries. In all the years that I was involved in working on science in Washington, D.C. and beyond, I have never seen a more incredible gathering of scientists and science supporters.

Science truly does touch everyone. At our event alone, speakers included a doctor, a marine biologist, a photographer, a religious leader, a pharmacist, a cancer survivor, and a child who would not be alive today if it were not for receiving a liver transplant.

Despite the incessant body shakes, weak knees, and fear of collapsing right there in front of all those people, I persevered. How did I do it? I know that I was able to finish that speech because of my tremendous passion. It was an incredible feeling to realize that I played a role in helping to make the world a better place.

It was the first time that I ever felt empowered from speaking. I actually got a thrill from doing it. All those other speeches did not contain the immense drive that came from deep within my heart like that moment I experienced at the March for Science. I may still have been scared out of my mind, but I allowed my passion to lead me to that instant because it was my duty. There was no other option for me.

That day, I looked out into the crowd of like-minded science supporters in my community and I felt comfort... I felt at home. Although it frightens me that science is being threatened, when the audience clapped for what I had to say, I felt hope deep within my soul. When I uttered those last few words — "I am so proud to be standing with you today. And I am even more excited to see each and every one of you working to support science! Thank you!" — I was overcome with joy and serenity.

Reaching that milestone goal of getting through a speech truly changed me. At almost forty years old, I learned that passion can ignite a flame in my heart to get me to do things I never dreamed possible. Since that time, I have led science advocacy group meetings and have broken through the wall of fear when it is time to talk about the issues that mean so much to me. I now believe in Desmond Tutu's words: "Hope is being able to see that there is light despite all of the darkness." The darkness that led to my speech is sure to lead to new opportunities and adventures. Who knows? Maybe someday I will even run for office.

~Sandi Schwartz

62

Unintentional Lessons

*We mothers are learning to mark our mothering
success by our daughters' lengthening flight.*
~Letty Cottin Pogrebin

There are lessons we intend to teach as a parent. And then there are unintentional lessons. My mother taught me to be a writer. Not actually, but accidentally. It happened the day I found her black binder.

It contained a story she was writing, privately, steadily, right under our noses. This was an enthralling discovery for a ten-year-old girl who was fiddling with notebooks and fiction. It gave me permission to start.

We never talked about it, but I watched her, placing my fingers on her typewriter when she wasn't looking.

My mother stopped writing at some point, pursuing other interests. I stayed with words.

I wrote for newspapers. I wrote in college. I wrote a play that won a competition. I wrote another that went nowhere.

Then I became a mother, one who wrote. I knew it was possible because my mother did it. I raised words alongside my toddlers, filling my own black binders.

Pursuing a childhood dream while raising children is awkward, which is why I didn't talk about it much with other people. I wanted legitimacy first — traditional, old-school, bookstore and newsstand legitimacy. I have learned the road to this kind of legitimacy is paved with rejection.

When my kids started school, things started to change. Slowly. Very slowly.

I started writing a column for the *Battle Creek Enquirer*. It felt good to see my byline again. It allowed me to use that wonderful word without blushing — writer. My kids even used it, which was a form of legitimacy.

My occasional column became a Sunday column. I gained publishing credits in literary magazines and anthologies. I had a few plays produced and was working on a book. Cairn Press published my first book, *A Teacher Named Faith*.

I am forty-four years old. I have three teenagers. I have finally made it.

My oldest daughter loves music the way I love writing. My experience has served me in several tight places with her because I really do understand the arts and how underappreciated they are. Pursuing one's passion is a blessing and a curse, something people will work another job to keep doing.

I do.

One day I was working one of those jobs, writing on my lunch break. When I got home, I found a note from my daughter on my desk.

She wanted to tell me about her mock college interview, the last lesson in her ACT Prep class. Apparently, the moderator had asked what book most inspired her. She mentioned my book.

She explained the book had taught her not to give up on her passions. It proved that she could make a career in music even if she wasn't a pop star at the end of college because her mom was "forty-some years old" and still making her dreams come true.

She ended her note with, "Now that's inspirational."

I bawled. Not for a minute, but ten.

I didn't mean to teach that lesson. I didn't know she was paying attention.

One day, my daughter will be the one teaching the unintentional lessons. The possibilities make me smile.

~Nicole L.V. Mullis

Sixty Loaves of Bread

In helping others, we shall help ourselves, for whatever
good we give out completes the circle
and comes back to us.
~Flora Edwards

I t all started with a single bag of groceries. My husband, son and I lived in a decent-sized, one-bedroom apartment. We were recovering from a financially difficult time in which we'd had to leave everything we had known due to unforeseen and very sudden circumstances. As we got back on our feet, we realized that although we didn't have a lot, we always had enough.

There was no need we couldn't meet if we put our heads together. Sometimes, that meant reaching out for a little help. It was a hard pill to swallow at first as neither of us had had to ask for such help before, but we'd swallowed our pride.

We found a freecycle/recycle group online that was local. Through this, we were able to furnish our apartment, and even find help with food for the short time we needed it. People were generous and willing to assist without question. Most had struggles of their own. Job loss and long-term illness in the family were two prevalent issues.

After our first month, we decided it was time to give back. I coupon shop and our pantry was well stocked, so I decided to put together a brown bag full of groceries to give away. It was the best feeling to be able to share with the community that had helped us so much.

During this time, I realized I often overcooked. Without an extra freezer, it was hard to store leftovers. We began plating up meals and offering up cooked meals at least once or twice a week, always including a homemade dessert.

Word got out. Suddenly, boxes of food started showing up at our door for us to share. Fresh fruits and vegetables that would have gone to waste at a grocery store and been discarded due to not being perfect showed up. Flour, sugar and other baking needs arrived as well. Orchards offered me the opportunity to glean, which meant I could collect all the fallen fruit for no charge.

Meals went out more regularly as a result of my posting, "For those in need or in need of a pick-me-up." I never asked their stories. I was happy to share and threw myself into my purpose. At the bottom of the bags, I'd place a list of local food pantries just in case their need was longer term.

During this time, we discovered I was pregnant. I'd had several miscarriages previously and was terrified as this was completely unplanned. I was due on Thanksgiving. Throwing myself into doing this kept my mind and body busy.

I knew after the baby I'd have to take a break from all the food prep I'd been doing. I grew fat, swollen and more tired by the day. My husband and I had just discussed me needing the break when he opened the door the very next morning to walk our dog and nearly tripped over the cases of zucchini.

"It's too much for you. Pass them on to someone else," he said.

This bountiful harvest was left in my care, and no matter how he tried to convince me, I knew I had to do something to ensure they were enjoyed over Thanksgiving to the fullest. So began the next four days of some of the hardest and most rewarding work I'd ever done.

One loaf of zucchini bread isn't hard to make, but imagine making sixty-plus loaves. I fell into a routine. Get up, prep all ingredients including grating a full case of zucchini, take my son to the bus, mix up and refrigerate dough, and then start the loaves four at a time in the oven. That oven went from 9:00 in the morning until 6:00 at night. The entire apartment building smelled heavenly. Neighbors knocked on the door for samples. I'm pretty sure even my husband and son smelled like zucchini bread as they left for work and school.

It was thirty-five degrees outside, but every window from kitchen to living room was open just to keep a comfortable temperature. I could hear people comment about the wonderful smell as they walked by our apartment.

I posted the loaves, explaining there would be an abundance. People stopped by hourly — some just families in need, some churches who planned on distributing or sharing the bread, and many single people who would be spending Thanksgiving alone.

I finished with a day and a half to go before Thanksgiving. I had two loaves left.

The exhausting adventure had left me practically glowing. My wrists and ankles ached, my back was sore, and my spirit was flying high. Still, one knows when the end of a good thing is near, and it was time. I posted one last time. I had a bag of Thanksgiving-themed groceries, a meatloaf dinner and a loaf of zucchini bread left.

In my post, I explained I would be taking a hiatus to finish my pregnancy and focus on my new baby when she came.

It was 7:00 when the knock came at my door. I will never forget the moment I opened it.

A father stood there with his head down, his arm around his daughter next to him. She was probably around ten or twelve. I'd never met them before.

I greeted them warmly, handing him the bag and her the bread. I could see her spirits lift right up. He raised his head, and his red-rimmed eyes met mine. "I don't know how we would have even eaten tonight had it not been for you. We... I..." He fumbled with his words as if an explanation was necessary.

Interrupting, I wished them a very happy Thanksgiving.

I realized the gravity of what I'd been doing. At the very beginning of the "I want, I want, I want season," I was addressing a real need — not just the basic need to eat, but a need to receive with a level of dignity and privacy.

Too often when we're in need, people demand our story. We have to provide proof, and it can be a humbling and demeaning process that can strip away our pride. Asking for help was something this gentleman had more than likely never had to do before, and I could see how grateful and appreciative he was. Thanksgiving for this family might not be a huge butter-dripping turkey, expensive desserts bought from upscale bakeries and wine, but it would be enough. Thanksgiving was not a day on a calendar for him, but a moment he knew he could feed his child.

Ingrained in my mind's eye to this day is his smile, the relief in his expression, and the restrained emotion in his eyes. I never knew his name, his story, or even how their life went after that. Yet knowing I'd helped even a little was all the reward I needed, and I still think of him and his daughter each year around Thanksgiving.

~Nicole Rook-McAlister

64

Making It Count

*All who have accomplished great things have had a
great aim, have fixed their gaze on a goal which was
high, one which sometimes seemed impossible.*
~Orison Swett Marden

I was set on the bumpy path to empowerment by the worst
thing that ever happened to me. I was determined to make
the death of my son count for something.

Bereaved parents who have lost a child are well acquainted
with devastation, helplessness and pure anger at whatever took the life
of the child they cherished. They often find themselves physically and
emotionally unable to do much of anything for a time — sometimes
months, sometimes years, and sometimes forever. When my Andy was
hit and killed by a drunk driver on the street in front of my house,
I began that long, horrible journey through a very real valley of the
shadow of death. Of course, I was sad — sadder than I had ever been.
My heart was an empty place where Andy had lived. I was also restless,
and I knew I needed to *do* something. My role in Andy's life had been
ripped away from me, but I still needed to be his mother.

"Go to MADD, Luanne," my brother told me after the funeral.
"They can help. I've seen them in action." As a career Atlanta cop, he
knew what he was talking about. However, when I investigated, I found
that our county didn't have a MADD chapter. It was not because we
didn't have a drunk-driving problem — we did — but because no one
had started one. That's where a woman named Mary came in.

Our children attended the same schools, we had many of the same friends, we even attended the same church, yet we had never met. She came to Andy's wake as part of a prayer group that included my sister-in-law, and I knew she had also lost a son to a drunk driver. I listened when she whispered, "Do what you want to do, not what everybody tells you to do." Mary's son, Tony, was hit by a drunk driver when he was just one minute from home. We began to spend time together, comparing our unspeakable tragedies, talking about our sons and lending support to one another. I was inspired by Mary's compassion and courage and by a unique idea she suggested.

"I don't know if you're interested, but I've been approached to start a Mothers Against Drunk Driving chapter here. I don't want to do it myself, but if you'd like, we could look into doing it together." I told her I would think about it, but I was already drawn to the idea. I was attracted to fighting what had hurt me so badly, to giving my anger an outlet, one that might help stop DWI from hurting others.

I also knew it wasn't going to be easy. When I asked them, most of the people I knew thought my grief had made me crazy. "You've just lost your son. You need to heal, not take on something this big." "You are already busy with your husband and a family that needs you…" And, finally, "You're just doing this for attention."

"Maybe they're right," I pondered. I wasn't altogether sure I could even accomplish anything. Could I do this? Even with Mary's help, could I put together a MADD chapter? Did I even have the energy to try? Someone had destroyed that sense of security and confidence I once had. He did it by making the terrible choice to get behind the wheel of his van after he had been drinking. Then he drove down my street and killed my son. Now it was time for me to take Mary's advice and do what I wanted to do, no matter what people told me I should do.

I knew I couldn't bring Andy back, but I truly wanted to do this work to represent him and his life on this earth. I wanted it in spite of all the sound advice from people who loved me and had my best interests at heart. Something told me I could do it. I thought I was strong enough and able enough, so I did.

In the months that followed, I became a woman I didn't know

I could be. Mary and I assembled a group of dedicated women, and some men, who worked tirelessly to accomplish our mission. We established a strong relationship with our District Attorney and his staff. We offered our services to victims of Driving While Intoxicated, and we took our place as part of a dynamic team of professionals who fought drunk driving every day.

We decorated Christmas trees with red MADD ribbons to create awareness, and we spoke at events for high school students and community organizations. We established an annual Law Enforcement Appreciation Luncheon to honor our local police, with keynote speakers that included Rudy Giuliani. We went to court with new victims who were just beginning to navigate the maze that is the justice system. We held judges, lawyers and lawmakers accountable, and we even worked to change weak DWI laws in New York. Honored nationally by MADD, we didn't rest on our laurels, but continued to work to achieve our goals, hoping that we were making a difference in memory of Andy and Tony and all the other loved ones who had been killed in DWI crashes.

> *I became a woman I didn't know I could be.*

One day, I realized we had not only empowered ourselves, but all MADD volunteers. We had committed to contacting a city official who was pushing for a shuttle to take revelers from one bar to another on busy nights. I inquired of him as to whether or not he intended for the shuttle to take them all the way home. "Of course not," he replied, "that's impossible. But it will boost the revenues of our city's restaurants and taverns, and that's important."

"MADD is all for a shuttle that takes drinkers all the way home," I said. "But if you are going to simply drop them off at their cars after drinking all night, you are putting the entire community in danger. If you pose this idea to the city council, MADD will oppose the plan vehemently," I warned, fearful that he would tell me, and MADD, to mind our own business.

Instead, the city council abandoned the idea. MADD had established a presence, and Mary and I and our team had found our power, accomplishing what we wanted to do, not what everyone else told us to do.

~Luanne Tovey Zuccari

65

The Gold Beads

*Surround yourself with only people
who are going to lift you higher.*
~Oprah Winfrey

I never expected in my worst nightmare to end up divorced with four children and no job. Because of reduced enrollment, I'd been let go from my job as a long-term substitute teacher at the worst possible time, with daughters in high school and college. The rent was late, and no matter how much I juggled the bills, I couldn't pay them. My electricity was getting shut off, and my children needed food.

Then a friend told me about the Women's Opportunity Center headquartered at the local YMCA, an organization that served displaced homemakers. She thought they would be able to help me.

It took me days to make that call.

When I first walked into the center, I was overwhelmed by the leader's kindness and compassion. The center provided food for families and business suits for job interviews. They provided computer training. They even helped with résumés.

Best of all, they introduced me to my mentor. Her name was Bonnie, and she had been struggling too, raising a son and a daughter after her divorce. She had returned to college and won scholarships to help achieve her dream of becoming a teacher. We soon became best friends. Bonnie was an inspiration, and she made me believe that I could also become a success. She encouraged me to return to college and apply for scholarships. Her motto was "Dreams 2 Reality."

At first, I hesitated. My confidence was so low, I couldn't imagine going back to college. I'd tried it over twenty years before and failed. Back then, all I cared about was spending time with my boyfriend and writing songs. I was more interested in getting married than getting an education. My grades suffered, and I dropped out in my early twenties. Soon I married my boyfriend and had four children. I became a full-time homemaker, and my dreams of college faded into the past.

Then I heard that the Women's Opportunity Center offered a motivational workshop. Since it was free, I decided to attend, because I needed all the help I could get.

I hid in the back of the room, feeling small and insignificant, listening to the instructor. I looked around at all the other women in the room. They looked so sad and defeated by life, exactly how I had been feeling for the past few weeks since I'd been laid off from my job. I was one of many displaced homemakers, searching for a way out of a life of poverty and mediocrity. Some of these women had even worse problems than mine — they had been abused, too. We all needed help.

"You have power to take control of your life," the instructor said. "You don't have to remain a victim." She encouraged us to take action to change our lives for the better.

I participated in the discussion afterward, and when I answered a question correctly, she strolled to the back of the room and laid a strand of plastic gold beads in my hand. They were cheap and gaudy, but they meant the world to me. They were a symbol of my way out.

After our session, I called Bonnie. "I've decided to apply for a loan and go back to college." It was a call that would change my life forever.

In my wildest dreams, I never imagined that months later I would be standing in front of a crowd in Trenton accepting the NJ Displaced Homemaker Scholarship. It was so exciting to be standing up there making an acceptance speech in front of news reporters. Bonnie was there beside me, accepting awards of her own.

On the first day of college, I showed up early for class. I sat next to a pretty blond girl.

She's probably the same age as my son, I thought. I was the oldest person in the room, and I wanted to shrink down in my chair and disappear. All the students were joking with each other, and I just sat there with nothing to say. I wondered what crazy notion had made me think I could possibly fit in.

Then my classmate smiled at me. "Would you like half of my pretzel?" I accepted it gratefully. Then, finally, someone my age walked into the room. It was the teacher.

I had no idea what I was doing. It had been years since I had been in a college classroom. Back then, I overslept, missed classes and couldn't focus. This time, things were different. I was determined to pass and get my degree. I studied diligently and bonded with my young classmates, who were star students. I sat up in the front of the class and participated.

Whenever I doubted myself, I would see those gold beads hanging in my room and smile. Bonnie had so much faith in me. My children were counting on me. It was time to stop being a victim of my circumstances, become empowered, and reach for my dreams.

Being an older student had its advantages. My favorite teacher often teased me when I knew things the other students didn't because they weren't born in the same era as us. I looked forward to coming to class and hadn't had so much fun in years. When our grades were posted, my jaw dropped in disbelief. I had A's in almost every class. My hard work had paid off.

If I could have focused in my twenties, my entire life would have been different. Yet I couldn't dwell on my past mistakes. There was no time like the present to change my life.

During my time as a middle-aged student at college, I wrote for the college newspaper and received many awards. On the day of graduation, I peered out into the crowd and saw my mother, Connie, beaming with pride, next to my smiling children. It was an amazing feeling to realize that I had overcome so much and become a college graduate.

That was only the beginning. Years later, I would achieve my lifetime goal of becoming a published writer. I hoped that my children now saw me as a positive woman who had overcome great challenges and was no longer a victim. Soon, my children graduated college too.

I had a lot of people to thank who helped me along the way. I couldn't have done it without the encouragement of my mentor and friend Bonnie, and the Women's Opportunity Center. But, most of all, I'd like to thank my workshop instructor, who still encourages women to take charge of their lives and make positive changes. I want her to know that I still have those beads, a symbol of empowerment, and will always treasure them.

~L.A. Strucke

66

Owning Your Space

What lies behind us and what lies before us are tiny
matters compared to what lies within us.
~Ralph Waldo Emerson

I come from a long line of women
Who suck in stomachs
And wear painfully large smiles
Who punish themselves at dinner
For eating lunch
Voices like wisps of wind
Silence that echoes down generations
Ever shrinking, they collect leaves and dirt
In matted hair from dragging themselves low
To make men feel taller on our family tree
That's why when I met you
I was scared to take up too much space
I tried to concave and let you grow from the hallowed ground
Of my hungry core
But you didn't mind that I filled a room
I was terrified to show you the hoarded opinions and dreams
I had stored in my back closet
(I had always meant to throw them out when I fell in love — to
  make room for yours)
But you just asked to see them
Now they occupy our walls like works of art

When I shrink
As is habit
You offer a ladle full of courage like a reminder
That the bigger I get
The stronger I get
The wiser
Healthier
The more I grow
The more we flourish
You say
The taller I stand
The more of me
you can see
"and baby I love this view"
You chuckle in the crook of my neck
I hope one day my daughters will smile and say
"I come from a line of strong-willed women who aren't afraid to
   own their space"
And the pictures on their trees
will start with you and me.

~Crystal Birmingham-Overmeyer

The Empowered Woman

Sticking Up for What's Right

67

It's Not Over Until
I Say It's Over...

The right way is not always the popular and easy way.
Standing for right when it is unpopular is a true
test of moral character.
~Margaret Chase Smith

I was the last person who ever expected to have a problem with sexual harassment. I was a forty-five-year-old widow with four teenage children. I was an average-looking woman, and on a sexually attractive scale of one to ten, I'd have rated myself a two. I was thirty pounds overweight, wore bifocals and didn't wear make-up.

I'd been a widow for ten years and had worked a variety of jobs to support my family. I didn't have any college or special job skills, and I took whatever jobs I could get. I'd been working two jobs, cleaning houses and working as a clerk in a small gift shop. When the gift shop closed, I needed another job to keep supporting my family.

I applied for twenty-three jobs and couldn't believe my good luck when I was hired at a jewelry store at a salary that would allow me to quit my job cleaning houses. Having only one job was almost like being on vacation.

That lasted six months, and then my boss started asking me odd questions about my personal life. Was I dating anyone, and why not? He was a sixty-five-year-old widower and had been pleasant to work with until then. Two men in their forties and three women in their twenties also worked in the store.

> **I told my children I was filing sexual-harassment charges against my boss.**

My boss began asking me out to dinner, and I refused. I explained I had four children at home and wanted to be home in the evenings with them.

A sexy novel and suggestive cartoons appeared in my locker at work. I couldn't imagine anyone else at work would have put them there other than my boss. Things escalated. He hinted I might lose my job if I wasn't nice to him. I began applying at other places for a new job. One day, he cornered me in the stockroom and tried to kiss and grope me. He said he would make me assistant manager if I'd "be friendly."

I called a lawyer, and he took my case on a contingency. If I lost, I wouldn't have to pay him anything. I told my children I was filing sexual-harassment charges against my boss.

My children's first reaction was: *How could any man be sexually interested in you?* Then they were embarrassed I was making this public. What if their friends heard about it? And finally, if I lost my job, how would we survive?

I was crushed. I hadn't exactly thought of myself as an innocent damsel in distress defending myself against the villain, but I had expected my kids to be sympathetic and supportive. Maybe they were right. Maybe I was making a fool of myself and humiliating my family.

Things were worse at work. The boss stopped coming into the office and appointed one of the men as temporary manager. The two men who worked at the store laughed at me and would ask me how my love life was. The women stopped talking to me at all. To say things were chilly at work was an understatement; it was like the North Pole. There was gossip about me, but what did I do to cause it? How far did I go with the boss? Had I encouraged or seduced him? Was it about the money?

I was fortunate to get a nice lawyer, but he was very young. I even wondered if I was his first case. He told me I was the perfect victim.

My boss had seen that and taken advantage of me. I was middle-aged, needed the job, and was the sole support for my four children. I didn't have any real job skills or training to make it easy to get another job. I was also quiet, shy and easily intimidated because I'd been bullied and abused as a child.

I told my lawyer that maybe it wasn't worth it. Maybe I should just give up. But he said he was sure my boss had abused countless women before me, and if I didn't stop him, he would abuse many after me. He said I had to be the champion who looked my boss straight in the eye and said not just "no," but "hell no!" He said he'd fight to the end for me, and it wasn't over until he said it was over.

My lawyer also got some good counseling for me that shed light on how I'd been timid and afraid my entire life. I'd tiptoed through life trying not to upset or offend anyone. I was feeling stronger and, in spite of the way I felt inside, I became brave on the "outside." I'd go to work every day whether anyone spoke to me or not. I would do my job and then go home to my children. I would see this through to the end, regardless of the outcome.

The case went to court. My boss did not show up, and the judge awarded me an amount of money that would have been equal to my wages for five years at the store.

I thought it was over. I'd survived. My lawyer said "no," it was not over, and I deserved more money. He wanted a written letter of apology and a good recommendation from my boss. It wouldn't be over until he said it was over.

I told my lawyer I didn't care about more money or the letter, and he said *he* cared. The judge contacted my boss and ordered him to produce a letter of apology and a recommendation, which he did.

The next week, my boss filed for bankruptcy — not because of my lawsuit, but because he hadn't been paying any of his debts for the past year and owed a fortune for jewelry, rent and income taxes. The store was closed and the inventory seized. My boss moved across the country. The people I'd worked with still wouldn't speak to me and blamed me for the store closing, even though I had nothing to do with it.

Going through the ordeal had been painful, embarrassing, exhausting and scary, but I came out of it stronger, smarter and no longer a victim. I faced the giant, and I won.

My boss died two years later, and my lawyer filed against his estate. Four years after I first filed my complaint, I got a check in the mail with the rest of the money I was originally awarded. There was also a note from my lawyer that said simply, "Now it's over."

~April Knight

By the Dawn's Early Light

If you have to do it, then you're doing the right thing.
~Kathy Valentine

"The colonel needs to see you," my flight commander said as I set my olive-green backpack down on my desk. It was a few minutes shy of 7:00 a.m., and a direct request from the boss usually meant one of two things: I was being promoted, or I had seriously messed up.

As far as I knew, I was definitely not due for a promotion. A bolt of panic shot down my spine, and it clearly showed on my face.

"Relax, lieutenant. I think she just needs you to run an errand for the promotion ceremony happening later this week," he said.

"Oh! Phew," I said, feeling my pulse return to normal as my shoulders inched away from my ears. And sure enough, when I reported to the colonel's office, she confirmed the request.

My orders were simple. Go down to the print shop, pick up flyers for the promotion ceremony, proofread them, and if everything looked okay, bring them back to her office.

As I drove to the printer, I couldn't shake a nagging feeling that something seemed off about this request.

"I'm one of our unit's technical writers. Of course, it makes sense that the boss needs a writer to proofread," I tried telling myself.

Sticking Up for What's Right |

But for some reason, I couldn't quite shake a sense of foreboding washing over me.

At first, everything went according to plan. The flyers had indeed been printed, the front cover was in brilliant color, and there were two packed boxes — an indication the order seemed to be correct.

Then I opened a flyer to read it. As I scanned the text, my stomach dropped into my shoes.

The sequence of events was accurate, the distinguished guest list was thorough and complete, and the ranks and names of promotees were all correct.

There was just one problem: A live singer had been listed to perform the National Anthem. I knew her personally. She couldn't carry a tune if her life depended on it.

In a military promotion ceremony, immediately after the official party arrives in place, the event always begins with a rendition of "The Star-Spangled Banner." Depending on the circumstances and rank of the person promoting, the anthem might be performed via a full brass and percussion band. Sometimes it's a live singer. And sometimes it's a pre-recorded instrumental version piped in over speakers.

The fact that a live singer was listed on the program wasn't the problem.

But *I* had been listed as the performer.

My first thought was there must be a mistake. Surely someone had, very incorrectly, given my Squadron Commander bad intelligence and told her that I could sing. *This cannot be happening,* I thought as I drove back to the office.

The boxes of flyers felt as if they weighed a hundred pounds as I lugged them up two flights of stairs and back to my commander's office. I peeked in the door, and she beamed and waved me in eagerly. Setting the boxes down did not alleviate the heavy weight that had fallen across my shoulders. I wasn't even sure where to begin.

"Everything look okay?" she chirped.

"Well, I… I did see one error," I started hesitantly. "Ma'am, did someone volunteer me to sing?"

I was one of just three women in my unit, and although we loved to play pranks on each other and had become as close as sisters, neither of them would have done something like this.

"Oh, don't be silly," she said. "Of course not. You're a woman, aren't you?"

When I signed on the dotted line to join the service, I had long ago braced myself for the fight and insinuations that I knew one day would surely come. Someone, at some point in my military career, would label me as "less" — less of a fighter, less of a warrior, less of a leader — simply because I was a woman.

But in all of the ways I had anticipated to fight sexism in the military, being on the receiving end of it from a woman floored me.

"Don't let fear get in the way," she chastised. "All women can sing. It's just mind over matter."

I fought to keep my jaw off the floor. I couldn't believe she had actually said that with a straight face! I stood frozen to the spot, too dumbfounded to move.

She offered a final, smug smile before turning back to her computer and clacking away at the keyboard.

I knew what I was supposed to do — what I was "expected" to do. Protocol told me I should have saluted smartly, turned on my heel, exited her office, and prepared to sing in just two short days.

Standing there, I pictured in my mind how the ceremony would unfold. The official party would file in. The snare drumroll would silence the crowd. And somewhere, behind a microphone stand, would lie my catatonic body, passed out from paralytic fear and shock.

In that moment, I did the only thing I could think of; I took a deep breath, locked my eyes on the floor and began to sing in my boss's office.

I made it all the way to "whose broad stripes and bright stars" before she stopped me. A look of sheer horror clouded her face as she realized I wasn't pretending. Had I attempted to hit the vocal scale needed for "the rocket's red glare," both the bombs and every window in the building would've been bursting in air.

Stunned, she mumbled that she would find someone else, and I was dismissed. I couldn't leave her office fast enough.

I learned two powerful lessons that day.

Admittedly, it does sound clichéd, but the saying to "trust your gut" could not be more sound advice. Our bodies can sense and pick up things that may not have yet registered in our mind, or even pick up on things that have not yet come to pass. My body immediately knew that something was wrong. Something, somewhere could sense that I had not been given the full story — and that instinct was spot-on.

And I realized in that moment that doing something simply because someone else thought I should was not fair to my own soul and spirit.

Now, whenever I have doubts or have a difficult day, I think back on that moment when I swallowed all pride and stood up for myself — in what very well could be one of the most humiliating ways imaginable. I was slowly appreciating my talents and skill sets, and I knew singing was not one of them.

The promotion ceremony went off without a hitch, although there was an emergency re-print of flyers to remove my name from the program.

I've heard the National Anthem many times since then. I can't help but feel a surge of pride remembering the day I had the confidence to stand up for myself and do a lousy job singing it.

~Kristi Adams

69

Don't Take My Wheels!

Take the power to control your own life.
Take the power to make your life happy.
~Susan Polis Schutz

My husband's 62nd birthday was only months away when he made an announcement. "I think I'm going to retire at sixty-two. I've given it much thought, checked into Social Security differences, and financially we can do it."

Ken's decision came as a surprise, but I liked the idea. Earlier discussions had helped us decide to move closer to where our grown children lived, back to a community where we had many longtime friends, but that plan was set for more than three years away. The "do-it-at-sixty-two" part came as something new, but after a long career in the banking business, Ken was ready for some leisure.

The next day, as I did household chores, I started thinking about what life might be like with Ken home full-time. Every day would be like a Saturday or Sunday. That might be nice. As I moved clothes from the washer to the dryer, a new thought stopped me with wet laundry in mid-air.

My dad had taken an early retirement, too, and he and Mom were joined at the hip from day one. The only time she had to herself was when he went to get a monthly haircut. Mom didn't drive, so Dad accompanied her on errands. No more public transportation for her. He helped in the house, pointing out new and better ways to do the

Sticking Up for What's Right |

tasks she'd done for close to fifty years. She went out to lunch, but only with Dad. They were inseparable by my dad's choice. My mother lost what little personal life she'd had prior to this new stage in their marriage. She hadn't asserted herself, bowing instead to Dad's wishes.

My own active life provided a good deal of enjoyment. I volunteered at a local hospital. I lunched with friends and belonged to several bridge groups. Would Ken want me to give that up? Would Ken expect me to put aside my freelance writing so that I could go to the hardware store with him? My stomach began to churn. I moved the vacuum cleaner with more force that day than I ever had, and my iron flew across the ironing board as I contemplated this new life filled with possible changes that didn't get my stamp of approval.

I kept my reservations to myself as we began to make plans for his October 1st retirement — listing the house, sorting through our belongings, and making moving plans. *I'll adjust,* I told myself. The only thing was, I didn't believe it. I kept thinking about my mother's retirement years with Dad. And then one night, Ken made a simple statement that left me with my mouth open and words stuck in my throat.

He said, "We'll sell your car. We can easily make do with one. It will be a big savings."

When I was finally able to speak, my words were blunt. "Absolutely not! I'm not giving up my car." I'd never even considered getting rid of one car. What could he be thinking?

There was going to be no argument since Ken just smiled and said, "We'll see."

I knew then that I'd fight for my independence. No matter how much I loved my husband, we both needed a life of our own. I would not turn into my mother who always stopped whatever she was doing to have Dad's lunch on the table precisely at noon. I realized after my father passed away that it was too late for Mom to create a full and happy life for herself.

We dropped the one-car subject, but it swirled around and around in my mind. I conjured up several situations. Ken would head out to the golf course and leave me stranded for five hours. Or I'd go out to do some shopping, and he'd say I needed to be back in forty-five minutes so he could go to wherever it is retired men like to go. My stomach started that churning again.

One afternoon, I sat at the kitchen table with a cup of tea and came up with a plan. I knew what I needed to say to Ken. After all, he was usually a reasonable man, although when it came to saving money, he could be stubborn. That evening, I made some of his favorites for dinner — steak grilled medium rare, baked potato with lots of sour cream, a salad full of our homegrown tomatoes and crisp Italian rolls. Earlier, I'd baked a chocolate cake to crown the dinner, and then slathered chocolate frosting over it. No harm in satisfying his sweet tooth.

After dinner, I brought up the car topic. "Let's start out with both cars and see how much we use them. Then we can go from there."

Cutting himself a second piece of cake, he agreed my proposal might have merit. While he ate, I gave him more food for thought. "You know how my parents were never apart once Dad retired." He nodded and took another forkful. "I don't want that to happen to us. I'd like both of us to have a life of our own. I'll do my volunteer work at the hospital, and you can find something of your own that interests you. I'd like to continue with my bridge clubs and my writing. And I'd expect you to play golf however many days a week you like and putter in the garden to your heart's content. Sometimes, we'll go places together, just not all the time."

Ken added a guideline of his own, one that would keep our life from a dreary routine. "I don't want to eat dinner at 5:00 or 5:30 every night like some seniors do." I readily agreed.

All that happened fifteen years ago. We still have two cars. We go our separate ways on a good many days, but we also do things together. If I'm home, I fix lunch for both of us. If I'm out somewhere, Ken makes his own lunch. At 5:00, we usually pour a glass of wine, watch the news on TV, and discuss our day. Then I fix dinner. It works for us. I have both a loving husband and my independence.

~Nancy Julien Kopp

70

Standing Alone

A woman with a voice is,
by definition, a strong woman.
~Melinda Gates

aul hired me on the spot during my interview for the accounting job. I would be starting the next day. He introduced me to the ladies I'd be working with — his secretary, Susan, whose desk was just outside his office down the hall from where I would be stationed, and then two others who were in their early twenties like me. Elaina, the fourth, was much older and would be training me to do the job she would retire from in about two months. Everyone seemed welcoming.

Back in Paul's office, we concluded the interview. As I rose to leave, I extended my hand to shake his. His fingers closed around mine. His other palm rested on my forearm for a moment and then began to glide upward and down, stroking me more intimately than I was comfortable with.

"You're going to fit in just fine here," he murmured, stepping toward me as I stepped back.

I thanked him, pulled away as politely as I could, and left. Once home, I decided to dismiss the whole incident. It was the early 1970s, and that sort of behavior was still quite common. I don't think the term "sexual harassment" even existed back then, but I was no stranger to it. Since puberty, I had been groped or had my bottom pinched and patted by strangers, and even had to administer the occasional slap to ward off unwelcome attention. But I had never experienced inappropriate advances by someone in power in the workplace.

The first few weeks went by quickly. Everyone was patient as I pushed past that novice learning curve. Within a month, I was relaxed and efficient at my job, but I began noticing that the atmosphere in our section seemed more subdued than other departments. Except for Elaina, who eagerly kept a retirement day countdown of bright red Xs on her desk calendar, none of my accounting colleagues seemed happy.

The reason became crystal clear the morning Paul returned one of my ledgers. He leaned over me to place it on my desk. As he pulled his hand back, his fingers deliberately brushed against my breast, while his other hand gave my shoulder an intimate squeeze.

Before I could react, he was gone. I sat there blinking in shock. I whirled around to check if any of my co-workers saw what happened, but everyone was focused on their own work. Again, I said nothing. I desperately needed my job. I had been unemployed for several months due to health issues, and my husband's job didn't pay enough to cover the bills that had mounted while I was ill.

Two days later, I was taking a late break alone in the company kitchen when Paul walked in. My heart started pounding when he smiled and eyed me up and down, stopping to focus on my chest.

"I like that sweater, Marya," he commented. "It shows off your lovely assets — both of them!"

"My break is over. I'd better be getting back," I responded nervously, reaching for my purse. I hoped I didn't sound as frightened as I felt.

To my shock, he gripped my wrist firmly as I tried to pass.

"Sit. Relax," he urged. "There's no rush. I know your boss won't mind if you're a few minutes late," he joked.

"I-I have a lot of work," I stammered, shaking off his hold and bolting toward the door. Behind me, I heard his taunting laughter.

During the next few days, there were no new encounters. I made sure I was never alone in the kitchen again, forgoing my breaks altogether if another employee wasn't present when I peeked in.

I started to see things with fresh eyes. Paul was inappropriate with all my immediate co-workers, rubbing their shoulders, kissing them on the cheek when they turned in assignments, patting their behinds when he passed them at the filing cabinets, and hugging them tightly and for far too long. His secretary, Susan, spent long periods in his office behind closed doors, often exiting with disheveled hair, her eyes filled with shame before she cast them downwards to straighten a skirt or blouse.

I began having trouble sleeping and became jumpy, stiffening when my husband spontaneously pulled me close for a random kiss. He noticed and asked why, but I couldn't confide in him. He treated me like his fragile princess, always protective and ready to do battle on my behalf. I was afraid of what he would do if I told him my boss was too familiar.

I knew it was futile to discuss the situation with the other girls. They were in the same predicament as I was. They needed their jobs, were bogged down with bills and responsibilities, and were afraid to speak out. Either way, it would have done no good. There was no help available all those years ago. We only had two options: to stay and tolerate the abuse, or to leave and go elsewhere, hoping things would be better. My co-workers had already made their choices.

Things came to a head about three weeks after the kitchen encounter. Paul called me over the intercom, directing me to come into his office and bring a file he needed.

My legs felt leaden as I made my way down the hall. Susan saw me coming and ducked her head, pretending to be intent on her typing. I walked into the room where Paul sat waiting in his chair with his feet up on his desk. He gave me another once-over, leering before insisting I close the door. I felt bile rise when he actually licked his lips like he was about to enjoy a feast. I left the door open and stood there waiting.

"How can I help you?" I asked, keeping my distance.

"I told you to close the door. Do it and get over here. I need a massage," he barked.

"I beg your pardon?" I asked, stunned.

"You heard me. I twisted my knee last night. I need you to rub it every day until it feels better. Now do as you're told. It's time you learned your place here. I'm getting sick of your prudish act!" he snapped.

I gasped in outrage at his gall. Fury replaced my fear of job loss. I was tired of feeling like prey every time I walked into work, and I wasn't going to tolerate it anymore.

"That's not in my job description! Go to a massage parlor!" I suggested with a newfound calm. "As for my 'place,' it's never going to be in some repulsive pervert's lap!"

With that, I put the file on his desk, turned, and walked to my desk. I retrieved my belongings and left the building, my dignity and pride intact. I didn't know what the future held, but I knew I'd face it with a newfound strength, courage and, most importantly, self-respect.

Eventually, I found another job where I felt safe and valued for my contributions and not my gender.

That day, decades ago, I stood alone. Today, I'm delighted to see women stand united, bettering the world slowly for females everywhere.

~Marya Morin

71

The High-Voltage Cage

Never be bullied into silence. Never allow yourself
to be made a victim. Accept no one's definition
of your life, but define yourself.
~Harvey Fierstein

I was working at AT&T. This was back when it ran the telephone business all over America, before the government broke it into pieces in the early 1980s. I'd started in a clerical position, like most women. Then, Western Electric, the manufacturing arm of AT&T, encouraged women to apply for jobs there in quality control. These were higher-paying jobs that had previously only been filled by men.

I signed up, as did a few other females, and the rocky ride began.

Inspecting wires can be a grueling and difficult job. Wire was often wrapped on huge reels that had to be rolled around the shop to get to the testing cage. The wire had to be stripped for testing, then attached to electronic testing kits, and this often led to voltage shocks.

My female co-workers and I learned the art of guiding huge reels of ocean cable by turning the reel while it was rolling, not while it was still. We learned how to strip a wire of its jacket and how to avoid shocks. We learned about injection molding, intermittent broken wires, conductors and the need to prevent them from touching.

The biggest lesson involved the high-voltage cage. This was where wires had to be tested in the water. Most of the wires we tested at Western Electric were used outdoors, and the wire jackets needed to be strong, to keep water from getting in and shorting out the wires. Some of the wires produced by Western Electric were even used under the ocean, to carry telephone calls from one continent to another.

The cage transmitted high voltage once the testing wires were attached, and the cage door was tightly closed and locked. The resulting electrical surge began when the tester pulled down the switch, which was, intentionally and for protection, *outside* the cage.

No one was to stay inside the high-voltage cage during the test. As long as the cage door was open, the switch could not be thrown. The tester would exit the cage after setting up the wire for testing, and then throw the switch from outside the cage, where huge amounts of voltage that could kill someone were sent through the conductors in the wire.

A few days earlier, a worker had been killed inside the cage. Employees in the shop would get a bit too confident and remain inside the cage during a test — a dangerous action. One such fellow was actually eating his lunch *inside* the cage while he tested.

That's the backdrop for my story, which is about the backlash we women were getting from a few or our male co-workers. There were five of us in a department of about thirty people. Most of the men were fair, kind, and helpful. But they didn't try to stop the few who were nasty. Sure, we were a little awkward as we learned our new jobs. We sometimes needed help from shop workers. We declared good wires as bad by mistake from time to time. But this happened to all the new male workers, too. With practice we would all get better and more confident.

A couple of childish males in the quality-control department thought it was a hoot to hide our tools, or to laugh at us as we struggled to roll cable reels with thousands of feet of wire upon them, or as we tentatively hooked up wires in the high-voltage cage. We were all sick of their boorish behavior.

One normal working day, my friend Betty came into our quality-control office, breathing heavily, pale and sweating. "Chuck locked the high-voltage cage," she told me, putting her arms upon the desk and taking deep scared breaths, "WHILE I WAS IN THERE!" I was shocked.

Betty had to stand in the middle of the high-voltage cage and scream for help. We were taught that if we were in that cage and the door got locked, we were not to touch anything, and were to call for assistance. Our co-worker Chuck and a few of the other guys thought it was hilarious to watch Betty get scared inside that cage, unable to move for fear of being electrocuted.

At some point, a shop worker unlocked the cage, and all hell broke loose. We'd been complaining to our boss about this boorish male behavior, but he just told us to "man up" — that the newness of it would pass, and the guys would get bored.

Meanwhile, Betty could have been killed by what Chuck thought was some kind of funny joke. I'd had enough.

"*60 Minutes*," I told our quality department's manager. "If this doesn't end, I am going on *60 Minutes* to tell our story."

The department manager fired our supervisor, which he deserved for ignoring that horrible situation run amok in his section. We got a new supervisor, and in due course all the men, as well as the females, asked that I run for union representative so we would have someone on the board who did what unions are supposed to do — protect the workers.

And I did! I ran for union rep. Many in the shop cheered me on and campaigned for me. They'd seen the horrible behavior of a handful of badly behaved males. Once elected, I got the union to approve transferring those males to the "wire shop." Females had not yet been assigned to that department, and perhaps the boors would be better off nowhere around female workers.

And as such things go, females learned the jobs and all the tricks of the trade over the years. The balance of males to females became more or less even, much like the general population.

It was time to take a stand, and I did. It wasn't easy, and along the way I made some enemies. But now, almost fifty years later, I recall the era of the maligned and mocked female worker, and how one person saying "Enough!" helped to bring about change.

~Patricia Fish

72

Grab Bag

I firmly believe that respect is a lot more important,
and a lot greater, than popularity.
~Julius Erving

tanding at her bedside, the doctor asked my seventeen-year-old daughter, "Piper, do you like school?" His crossed arms revealed his agenda to discredit her physical complaints and discharge her from the hospital. It wasn't our first experience with this line of questioning.

I knew what he was implying, and as her mom I ached to jump into the conversation to protect her, but I needed Piper to answer for herself. After all, I wouldn't be able to safeguard her from such accusations all her life. I waited for her reply. *Don't raise your voice,* I thought, *or he'll accuse you of defiance. Don't falter, or you'll appear unsteady, anxious. Don't cry, or he'll label you depressed. And, most importantly, don't give him approval through silence.*

She made eye contact with the man in the lab coat looming over her, and she said, "Of course I like school. I take advanced placement classes at a private school to challenge myself, so I can get into a top university after I graduate."

That's my girl, I thought. *Nice defense.*

But the doctor refused to back down. "Do you find yourself missing a lot of classes?"

"Are you kidding?" she said. "In AP classes, missing one day is like missing a week. I've only missed two days this entire school year.

I hate to fall behind." She looked at me, and I smiled because she remained self-assured.

She could've told him how she darted from classes throughout the day to vomit in the restroom and then quietly returned to her desk as if nothing had happened. Or she could've mentioned that before the first bell, while her friends chatted about last evening's events, she marched to the nurse's office to give herself a heparin shot in the stomach. And that during lunch, she returned to the nurse to swallow one of the many handfuls of pills she had to choke down each day that enabled her to attend school in the first place. But she knew better than to provide him ammunition. The more facts she reported to the man in white, the increased likelihood of being labeled a malingerer, a faker. She had learned to say as little as possible.

"Maybe it's just your monthly visitor," he blurted.

Stunned, I looked Piper in the eyes and saw a flicker of temporary confusion turn to disbelief.

Obviously, he thought her weak, unable to handle pain.

If only he'd witnessed Piper's disappointment when she couldn't pass the ROTC physical. How bravery and courage fueled her desire to defend our nation, but migraines, seizures, joint pain, numbness and tingling in her arms and legs, blurred vision, dizziness, shortness of breath, chronic fatigue, memory loss, and vertigo dashed any hope of donning a military uniform. Denied a future as an Army warrior, she still possessed a warrior's spirit.

I stepped in to teach my daughter yet another lesson in handling misogyny.

"Do you really think she'd go to the ER for her period? You realize she was transported here by ambulance from another hospital, right? If it were her menstrual period, the other hospital would've laughed at her and sent her home. They thought her condition severe enough to admit her here."

I waited for our punishment. How dare I question a doctor? A male doctor at that.

"Well, they were wrong. She can go home."

I flinched. "Does she get the courtesy of a proper diagnosis?"

"I think it's a flu bug," he muttered.

"She's been vomiting for months. Does the flu last that long?"

I braced myself, knowing I'd crossed a bigger line by challenging his diagnosis. But what did we have to lose?

He shook his head.

"Could you at least palpate her abdomen to see where the pain is coming from? Like I said, this has been going on for months."

He glared at me. "That won't be necessary. She can get dressed and go home."

He handed her an eviction notice.

I turned toward Piper, who was on the verge of tears, and gave her the don't-give-him-the-satisfaction-of-crying look.

And home we went: a place devoid of judgment, sarcasm, eye rolling, and degradation.

Knowing that she had a chronic disease and would have more encounters with indifferent medical doctors in months to come, Piper and I developed a plan.

"Can we just get up and leave when they're so rude?" she asked.

That thought had never occurred to me, being raised by parents and grandparents who held doctors in high esteem. With this question, I realized she did not believe that doctors were almighty and all-knowing. Why not leave? As paying customers, weren't we entitled to respect? Why would I continue to allow healthcare professionals to belittle, chastise, or question my daughter's character? Or to infer she faked an illness when she suffered every day, all day?

We devised ground rules: We would no longer entertain their talk of a school phobia, hints of gender weakness, accusations of malingering or faking, or the labeling of a mental health diagnosis without sufficient cause. The most important rule: We wouldn't be rude or disrespectful in return. We would uphold our dignity.

"I'll follow your lead," I suggested. "It's your appointment, so I want you to call it when you feel the doctor crosses a line. Your line may be different from mine."

"Let the games begin," she said.

First up, a visit to a gastroenterologist for her continued nausea and vomiting.

"It could just be related to ovulation or, perhaps, anxiety." Wow. A double whammy.

I watched for a signal. Piper reached over, grabbed her school bag and stood.

The doctor's eyes widened.

"Thank you for your time," she said. "Mom, are you ready?"

I followed her lead and plucked my purse from the ground. "The only anxiety she has is when a doctor doesn't take her pain seriously. And I don't think she's been ovulating every day for months. But thank you."

As the doctor tried to process our boldness, we walked away with confidence in our decision. We no longer rewarded disrespect. We no longer paid for incompetence. We no longer argued against an archaic establishment that continued to blame the chronically ill who sought help in hopes of alleviating their pain and suffering.

Next up, an allergist. "So, you've had Lymes disease in the past?"

Ouch, I thought, and waited for Piper's decision. She grabbed her bag, signaling the end of the appointment. "It's Lyme disease. Not Lymes. If you don't know how to say it, I don't know that you can treat it. Besides, there's no cure, so I still have it."

The doctor straightened and looked at me for a second opinion, and I nodded. Piper and I high-fived all the way to the car.

We now treat the first doctor's visit as an interview, deciding if the physician's views and knowledge of Lyme disease are compatible with Piper's needs. Based on the interview, we either hire or we fire. Our treatment for curing a doctor's arrogance and rudeness? We grab our bags and take our dollars elsewhere.

~Cathi LaMarche

73

My Name Is Not Et Ux

Doing the right thing has power.
~Laura Linney

I was summoned to the school office to take an "important" phone call while the principal himself covered my fourth-grade social studies class. "It's your bank," the secretary informed me before handing over the receiver. "They're verifying your employment for your house loan."

"It seems we have an... irregularity... in your paperwork," the voice on the phone informed me. "Do your children live with you full- or part-time?"

"I have no biological children," I replied. "My husband has two children who live with their mother, and they visit him every other holiday and a few weeks each summer."

"But it says the co-borrower pays child support," she continued.

"That's right. I'm the borrower, and my husband is the co-borrower."

"That's highly irregular," she said.

"He's a commercial fisherman," I told her. "My teaching income is the one we wish to base the loan on. It's more dependable. His income fluctuates with the fish."

"Oh, my," she stammered. "I've never seen paperwork with the wife listed as the primary borrower before."

I laughed. "Get used to it. It's 1984. I guess I'm just blazing the trail here."

"But what if you get pregnant and take a leave of absence?" she asked.

My hackles clearly rising, I said, "I'm pretty sure it's illegal for you to ask me that."

She cleared her throat. "In order for us to approve this loan, we have to take everything into account."

"My husband and I could both quit our jobs tomorrow," I replied, my voice going up an octave. "To ask me if we plan on having children is completely out-of-line and offensive, and…"

> **"I am listed as the borrower because I am, and always will be, the primary breadwinner."**

I stopped speaking abruptly when the school secretary put her hand on my shoulder. She leaned in close to whisper in my ear, "You want to get a loan or not?"

"Ma'am?" asked the loan officer. "Ma'am? Are you still there?"

"Can we start over?" I took a deep breath. "I am listed as the borrower because I am, and always will be, the primary breadwinner. I saved up all the money for the down payment myself out of my own income while also supporting my husband and paying the child support for his two children."

"I see."

"I sincerely hope you do. I've worked hard to be able to buy a house, and I'd like to buy this one with a loan from your bank. How can we make that happen?"

Fortunately, we were able to make my dream come true, and I was elated — until the day the official bank papers arrived. Printed at the top of each payment coupon was my husband's name and "et ux" printed behind it.

I called the bank and asked to speak to our loan officer. "Et ux?" I asked, bewildered. "What in the world does that mean?"

"It's Latin," she replied. "It means 'and spouse.'"

I could feel the heat rising up my neck. "It's my loan, my house, and my payment coupons," I began softly, "and my name is not 'et ux.'"

"It's policy for us to issue the coupons in the name of the borrower and…"

"We've been all over this," I said through clenched teeth. "I am the borrower, not my husband. Unless you want to receive checks signed 'et ux,' you're going to have to reissue these coupons."

It took some time, a few more phone calls, and a personal visit to the bank president, but I did, indeed, get my name listed on the coupons. And they did, indeed, have both our names at the top — except his name was listed first.

I called the bank and asked to speak to our specific loan officer, but she was away from her desk, so I was connected with another bank employee whom I was told could help me. "Could you please explain to me why my husband's name is listed before mine on my payment coupons?" I asked politely when the call was transferred.

"We always list the man's name first," he replied, "since the man is the primary borrower."

Wrong answer. If he had said the names were listed alphabetically, I could have let it go. But once again, I had to explain that I was the borrower, and he was the co-borrower.

"That's highly irregular," the bank employee began.

I started to laugh uncontrollably. "Irregularity seems to run rampant at your bank," I finally choked out. "It's 1984, and I'm determined to eradicate this old paradigm once and for all."

"Perhaps you'd like to talk to the bank president," he said.

"Perhaps I would," I agreed. "I've got trails to blaze."

The third time was the charm, and the new payment coupons, with my name listed first, were issued the following week.

~Jan Bono

I'm the Hero of This Story

The whole story is about you. You are the main character.
~Don Miguel Ruiz

"**L**isten, I don't think you're happy here."

I looked up at my boss, Chip. "I beg your pardon?"

Chip smiled coolly. "I said that I don't think you're happy here."

It was my turn to at least try to smile. "What makes you say that?"

Leaning against a bookshelf, Chip crossed his arms over his chest. "Let's talk over coffee."

"All right," I agreed. I followed my boss to the break room where he poured each of us a cup of coffee.

"What's up?" I managed to ask after taking a very small sip of the bitter coffee.

"I'm thinking that you'd be much happier working somewhere else."

"Just what are you saying? Are you firing me?"

Chip leaned back, hands flat on the tabletop. "Firing you? Of course not. I'm just suggesting that you look for another job where you might be happier."

"I don't understand why you think I'm not happy. I am happy, Chip. I like my job, and I need my job."

"There are a ton of jobs out there. I'm sure that if you applied yourself, you'd be able to find something that you'd really like." Chip got to his feet. "Think about what I said, okay?" He tossed the rest of his coffee in the sink and then threw the Styrofoam cup into the wastebasket. He left the break room, whistling as he shut the door behind him.

I knew my mouth was hanging open, but I didn't seem to be able to shut it. I couldn't lose this job. That's all there was to it. Numbly, I returned to my desk, avoiding eye contact with anyone else in the office. At the end of the day, I waited until Chip had left before heading for the parking lot. I was almost out the back door when Audrey, another employee, stopped me.

"What did Chip say to you?" Audrey questioned.

"He thinks I'd be happier if I started looking for another job."

Audrey's eyes widened. "He fired you?"

"No, he wants me to quit."

"That creep! You know why he's doing this, don't you?"

I shook my head. "No, I don't. I thought I was doing a good job. Everyone seems to like me, and I always get positive work reviews."

Audrey cut me off. "It has nothing to do with you or your work." Gesturing toward an empty desk in the corner of the office, she said, "It's all about her."

I looked at the desk. It was where Destiny sat, a young woman with dark brown hair and clear blue eyes. "Destiny?"

"Chip wants you to leave so he can give Destiny your job without any repercussions. Don't make it easy on him. What he's doing isn't exactly illegal, but it's completely unethical and totally unfair to you. Don't let him get away with it."

Anger mixed with disappointment, and I felt a wild urge to walk out the office door and never return, but I knew that such an over-the-top gesture would feel good for about five minutes before reality kicked in. "What can I do?" I questioned. "If he wants to, he can make my life pretty miserable here."

"Just don't quit. Fight it. I know that's easy for me to say, but that's what I'd do if I were in your shoes. I'd fight every step of the way. This is your job. Fight for it. You have to be the hero of this story because no one else can fight it for you."

"I'll try," I promised, knowing that it wasn't going to be very pleasant to go to a job every morning knowing that my boss didn't really want me there.

My prediction was right on the money. The next few months were pretty miserable. After seeing that I didn't plan on quitting, Chip tossed more and more work on my desk. But it wasn't until someone started leaving employment ads in my mailbox that I finally lost it.

"This has to stop," I said after marching into Chip's office and dropping the latest help wanted ad squarely in the middle of his desk.

"What are you talking about?" Chip questioned.

"If you think you can scare me into quitting, you're wrong. I need this job, Chip, and if you want me to leave, then you're going to have to fire me. And if you fire me, I'm going to file for unemployment and see a lawyer about an unfair dismissal because we both know you have absolutely no grounds to get rid of me. Now is this harassment going to stop?"

For several long moments, Chip and I glared at each other, but I refused to be the one to back down. Chip finally looked away. "I don't know what you're talking about," he mumbled.

"I think you do," I told him coolly. "If we're through, I'll get back to work. I have a lot to finish." I left Chip in his office, and even though he hadn't admitted anything, I had the feeling that the fight to keep my job had finally been won.

A few months later, I found a better job with higher pay and more perks. It took me less than five seconds to accept.

"Great. I know you'll be happy with us," my soon-to-be-boss told me.

"I know I will be, too," I replied since I had learned that I could be happy anywhere as long as I continued to be the hero of my own story.

~Nell Musolf

75

Chicken Soup
for the Soul

It Started with Potatoes

The best protection any woman can have… is courage.
~Elizabeth Cady Stanton

It was late afternoon as I left the schoolyard. My friends and I had been engrossed in our favorite pastime — skipping rope. Even though it was December, we never felt the cold.

The time slipped away from us. Most of us were latchkey kids, and our moms didn't worry about us as long as we came home by dark. That day, we'd been having so much fun we never noticed that the sun had gone down.

At last, we said our goodbyes and went in different directions. I had about a six-block walk through the streets of Long Island City, New York. Although I was shy socially, I was not afraid to walk alone, even after dark. I knew my way around. I came this way every day while attending junior high.

New Yorkers do not let their fear or anxiety show. If we act like we know what we are doing, we are less likely to be harassed.

But that evening, leaving the schoolyard, I got an eerie feeling. Something was wrong! The streets were deserted. I didn't see a soul, but I felt I was being watched. From between parked cars, a shadowy figure suddenly emerged in front of me. It was a man about fifty — old to me — in a black raincoat and a blue baseball cap. I tried to circle around him, but he blocked my way. When the streetlight shined down on him, I could see him clearly. The best way to describe him in my then-teenage way was that he was creepy. He sneered at me, saying, "Hi ya, kid," and proceeded to make lewd sounds and gestures with his mouth.

If that weren't repulsive enough, he then opened his coat. For a fleeting second, I thought I was going to be sick. I had never been exposed to something so vile before. I was terrified! As soon I regained my composure, I fled. I ran all the way home, turning around only once to see him following me. But he was blocks behind and had a hard time keeping up. He was huffing and puffing. I was young and could outrun him easily.

When I got home, I went straight up to my room. I wasn't sure how to deal with it. I felt soiled. I never told my mother a thing. I was too embarrassed and appalled.

If I can forget it, maybe it will just go away, I thought.

The next afternoon, my friends and I were in the schoolyard again. This time, it had been snowing, and we were building snowmen. It was a competition for the biggest and best snowman. It started getting dark, but the snow was still coming down. It only increased our enthusiasm. Then I remembered the previous evening's unpleasant incident, so before it got any later, I said goodbye to my friends and left. But not before I warned them of the obnoxious man on the loose.

"Go home early and stay safe!"

I had to stop at the grocery store to pick up some potatoes for my mom. After making the purchase, I headed home. I had to walk past the schoolyard again.

Several girls were still there building their snowmen. I was wishing they would go home. In the back of my mind, I was remembering my unnerving experience the previous night.

Suddenly, it was *him* again — the revolting man! I'd have recognized him anywhere. He was wearing the same cap and raincoat. He was walking in front of me toward the school. He hadn't seen me. He appeared to be playing with the buttons on his coat, as if ready to open them.

My first instinct was to run home quickly, but then I remembered my unsuspecting friends. We were all about twelve or thirteen, but some of the girls were smaller, more delicate and appeared to be more vulnerable.

It dawned on me suddenly that although I was just a girl, I didn't *have* to be afraid of him. I was young, but I was tall and strong. I decided to take matters into my own hands.

I still remember his shocked expression when he noticed me and realized I was running *toward* him and not *away* from him. I didn't chase him as fast as I could because I didn't know what I would have done if I caught him. I just wanted to scare him away.

Suddenly fearless, I started yelling at the top of my voice, like the spunky New York girl that I was.

"You dirty bum!"

"You filthy rat!"

I yelled at my friends to alert them. "Watch out for the scumbag!"

The potatoes we were supposed to have for dinner came out of the bag as I started flinging them at that vulgar lowlife. One hit him in the back. It felt good to fight back. I wasn't a helpless little girl after all.

When the girls noticed what was going on, they quickly got into their gutsy New York City girl mode. No shrinking violets were we! The snowmen they had been building were quickly transformed into snowballs. Soon potatoes and snowballs were being hurled at the predator from all angles.

I am a female, but not powerless.

The creep was getting bombarded. We had surrounded him. It felt good to be defending ourselves. I almost felt sorry for him — but not really.

Then one of the potatoes or snowballs must have hit the school window because the lights went on suddenly, and the custodian came out with his helper. One of them ran after the perpetrator as he tried to run. A short chase ensued as the man almost got away. Eventually, he was apprehended a few blocks down because some quick-thinking citizen had alerted the police.

When I got home, I had to explain to my mom why there were only two potatoes left from a five-pound bag. She said I should have confided in her sooner about what had happened to me. She also made it clear that I should have reported the pervert to the school authorities right away. But then she added, "I am so proud that you had the presence of mind to take matters into your own hands when you needed to."

As I grew older, I realized more and more that my gender doesn't define me. I can be anything I want to be. I am a female, but not powerless. I have a will, a voice and the ability to help myself and others. And, if necessary, it's all right to ask for help.

If all else fails, I can still resort to potatoes and snowballs.

Today, the words "I'm only a female" would never enter my mind.

~Eva Carter

76

Road Trip for Rights

*We are struggling for a uniting word, but the good
news is that we have a uniting movement.*
~Emma Watson

earing my name called, I stepped timidly up on stage. Steadying my trembling hands on the podium, I looked out at the sea of people and wanted to run away. I swallowed hard to settle the knot of nerves in my stomach. *Just remember all it took to get here,* I thought. With an audible quiver in my voice, I dived into the speech that I had practiced diligently, nervous but determined to make my voice heard.

It all started with an impassioned essay I had written in response to a radio host's slanderous comments about women's rights. I had stayed up for days researching information to discount his claims. Content with the final product, I submitted it to my boss for publication. Later, I received a text stating that he chose not to publish it because the subject matter was "too controversial." Hurt, I replied impulsively with my two weeks' notice.

In a blind fury, I began submitting my story to others. Someone had to be willing to get it out while the subject was still topical. After days of "thanks, but no thanks" responses, I felt disheartened. No one was interested in a no-name writer with a strong opinion that opposed that of a celebrity. Had my boss been right?

Finally, I received a resounding "YES!" from a small, yet powerful online blog that was controlled by and focused on women. The editor explained apologetically that they could not pay me. Not concerned about compensation, I felt validated.

"Mom, have you seen this?" My daughter woke me up. "You've gone viral," she yelled, hugging me. Confused about what that even meant, I sat up and turned on my computer.

My story had thousands of views. Women (and like-minded men) were sharing it everywhere, from all over the country and the world. People I didn't know were touting me as the "voice of the next feminist generation." My e-mail was flooded with responses, including death threats. I was bombarded with "congratulations" and "I loved your story" texts from friends. In less than a day, my world had changed. Life became a blur of activity. People were listening.

"Hello, Ms. Thomas. I am with the grassroots 'We Are Women' movement. I was lucky enough to see your speech in Tallahassee. I would like to know if you would be interested in speaking at a rally that we are planning in D.C."

My eyes teared up in disbelief. The e-mail went on to explain details, but all I could focus on were those first few sentences. Me? A middle-aged single mother from Florida with only a high school education? What did I have to say that could change the world? Who would even want to listen? Not willing to give up such an opportunity, I agreed hastily.

Then reality sunk in. It was just me, the unemployed writer who had just typed out her opinion. Who was I to tell anyone what to think and feel? What on earth did I have to say that would be worthy of such an event? More importantly, how would I pay for the trip? And I really needed to find gainful employment, not focus on a rally that was hundreds of miles away. Similarly disheartening were the reactions of friends, excuses for why they couldn't go to the rallies in their own areas much less Washington, D.C. The general "we need to stand up but can we really change anything" ambivalence was depressing. For weeks, I fought with myself, ready to reply with the myriad reasons why I could not attend their rally. My inner dialogue sounded like the justifications of those who had been frustrating me.

Still unsure of what to do, I called my kindergarten teacher. She had taken on the mother-figure role after mine had passed away. As always, her advice was the pep talk I needed.

How was I going to get there? "You could hitchhike," she joked. Not a safe way, but it did plant the idea in my head. I was going to do this trip! And I wasn't going to spend a cent — a huge ideal that I was determined to make happen. There was a point to be made. If we put our minds to something, we can accomplish anything. Fervently, I began contacting everyone I knew on the path from my house to D.C., explaining what I was doing and that I needed a ride. I set up a website for my "Road Trip for Rights." Small donations for my trip started rolling in. The resounding enthusiasm from my friends and strangers gave me hope.

Armed only with my computer, phone and a backpack of essentials, I began my adventure. A friend drove me to be picked up by an ex-boyfriend. He then drove me to a one-time roommate who then drove me to stay with a man I had befriended because I had written a story about him. And so on. As usual, the best-laid plans often go awry. Stranded, I frantically turned to social media. Eight hours later, a woman I had never met who had been watching on the website pulled up. She and her disabled daughter were heading to the rally themselves and were kind enough to take a four-hour detour to save me. Back on track, we arrived safely in our nation's capital. She dropped me off at my hotel (I was staying with the woman running the event), and I was finally able to relax before the big day.

After the most amazing day of my life, I returned to my hotel.

Not looking forward to facing the pilgrimage home in reverse, I had begun to doze off when the front desk informed me that I had a package delivered. Not expecting anything, I shuffled downstairs to be handed an envelope with my name written on it. Inside were a train ticket and a note that read, "Thank you for being a voice for those of us who cannot speak." Tears welled as I searched for some clue to the identity of my anonymous benefactor. Realizing that I had done what I had set out to do, I boarded the train, grateful and exhausted.

Since then, I have been to many rallies and marches. Each time, I did it on my own terms. In 2017, I made the trip back to D.C. to march with my best friend, my kindergarten teacher and 500,000 of our closest friends. This year, the three of us reunited to attend the march in our hometown.

The magazine and the blog that agreed to publish that story may no longer be in existence, but the journey of self-discovery they both led me toward will never be forgotten. And I will always be thankful for that blow-hard radio host whose vitriol ignited a passion in me to find my voice.

~Jodi Renee Thomas

77

Young and Brave

*I have learned over the years that when one's mind is
made up, this diminishes fear; knowing what must
be done does away with fear.*

~Rosa Parks

s a mother of four children, I spend a lot of time thinking about the values I want my children to find important. I want them to not only respect others, but also be brave enough to stand up for themselves when something is affecting their wellbeing or moral compass. I always hoped they listened as I got eye rolls and cheeky responses, but it was the day my daughter told me she was assaulted by her teacher that I realized just how important it would all be.

A few days before Christmas break, I picked up my youngest child from middle school. When she got in the car, the usually bubbly girl didn't say anything, and her head was hanging down. We started to drive toward home, and that is when she finally spoke. Through teary eyes, she said I would be getting a phone call from the principal that evening.

My first thought was, *What did you do?* Then more tears started, and I could tell this was much deeper than a simple late-to-class or dress-code violation. My daughter told me the events of the day, and I was simply speechless. She had gone into the science room before class to ask a question. While standing at the desk, the teacher attempted to run his hand up her shirt. When she tried to back away from him, he grabbed her by her belt buckle so she couldn't get away. Luckily, the door was open, and another student witnessed the events and ran to get the principal.

An investigation started immediately, and it was a Pandora's box. This had been going on since the first day of school, and not with just our child. He had been inappropriate with eight girls. The school and police acted swiftly, and we are grateful. He was initially charged with twenty-six counts, three of them felonies. Unfortunately, some investigative compromise occurred, and all charges were dropped except for two felonies: our daughter and one other girl.

> *She not only would testify, she wanted to testify.*

We had a long talk with our daughter, as we were concerned that a trial would be hard on her. She was only fourteen, and the town was already taking sides. She didn't even need to think about it. She told me he needed to be stopped, and if it would keep him from hurting another girl, she not only *would* testify, she *wanted* to testify. I realized she was wise beyond her years.

The court process was long with many court hearings. Our daughter gained new strength with every court hearing. Being able to tell her story and seeing her former teacher face charges empowered her. When he was sentenced by the judge, I could see the satisfaction in her face. The judge made sure he would not be around children again and also mandated that he go through extensive therapy for many years. These were two things that our daughter wanted because she felt it was the best way to stop him from resuming his behavior.

This story started with a girl who was victimized, and as a victim felt powerless. However, by her own strength and courage, she took back her power. She made sure her teacher knew his behavior was unacceptable, and she was not allowing him to hurt her or anyone else. This empowered woman will carry this strength with her for the rest of her life.

~Michelle Bruce

78

Don't Look Back

*We all have a story. The difference is: do you use the
story to empower yourself? Or do you use your story
to keep yourself a victim? The question itself
empowers you to change your life.*

~Sunny Dawn Johnston

I was in high school, and I was a slave. I was Cinderella. If I
described the conditions that I worked under, I'm not sure
many people would believe me. It was a modern-day nightmare that ended between 1:00 and 3:00 in the morning and
started again when I came home from school the next day. It was an
unending cycle with weekends being a special kind of hell.

My dad and stepmother owned a restaurant in a busy resort town.
Instead of hiring a dishwasher while I was at school, they let the dishes
stack up for me when I got home. I would put down my bag of books
and start in on trying to catch up the second I walked through the
doors that were kitty-corner to my high school.

Never mind that I was underage; after the dinner rush, I did
double time as a waitress and served drinks to the rowdies from out of
town who came to fish and visit the pristine lakes. Once they stopped
coming in, the cook and I were the only ones still on staff, and we'd
finish the dishes and set up things for the morning. I was running on
fumes, but I'd always gotten good grades, and I did my homework
when I was finished. Sometimes, I didn't get to sleep at all except when
my head hit my desk in class. I dropped a class, stayed on the honor's

list and slept in the nurse's room on my now free period.

I survived.

One day, it was so busy in the restaurant that the cook asked me to go to the adjoining house to ask my stepmother to help out. It was after the supper rush but still busy, and she hadn't come into the restaurant since I had come home from school.

I went inside and knew something was wrong; the only sound I heard was water running in the bathtub. The lights were all turned out, and water was seeping out into the hallway. I went into the bathroom and saw my baby half-sister lying face down in the overflowing water!

I had been a Girl Scout before my stepmother and her drinking had broken up my life, and I knew pediatric first aid. I grabbed my sister from the tub and, after a few pumps on her chest, she opened her big blue eyes and looked around her with fright. I shut off the tub and wrapped her in a big towel.

I went into the living room where my stepmother had passed out on the couch. Her daughter would have been dead if I hadn't come in to ask her to help. Groggily, she raised her head and looked at me with a goofy, drunk grin on her face, "Hey, what's going on?"

I pushed her daughter into her arms. "You nearly killed your daughter. That's what's wrong."

The little girl tumbled gently from the drunken woman's arms onto the couch and the blankets that were tangled up there. My stepmother shook her head. She tried to run her fingers through her hair, but they got stuck in the mad nest of hair.

"No, no," she denied. A wicked gleam came into her eyes. "You. It was you. *You* nearly killed her."

She only struck me once, but it was all I needed to pry her fingers off my neck and walk out the front door. I stopped long enough to get my schoolbooks, which I never forgot. My dad came home, too late for me, like he had always been too late for me since I had become a teenager. My books were in the basement of the restaurant where I lived alongside the mice and other vermin that lived in the cellar of the restaurant.

"What's going on?" he asked. He was a behemoth presence in my life, but he held no power over me anymore. He had not only allowed this to happen, but he had encouraged it. He was as responsible as my stepmother.

"I'm leaving," I said. He stepped forward, arms raised to grab me, his large body ready to block my path.

They barely fed me, and I was just over five feet tall, but my finger didn't shake when I raised it and pointed it at him. My voice didn't falter. "Don't you lay one hand on me, or you'll wish you'd never been born."

The cook watched. He didn't know what was happening, but he'd always been my friend and ally. "Bob, call the police if he tries to stop me. I'm going to get my books, and then I'm leaving this place, and I won't ever be coming back."

I turned to look at my dad. Our eyes were the same shade of blue. His were bloodshot with rage; mine were bright with defiance and joy. Our gazes met and clashed, and our wills collided. He stepped aside.

I don't remember packing my books. I do remember that I only took what I needed for school. The rest of it could rot in the prison they'd left me in. I was underage. I was a runaway. I was free.

Was I irresponsible? A teenage runaway? The social worker who handled my case thought I was. I read her notes years later. She predicted that I didn't know the consequences of living in the "real world," and that I would quickly return home. They didn't believe me when I told them how many hours I worked with no pay, and with barely any food or sleep.

I wasn't irresponsible. I finished grade twelve on the honor roll and got a scholarship to go to university, but that's a whole other story. The social worker didn't understand the wonder that I experienced each day when I went to work and received a fair hourly wage as a short-order cook. I only worked between four and eight hours, and I got breaks. They fed me for free, and the food was good.

I didn't have much, but what I had was mine. I fried eggs in a wok and made soup in the same wok because I could only afford one secondhand pot. I put up my first shower curtain, a cheap plastic thing that I had to be careful not to tear with joy after showering for a month without any curtain at all.

I had help. I had friends. The cook, Bob, was a friend to the end. He helped me rent a place and never once tried to take liberties with the little ragamuffin he'd helped out.

If I could have afforded it, I would have framed my emancipation paper when my parents were forced to free me from their ownership. I was free. I saw wonder and beauty in the world again and used my freedom to do good things.

My dad told me years later that he never imagined I'd run away. He said, "You'd always been such a good girl. I just always thought you'd be there."

He never understood why his "good girl" left. But I never regretted it.

I have never looked look back. Freedom lies ahead, not behind.

~Virginia Stark

79

Enough with the Flowers Already

*Remember, Ginger Rogers did everything Fred Astaire
did, but backwards and in high heels.*
~Faith Whittlesey

They sent me flowers. I saved them millions of dollars and they sent me flowers. I know they meant well, but really?

I was a Wall Street analyst, and I was very good at what I did, figuring out which stocks were going to rise and which were going to fall. There was a company I knew very well, one whose stock I had recommended for years. Its price had gone up, but then I had decided that it was overvalued and it was going to go down.

I told a few of my clients, big professional investors, and got the ones that owned that stock to take their profits and get out.

And that's why I got the flowers. Because that stock went down and one of my very nice clients wanted to thank me for getting him out before he lost all his profits. But I would rather have gotten more money in commissions than receive a big bunch of flowers.

It was okay though. They were nice guys and they did pay me as well. But there's no way a male analyst would have received flowers… for the same great work. And I was pretty sure a man would have been paid more.

Paying analysts for their stock picks was basically done on the honor system, with the clients deciding how much to pay via brokerage commissions. Time after time, stock pick after stock pick, it seemed that I was earning less than my male colleagues.

I decided to start my own hedge fund, so I would be in charge of what I made. When you run a hedge fund, it's all math. If your portfolio goes up, you get twenty percent of the profits. It doesn't matter if you're male or female or an iguana. Math is math.

So I ran that fund for a few years and never had a down quarter. I got my twenty percent of the profits and made a nice living while working from my house and being there for my young children. I only had one run-in with a male chauvinist that I remember. He called me one day to complain about something — I don't know what — and accused me of running school bake sales instead of my hedge fund. I had a policy. I got to fire one annoying client each quarter — by sending him back his money. So I sent him all his money immediately, and then he begged me to take him back. But I was working too hard to make money for someone I didn't like. I didn't let him back in.

> They saw a petite, pretty, blond woman and thought I was some kind of bimbo.

There was a lot of male chauvinism on Wall Street but I navigated my way through it. Sometimes I could use it to my advantage. Guys didn't expect me to be smart. They saw a petite, pretty, blond woman and thought I was some kind of bimbo. I would actually get a lot of information out of them, sometimes figuring out stuff that no one else knew. I was written up in *Forbes* magazine for being the first analyst ever sued by a New York Stock Exchange company — for exposing the massive accounting fraud perpetrated by their CEO and other top officers. I had figured that out using two things — my ability to get men to talk to me on the phone... and math. When their own accountants finally conceded that what I had been telling them was true, the top management was fired and their stock went to zero. Their lawyer ended up apologizing profusely to me during a deposition when I proved to him that his clients were crooks. Oh well, guys. The little blonde got you.

Then I got the coolest job. I kept running my hedge fund but also joined the management team of an exciting new start-up telecommunications company. I was the Executive Vice President of Strategic Planning. It was a company with huge potential. When I joined them they were out of cash, but because of my reputation as a straight shooter on Wall Street, there was a hedge fund that was willing to invest six million dollars in the company as long as I was on the executive team.

Things were looking up! It was my presence that brought in the crucial cash infusion. For the next two years, I was a critical member of the team and we raised tens of millions of dollars and grew the company like crazy. I felt like I was getting respect. The environment was definitely getting better for women in business, and I was the company's representative to Wall Street. I talked to all the investors and kept them up-to-date and interested in our company.

I was always part of the team that presented to institutional investors as we raised money to fuel the company's tremendous growth. I was at the front of the ballroom or sitting at the conference table, explaining the PowerPoint slides. When you raise money for a big company, the investment bankers take you around the country on what is called a "road show."

On one road show, we were in Denver for breakfast and had a big lunch meeting in San Francisco with fifty important investors. Our flight was canceled. This was before smartphones. My colleagues and our investment bankers just stood there at the gate looking lost. I ran over to one of those airport phones that they use to page people and asked the operator to put me through to whatever charter jet service existed at the Denver airport. Then I chartered a jet with my credit card, rushed everyone to the other side of the airport, and we took off for San Francisco. The pilots arranged for limos to pick us up planeside when we landed and we made it just in time for the lunch meeting.

The biggest deal I was involved in was a $225 million capital raise. That time we didn't fly commercial. We did the whole road show on private planes, flying from city to city with limos meeting us right on the tarmac and speeding us to our next meeting. Sometimes we saw investors in two cities in two states on the same day.

The CEO, COO, Vice Chairman and I were on the plane one night, along with a few investment bankers. I actually felt like "The Grownup on the Gulfstream" as the men watched some stupid movie that involved Eddie Murphy and fat people sitting around a dining room table passing gas. These captains of industry were in hysterics. So were the investment bankers. And I thought, *Wow, if people really knew*. But that was just a male/female thing.

Anyway, I presented to the potential investors at every meeting. I was one of only four people who reported to our CEO, and there were thousands of employees by then. I felt like I had arrived — the only female on the plane and an integral part of the team that had a successful road show and raised $225 million for the business.

We closed the deal, and I was thinking, *There isn't a single institutional investor in this company who isn't in at least partly because I've talked to them. The road show was great and I'm one of the guys... except for my taste in movies.*

A few days later, we were back at the office, victorious. Then, to express their gratitude to us for making the deal a success, the gifts arrived from the investment bankers. The CEO, COO, and Vice Chairman each got a six-bottle case of Dom Perignon champagne. I love champagne!

Guess what I got?

A vase filled with flowers.

~Amy Newmark

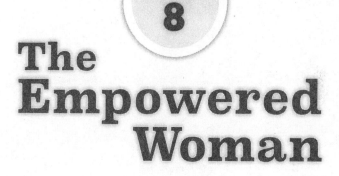

The Empowered Woman

Chapter **8**

Time for Me

80

Spontaneous Spirit

I learned that courage was not the absence of fear,
but the triumph over it. The brave man is not he who
does not feel afraid, but he who conquers that fear.
~Nelson Mandela

Anyone going to an amusement park might have seen the likes of me. I was the gray-haired lady with sensible shoes. I held purses, cellphones and sunglasses while my loved ones hurled themselves through space on roller coasters. Afterward, flushed with excitement, they'd pose for selfies to celebrate their latest flirtation with the Grim Reaper.

I admired their bravery, but refused to challenge my own limitations. Sitting it out worked for me, and that's exactly what I had planned to do on that pleasant spring morning twelve years ago.

To celebrate my husband's sixty-fifth birthday, we'd driven an hour south to Skydive Miami in Homestead, Florida. As a young man in the Army, Joe had logged hundreds of jumps with round parachutes, and he wanted a closer look at the newer wing style. Watching those young people swoosh in to a perfect, stand-up landing reignited memories of his youth.

"Sure looks like fun," he hinted.

"Like the best birthday gift ever?"

His eyes twinkled with mischief. "Exactly like that."

"So much for the new tie," I laughed.

We high-fived and headed for the skydiving office. My mind was racing. I visualized Joe suited up on the tarmac. I would shoot video as the plane took off. Then I'd rush over to the drop zone to capture the landing.

Knowing my adrenaline-junkie husband, I wondered if this might become a recurring event. I saw our weekends planned out for the next few years. Joe would skydive while I took pictures. He would struggle to describe the sensation of flying, and my imagination would strain to fill in the gaps. If fear kept me sidelined, I'd never fully understand.

Not this time, I decided. I didn't want to hear about it. I wanted to see and feel it for myself. When he approached the sign-up window for an application, I squeezed his arm.

"Why not make it two?"

"You're kidding," he grinned. "You'd do that?"

"It's a once-in-a-lifetime offer. I want to share this with you."

Chuckling in disbelief, he held up two fingers. We filled out paperwork and signed liability releases. Joe paid extra for a video of my first jump.

After zipping ourselves into electric-blue jumpsuits, we filed into the training room. Using a mock-up of an airplane door, we learned to roll out, maintain a stable free-fall position, and lift our feet at landing. In the tiny, windowless classroom, everything seemed easy. I repeated the steps with my instructor, Pete. Joe beamed with pride at his remarkably confident wife. Our trainers dispensed altimeters, helmets and goggles, and strapped us into heavy black tandem harnesses. My videographer taped a pre-flight interview in which I laughed with ease.

When our flight was called, we boarded the small Caravan airplane where we sat cross-legged in pairs on the floor, instructors directly behind their students. Pete clipped his harness to mine as the plane roared down the runway. Through the clear, roll-up door, I watched the treetops fall away.

My stomach lurched as two realities hit me: This was actually happening, and I'd made a terrible mistake.

My mouth was dry as the Sahara, my palms sweaty. I couldn't do this. What was I thinking? I belonged on the ground taking pictures, not in the center of the action. I glanced at Joe, who was chatting away with his instructor. The animated look on his face did not calm my nerves. My husband was afraid of nothing. He'd done this hundreds of times without an experienced jumper strapped to his back. Crazy fool probably wanted to go solo.

At 13,500 feet, the jumpmaster gave a thumbs-up, and to my horror, the clear door slid up like a roll-top desk. This could not be right. Flying with an open door was dangerous! Didn't they realize someone could fall out?

Oh, yeah. That's why we were here.

On cue, Joe and his instructor shuffled like chain-gang prisoners toward the deadly aperture. I watched in disbelief as they nodded three times in unison and tumbled out. There are things in life we can prepare for, but seeing one's husband fall out of an airplane is not one of them. My heart was in my throat.

I was reeling with shock when Pete lifted me to my knees and nudged me toward the gaping hole. To steady myself, I clung to a metal bar overhead. Pete tried to pull my hands away, but I refused to let go of the one solid object between me and certain death.

As impatient jumpers piled up behind us, I realized I had a choice. I could refuse to jump and ride back with the pilot. I played it out quickly in my head. The waste of non-refundable money. Joe's face watching my instructor land without me. My shame at letting fear win out once again.

No way! That was not going to happen. I took a deep breath and released my death grip on the bar. Following our pre-flight instructions, I crossed my arms over my chest and arched my back. Pete rolled us out of the plane.

The sense of falling lasted only seconds until we achieved the welcome stability of terminal velocity. Pete tapped my shoulder, the signal to spread my arms like wings. Just as Joe had described, the wind resistance at 120 mph was so powerful, it felt like a cushion of air supporting us. The noise was deafening, and G-forces assaulted my face, making my smile feel more like a grimace. I remembered to make eye contact with the videographer flying directly in front of me, documenting my final moments for the next of kin. "Hi, Mom!" I mouthed, although in space, as they say, no one can hear you scream.

Pete checked his altimeter at about sixty seconds and then waved off the videographer. He reached back to deploy the parachute, and our free fall came to an abrupt end. Our bodies jackknifed from horizontal to vertical, legs flying out in front like two rag dolls as the harness held tight and the chute flared open. It was peaceful then. Quiet enough to talk. We drifted through the air like a giant butterfly. Pete pointed out landmarks on the horizon, and I admired the beautiful patchwork of the surrounding farmland. As we soared gently toward the earth, my only regret was that we couldn't stay up longer.

> *It's my choice — sit it out or try it out.*

Skidding into the drop zone, I lifted my feet and let Pete nail the landing. When he uncoupled our gear, I ran into Joe's arms. Our celebratory embrace was captured by the videographer. The look of admiration on my husband's face said it all. On the way home, we both had stories to share.

Years later, reliving the memory still makes my heart race. When faced with an opportunity that scares me, I remember that open door on the airplane. "Why take a chance?" my doubting voice says. "Why jump out of a perfectly good airplane?"

"Because I can," my adventurous voice replies. It's my choice — sit it out or try it out. I choose to push through the fear and seize the adventure that lies beyond.

~Linda Barbosa

81

Single Mom Saved by Single Flower

*No woman can control her destiny if she doesn't give to
herself as much as she gives of herself.*
~Suze Orman

"Y ou're better at jumping off cliffs in life than anyone I know," a friend once told me. "Sometimes
you land on a bush," he added, "but you always
land somewhere."

In the summer of 2007, I jumped off the ultimate cliff—adopt-
ing a baby boy from Guatemala. I was fifty-one and single, and my
family lived 400 miles away. There was no bush big enough to catch
me this time.

When my son arrived, the avalanche that hit my life took two
forms. I was swept away by a volcanic love that was like nothing I
had ever experienced. And I was flattened by the completely confining
nature of my circumstances.

I called it the "Love Lock Down." There were nights when, after
putting my son to bed, I would simply sit in the darkness and listen
to my breathing. It was that overwhelming.

In the best circumstances, six people are working on behalf of a
young child's life: two parents and two sets of grandparents. I had to
be all six, every night and every day.

I was proud that I could hold my son in one arm when he weighed twenty pounds. Two years later, when he weighed thirty-nine pounds, I laughed that I had ever thought twenty pounds was a challenge. I had to become that strong — my arms were the only ones available.

People would look at me with wide eyes and say, "Do you have enough support?" I didn't even know how to answer.

Chop wood, carry baby. I put my head down, loved my son and made it through every tiring day with as much aplomb as I could muster.

By the spring of 2010, he was toddling, and I was completely exhausted. Worse than my physical fatigue was my sense that I had no time for anything I wanted to do, and hadn't for three years.

In my pre-mama years, I had loved working on the small garden in front of my home. But the area had been reduced to a patch of green confusion after three years of neglect.

"Rescue me," it would say every time I looked at it.

"I can't right now," I would have answered if I had the time to say anything.

Still, that garden kept calling.

So, one day, I bought a six-pack of summer flowers, and when I returned home from the store, I dug a hole and planted one flower. Just one.

I knew I had no time to "garden," but I was feeling defiant that day. And heck, I thought, I can plant one flower!

I left the rest of the flowers sitting on the grass, and then went inside to attend to the many things that needed my attention.

But something unexpected happened: For the rest of the day, I could feel that one flower singing to me. Somehow, that one flower had gotten inside me and was singing a new song of possibility.

What had happened? I wasn't sure. Somehow, the simple act of planting a single flower had made something click inside me and put me back in the flow of things. I still didn't have time for "gardening," but I did have time to make one simple gesture a day.

Thus, step by step, flower by flower, and day by day, I kept at it. Over the weeks, I created a garden that knocked me out with its beauty. Pale pink impatiens sat in dappled light in front of big-leaved hostas. Lily of the valley bloomed everywhere, and dark red astilbes added jolts of color that cried out, "Be gutsy. We are."

The radiance of my garden became the single most sustaining element of my world that summer.

I never spent more than ten minutes on it because I never had more than ten minutes. Nonetheless, its beauty soothed and inspired me. I would look at it — the garden I thought I had no time to create — and be reminded that I actually could do things if I did them in tiny steps each and every day.

The flowers became my inner cheering squad. I no longer felt at the mercy of my situation, and the joy I experienced inspired me to apply this technique to other corners of my life. As a result, rooms got painted (a square foot at a time), furniture got reupholstered, laughter was rediscovered, and, ultimately, a sense of balance slowly returned to my life.

It was a quiet, daily revolution — a tiny shift in the way I did things that taught me some gigantic lessons, such as:

- Ten minutes a day adds up to more than an hour a week and over sixty hours a year.
- Time is elastic. When we bring complete focus to whatever we are doing, we can get a surprising amount done in a small amount of time.
- To do things incrementally is to act in the way that nature acts. All we have to do is fold this knowledge into our own human nature to reap the benefits.
- When the tortoise goes up against the hare, the tortoise always wins. Be the tortoise.

Looking back, it seems that I did land on a bush — that single flower. It was small and pink, yet somehow large enough to catch me.

~Lorne Holden

Dr. Nanny

*It takes courage to examine your life and to decide that
there are things you would like to change, and it takes
even more courage to do something about it.*
~Sue Hadfield, Change One Thing!

My dream was to earn my doctorate at St. John's
University in Queens, New York, where my father
was a professor. But during a visit to the United
States Military Academy during my junior year in
college, I was escorted around the post by a handsome "cow," a cadet
in his junior year at West Point. Soon after, my doctoral dreams took
a detour.

After graduating from college, my cadet and I married. For the
next thirty-two years, we raised our five children. I stayed at home
with the kids and wrote nonfiction books for young adults, *Chicken
Soup for the Soul* stories, and features for my local newspaper. Those
were glorious times.

When my two youngest were in high school, my oldest daughter
chose to pursue her doctorate in psychology. Additionally, my niece,
my college roommate, and my brother-in-law were all engaged in
doctoral studies. I was so proud of them, but I also felt envious. I
became determined to go back to school.

I searched the Internet and found the perfect Ph.D. program for
me. It was a combination of classes in writing, literature, and teaching.
Actually, I wasn't planning to teach, but the other courses would serve

me well. The university was a two-hour drive away in New York City, which presented a worrisome obstacle to me because I suffer from panic disorder.

When I was in eighth grade, I spent an entire month in my home, unable to leave, paralyzed by fears. With the help of a talented psychologist, I learned relaxation and visualization techniques that helped me cope with my panic attacks. He taught me to break activities into small bits and deal with them a little at a time. "Just concentrate on this moment," he told me. "Don't worry about the future, about the 'what-ifs.'" I soon got back to school and back to life. Even though I now know how to handle my panic, I still experience anxiety daily.

> **At fifty-two, I was the oldest in the classroom.**

I took a deep breath and broke my doctoral goals into little, manageable pieces. I wrote my admissions essay and gathered recommendation letters. I took my Graduate Record Examination — twice. Remember, I hadn't done geometry in over thirty years. When my acceptance e-mail arrived, I danced around the kitchen island. Then I signed up for my courses.

Each day of class, I gathered my courage anew and jumped into the car. I found myself enjoying the ride, singing aloud to the songs on the radio. I felt like a cosmopolitan woman as I crossed the city bridges and saw the Empire State Building in the background. At fifty-two, I was the oldest in the classroom, and a generational divide sometimes appeared. One afternoon, we took a tour of the microfilm area of the university library. One of my fellow students noted a tall wooden cabinet recessed into the wall. "I wonder what that is," she said to me.

"It's a telephone booth," I told her with a smile.

Despite some generational differences, my youthful colleagues challenged and energized me with their intellects. One time, a young man who was writing a project about teaching pedagogy asked if I could suggest a theorist to research. "You should check out Bell Evans," I told him sagely. Immediately, he plugged the name into his iPhone and thanked me profusely.

On the drive home, I felt amazed at how quickly the theorist's name had sprung from my middle-aged brain. I congratulated myself for taking the young man under my wing. Then I realized that Bell & Evans was the brand name of my favorite chicken breasts.

Over those years, my classmates — most of them younger than my two oldest daughters — became my friends. We were facing this doctoral marathon together. I made it through my required classes, six months of studying for my comprehensives, and the oral comprehensive exam.

Suddenly, my goal was diverted again. I underwent coronary artery double bypass surgery. My cardiac surgeon said I had to skip a semester to recover. For those months, I attended rehab and refreshed my knowledge of French for the translation exam.

When I returned to school, I was required to teach writing and literature for two semesters. I had not held a job outside the home since I was a camp counselor as a teen. Could I meet the responsibility? After all those years of writing silently in my home, would my students be taught by a mime? Class by class, I realized that I loved my students and enjoyed being an educator. The students even laughed at my jokes. An unexpected career opened before me.

Finally, I researched, wrote, and defended my dissertation, "'What's So Funny?' An Analysis of James Thurber's Humorous Writing." At St. John's University in Queens, New York, on May 19, 2016, my mentor slipped the doctoral hood over my head. Yes, after the deferral of my dream, I received my Ph.D. from the very university where my father had taught and I had hoped to earn my doctorate thirty-six years earlier.

My husband and children sat in the audience to watch me graduate, with the exception of my oldest daughter, who had recently given birth to our first grandson. That evening, I was a doctor and a grandmother; I was Dr. Nanny. My next challenge would be to fly to Florida to hug that grandbaby. During my semester break from teaching at Marist College and The Culinary Institute of America, I would be on a flight. Anxiety had kept me from flying for thirty-four years, but now I had confidence that if I took the next adventure a little at a time, I could do that, too.

~Marie-Therese Miller

Saying "Yes" to Myself

Sometimes, we have to say no so
we have more time to say yes.
~Suzette Hinton

"Will you do a favor for me?" someone would ask.

"Of course, I will. What do you need?" I would always answer, agreeing to do the favor before I even asked what it was.

I would never have dreamed of saying "no" to anyone. If anyone asked me to do anything, I'd do it. Saying "no" was never an option. I wanted to be a good person. I wanted to help people. I wanted people to like me. I wanted people to love me.

I was a good, obedient child and grew up to be a responsible adult. I married a dependable, hard-working man whom everyone said was perfect for me.

I had four children, and I was always the "room mother," helping with class parties and taking cookies to every school event. I helped with the Girl Scouts, Boy Scouts, charities and fundraisers. Nothing was too much trouble.

After my children grew up and left home, and my husband passed away, people thought I needed things to do to fill what they felt was my empty life. I volunteered at the hospital and a nursing home, and I taught a Sunday School class.

I was free labor. I'd drive people to the airport and go back and

Time for Me | 299

pick them up when they returned from their vacations. Your mother-in-law needs a ride to the airport at three o'clock in the morning? Sure, no problem.

I was spending time and money I couldn't spare, and I often didn't get thanked. I didn't do things to be "thanked," but I would have appreciated some sort of acknowledgment. I was "busy" being "busy." I was exhausted, but I was afraid to say "no" because I thought people wouldn't like me anymore.

I had to have back surgery, and I told everyone I would be confined to my home for at least a month while I recovered. No one offered to drive me to the hospital or drive me home. I didn't want to inconvenience anyone, so I took a cab. No one visited me in the hospital, and no one brought any meals to me after I got home.

No one called to ask if I had enough groceries or if I needed a prescription filled or if I would like some company.

I'd always filled out certificates of appreciation for people who contributed to the zoo, and when the man in charge of the zoo called and asked if I could prepare 100 certificates, I told him "no." I wasn't well, I explained, and I would not be doing the certificates in the future. He'd have to find someone else. He was shocked.

"Do it for the animals," he said. He offered to drop off the certificates at my house where I could fill them out. He'd come back and pick them up. He couldn't believe it when I said "no."

A lady at church asked if she could drop off her cat for me to take care of for a week while she took her family to Disneyland. I explained I'd had back surgery, and I couldn't take care of her cat. "But you always take care of Fluffy!" she said. "He's really no trouble at all."

The truth was Fluffy was a lot of trouble. I had taken care of him twice while she'd gone on vacation, and he'd gotten hair on everything, climbed my drapes and pulled them down, and didn't always use his litter box. I told her I was sure she'd find someone else to take care of Fluffy, but I couldn't do it anymore.

The church secretary called, not to ask how I was feeling, but to ask when I could start teaching the Sunday School class again. I told her someone else would have to take over. She asked if I had any notes for the classes, and I said "no." I thought whoever took over the class would want to teach it their own way, and I was sure they'd do a great job.

I have the right to say "no," without an apology, explanation or guilt. The world didn't end when I started say it, and much to my surprise, things got done without my help. Other people stepped in and did the things I used to do.

> *I have the right to say "no," without an apology, explanation or guilt.*

People say I am not the same person since I had my back surgery. They are right; I'm not the same person. I was laid up for a month with a painful back, and during that time I found my spine.

People haven't really missed "me"; they have missed the services I provided. I had allowed people to use me, thinking they would like me, but when I needed help, no one was there.

I don't volunteer for anything anymore. I spend my time doing things I never seemed to have time to do before. I'm taking an art class. I go for walks in the park. My time is my own.

It's hard to say "no" when I've been a "yes" person all my life, but I feel powerful for the first time. I don't have to make up excuses or lies or explain or apologize. "No" is a complete sentence.

My time is the most precious thing I own, and for years I let people steal it from me. I don't blame them; I blame myself. I was a doormat, and I let people walk all over me. I was trying to earn friendship.

Some people might say I've gotten "hard," but that isn't true. I've just gotten strong. I don't like people less; I like myself more.

I saw a bumper sticker on a car that said, "I don't regret the things I've done wrong as much as I regret the things I did right for the wrong people."

Saying "no" to other people is saying "yes" to myself.

I feel so free!

~Holly English

84

Already Possessing the Answers

We all have within us a deep wisdom,
but sometimes we don't know we have it.
~Shakti Gawain

"No matter how hard I try, I just can't seem to keep up," Julie confessed, and then she began to cry. "I'm exhausted, physically and mentally. Charlie was up most of the night last night. There are piles of laundry all over my house. I haven't showered in days. And I can't remember the last time I looked into my kids' eyes — really looked." Her voice trailed off as tears streamed down her face.

I passed Julie the box of tissues. I had explained earlier that night, before the retreat's Faith Sharing segment, that several groups had dubbed the box of tissues the "Talking Stick." Inevitably, when it came time to share, the tears came, too. Julie had refused the box, saying she wasn't one to cry. But she accepted the tissues now with gratitude.

This was the fifteenth retreat I had run for mothers of young children. I could count on just one hand the number of moms who hadn't cried when it was their time to share. Goodness knows, I wasn't one of them. I don't cry often, but I've cried more in motherhood than in my entire life combined.

Five years before, I had done just that for an entire week. My kids were then eight, six and two. They were typically good kids, and I did an okay job as a mom, but neither applied that week. Their mistakes aligned with my moodiness. It was like the perfect storm. I felt like a complete failure as a mother and as a person. I wanted to run away from my life forever!

That Saturday, all those years ago, my husband saw the desperate state I was in. "Go," he said. "Just go out, anywhere, for as long as you need. I'll hold down the fort here." He didn't need to say it twice. I grabbed my journal, Bible and car keys, and ran out the door.

I ended up at a retreat center twenty-five minutes from my home. It wasn't that I had decided to go there; it was more like I was led. I only went inside the building to ask permission to be on the grounds.

> *I felt like a pressure cooker whose release valve had finally been opened.*

Then I spent the rest of my time there wandering around in all of God's beauty.

I walked the outdoor labyrinth, weaving in and out of the pattern, just like my thoughts. I meandered down the hiking trails, barely noticing the lush trees and plants everywhere. My final destination was the outdoor chapel at the water's edge. As I sat facing the cross, with Lake Cochichewick as the backdrop, I cried, journaled and prayed. Then I cried, journaled, and prayed some more.

I felt like a pressure cooker whose release valve had finally been opened. For three solid hours, I sat on that bench and let all those feelings of frustration, desperation, confusion, and disappointment pour out of me.

When I walked back to my car, I was shocked to find I felt as light and free as a bird. I couldn't wait to go back to my life as a mom, despite having literally run from it just hours before.

Driving home, it occurred to me that every mother out there needs what I had just experienced. But motherhood can be so busy; most moms don't have the time or the energy to plan that getaway. That's when I realized I wanted to be the one to create that for them. So began my MOSAIC of Faith ministry.

Over time, MOSAIC of Faith has branched out in many different directions. But the evening retreats for mothers are definitely the most empowering branch. The secret to their success is the Faith Sharing.

After I provide the content for the evening, as well as a guided meditation to de-stress the moms, I send them all off to their own rooms to reflect. When they return, we Faith Share: Each mom shares her thoughts and feelings *uninterrupted*. When do we moms and women ever get to talk uninterrupted?

Women *always* interrupt each other. We do so usually with the best of intentions: to affirm, to give advice, to share our similar stories as a way to prove we've been there and understand. But when we interrupt, we derail the talker in her journey toward discovery.

I truly believe we already possess most of the answers we need deep within ourselves. But life's busyness and noise drown out those whispers. If and when we are fortunate enough to find some peace and quiet, we're so beaten down that we lack the self-confidence to believe the answers we hear.

That's why it's so important to speak those answers out loud. Talking, uninterrupted, lets us flush out the strong emotions. In doing so, we become more objective; we see things more clearly. Suddenly, everything makes sense. Not only do we see the solutions to our problems, but we see why we had the problems in the first place. Best of all, we recognize and appreciate both the problems and the solutions as necessary aspects of our own journey.

Things were no different for Julie. As she continued to share, uninterrupted, her tears grew fewer, and her vision grew sharper. With no help from us, except for our sincere acceptance and deep listening, Julie stumbled upon idea after idea for how she could approach her daily life differently. With every thought she gave voice to, her voice grew stronger and more self-assured. Soon, the tears in her eyes were replaced with glimmers of hope and confidence.

Later, as we were gathering our things to leave, Julie came over and gave me a hug. As she pulled away, she said, "You know, I really had no idea all those awful emotions were inside of me. I knew I was struggling, but I didn't know I was struggling that much. Thank you for creating the space for me to figure it all out, face it, and get rid of it. I'm leaving here tonight believing I can really do this mom thing now, and actually be good at it. Thank you for helping me to see that."

"You're welcome, Julie," I said, with all sincerity. "Thanks for digging so deep and trusting me with everything. It was an absolute honor to witness you finding the answers you already possessed deep within."

~Claire McGarry

85

Beyond the Gold Watch

The best way to predict the future is to create it.
~Abraham Lincoln

Well, I got the gold watch — figuratively, that is. In reality, unless someone was on the board or a department manager, they just left. There was no gold watch for retiring.

I had turned sixty-five the year before, and my co-workers started asking: Where was my place in the sun? Tucson? Tampa? They said I was so lucky that I wouldn't have to get to work with two feet of new snow on the roads.

I started to wonder if they were hinting. If I left, my spot was a chance for a move-up for someone else. To quiet speculation, I said, "Fourth of July." And I regretted it later when that date kept creeping up on the calendar.

They threw a party for me, a "surprise" on July 3rd during lunch break. I got a cake and a beach umbrella — for that dreamy beach, I suppose. At the end of the day, I received a few hugs, pats on the back, keep-in-touch comments, and a couple of tears from those who had become real friends during my fifteen years there. I hoped they would still include me in the card games and dinners out we sometimes had.

The kids were grown and gone. There were grandkids, but since everyone lived a state or two away, I couldn't just drop in.

July 4th, of course, was a holiday, so it was normal to sleep in, plan a family picnic, or have a "paint-the-kitchen day." The 5th was a breeze, too, being as it was a Saturday. Church was on Sunday, so nothing changed in my routine.

Monday, I woke at the usual time, despite not setting the alarm. The neighborhood of working blokes was empty. Everyone else had gone to work. So I sat in the kitchen, lingering over my second cup of coffee.

My eyes still flicked toward the clock every few minutes. My body tensed as I fought the urge to leap up for a shower and dash out the door. My brain panicked when I got to the point where I would be late.

I had no plan. No retirement dream beach. I had no friends to call; they were all hurrying to work. Oh, yes, financially I would be fine. *That* much was planned. I had gone to the seminar and set up a wise plan for "when I retired." But my mind was not prepared. My mind kept saying, *You're unemployed. What will you ever do?* I had the education, résumé and know-how for my job. Who was I now?

I was glad for the knock on the back door. It was the gal next door, Jenny-something. She was in jeans and a T-shirt. "I hate to ask, but could you possibly drive me to drop off my grandson? My car won't start, and I need to have him there before nine."

It turned out that her grandson was in a preschool program not far away. I agreed.

I didn't know her well, even though she and her husband lived next door for a few years. I didn't even know her grandson was four years old until he got into my car and told me. He also told me his birthday was in August; he had the same name as his other grandpa, Colin; he was going to New York at Christmas time to visit said grandpa; and his grandma had packed a peanut-butter-and-jelly sandwich because they were having fish sticks for lunch at school, and he hated fish.

"As you can tell," Jenny said as we drove along, "he's rather shy."

She added that she knew I worked, so wasn't it fortunate I was at home that day to so graciously give her a lift. I gave her the abbreviated version of my retirement, which ended as we pulled into the school parking lot.

It was a nice building, though obviously used for a business before it became a preschool. The sign above the door said: Daybright

Preschool for Exceptional Children.

Jenny laughed. "Because they believe *all* children are exceptional."

"I like that," I replied as they got out.

"Come in and have a look for yourself," she said, as Colin galloped across the lot toward the door. I followed.

Children's art lined the hallway, and I could hear young voices singing in one of the classrooms. I followed Jenny as she took Colin to his room, and he quickly joined his classmates as they sat in a circle on the floor while the teacher outlined the day's activities. The children interrupted with questions and unrelated subjects, but it seemed somehow organized. The teacher asked what song they would like to sing to begin their day, and after a short burst of suggestions and a quick vote, they decided on "Tomorrow." Then they all stood and happily sang, some out of tune.

I liked what I saw.

As Jenny and I were leaving, we met the principal, and I was introduced. A former elementary school teacher, she had started this preschool after noting that so many children were not prepared for school, for the change from home to the stricter routine of the classroom.

I spent my next days organizing closets, sweeping the garage floor, and picking out paint for the bathroom.

"What's wrong with the color we already have?" my husband asked at dinner. I didn't know. I admitted that, as a retiree, I was still in working mode and had the urge to do something.

I spent another week painting, cleaning, and going out to lunch with my former co-workers — and became totally wretched.

"Retirement isn't working," my husband finally said to me. "Take some time. Figure out what you really want to do — I know it isn't painting the entire house — and *do* it."

I found my niche. I now fill my days with my new calling, and have no time for painting walls or sweeping garages. Yes, I went back to Daybright, talked at length with the principal, and am using hidden skills as a story lady. I am reading to the children, listening to them read, and then discussing what they liked or didn't like about the story.

My new young friends have such unique observations of the world I thought had grown old and stale. I feel awakened.

Retirement is glorious when we follow a passion.

~NancyLee Davis

86

Old Maid?

*No one is in control of your happiness but you;
therefore, you have the power to change anything
about yourself or your life that you want to change.*
~Barbara de Angelis

y the time I turned twenty-eight, I had been teaching for seven years, held a master's degree in education and was buying a home. I was surprised by my home-buying experience. As I signed my loan documents as an "unmarried woman," I somehow felt I'd failed. I'd been so busy racking up accomplishments, I forgot to get married.

Handling this minor oversight in my usual direct manner, I fell in love with a suave engineer. We met in the fruit section of the super-market — he in an expensive suit and me in my typical weekend attire: sweatpants and a T-shirt. I noticed the waves in his thick black hair and caught his twinkling eyes studying either me or the grapes I was holding up for closer inspection. Embarrassed by my sloppy appearance, I moved on, only to run into him in several other aisles. Finally, he vanished, and I checked out, glad that my Oreos had been concealed from the well-dressed man by the three rolls of paper towels I was buying.

Parked next to my box-shaped car was a sporty 280Z. Leaning comfortably against the passenger door was my now grinning Adonis, who introduced himself and asked if I'd like to meet for coffee sometime. "Meet" and "sometime" sounded non-threatening, so I agreed to meet him after school the following Tuesday.

Nick was absolutely charming for the next six months… until we got engaged. The heart-shaped diamond he placed on my finger served as a beacon for friends, co-workers and mere acquaintances to offer congratulations. My parents were ecstatic. It had been over a decade since the last of my three older sisters had wed, and they were eager to see me follow in their footsteps. A twinge of disappointment struck me at the thought of this event earning a ticker-tape parade while my hard-won master's degree caused barely a ripple in the placid lake known as my family.

Nick's charm faded as he began to voice new criticisms about the way I dressed and cleaned my house. I have to admit that his apartment was spotless, but I wondered why he spent so much time at my place if it wasn't up to his high standards.

Our love boat really got rocky when he worked out a budget for me — a list of things I could cut out. Me, the one who could make a week's worth of meals out of one chicken? Me, the one who bought a house on a teacher's salary? Suddenly, I resented his sports car,

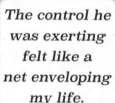

The control he was exerting felt like a net enveloping my life.

Italian shoes and $100 cologne. Despite making more than twice what I did, he'd maxed out two major credit cards and was working on his third. I asked him what he planned to cut out, but was rebuked because he "needed" certain things to maintain his position. The only desire I felt at that moment was to cut and run. The control he was exerting felt like a net enveloping my life.

Children were a big topic between us. He wanted a soccer team of boys. Like my sisters before me, I wanted to be a stay-at-home mom. Since the money issue had already reared its ugly head, I shouldn't have been surprised to hear we'd need both of our incomes. His idea of the upside? As a teacher, Nick assured me I could deliver our babies during the summer without missing any work.

Normally cheerful, I was noticeably depressed. The same people who initially *oohed* and *aahed* over my flashing diamond ring now seemed determined to see this wedding through. When I expressed the doubts that were multiplying daily, I was assured that every bride has pre-wedding jitters and was advised to shake them off.

On the night before the wedding-dress shopping trip I'd planned with my mother, Nick dropped the proverbial straw that broke this camel's back. He announced that he was building a pen to keep my two dogs confined in the yard. This would open my large back yard for barbecues and entertaining. My jaw dropped. I'd chosen this small house with its big yard for Bunny and Fluffy to enjoy! All the controls Nick had been pushing at me paled as I realized I wasn't the only one who would be hurt if we married.

I called my mom to cancel our wedding-dress adventure, and while I was at it, the wedding. I was delighted that she didn't remind me of my "advanced" age or try to talk me out of making a hasty decision. It wasn't really hasty anyway... it had been coming for months.

Had I failed at achieving my most recent goal? I like to think that this was my version of jumping off the tracks while a fast-moving train approaches. Because I made that leap, I was free to travel on life's journey, seeking a better destination.

~Marsha Porter

87

An Accidentally Funny Life

Keep your face always toward the sunshine —
and shadows will fall behind you.
~Walt Whitman

I was out of breath when I finally made it to my seat near the back of the airplane. I had run from one end of the terminal to the other, dragging a heavy bag behind me, my husband so far ahead that I couldn't make him out in the crowd. It was impossible for me to keep up with his long legs and willingness to plow down anyone who got in his way. My having to say, "Excuse him, he was raised by hyenas" to all the folks in his path of destruction slowed me down even more.

But my breathlessness that afternoon wasn't simply my body's response to unusual feats of exertion and apology. What Paul and I had done earlier that day — signing papers to buy a house in Oregon while on vacation — was enough to suck the oxygen out of anyone's lungs. It also made me have to pee. I must have gotten up to run to the tiny outhouse in the sky twenty times during our flight home.

As I sat in the on-board bathroom on one of my treks, I noticed my hands were shaking. What had we done? To be more specific, what had *I* done?

You see, I was thirty-five, while Paul was only twenty-six. Clearly, I was the adult in the relationship, right? But here we were, facing a future in which neither one of us had jobs or knew anyone. This wasn't as big of an issue for Paul because he was always teetering on the brink of being fired from his first real job out of college. But I had been at my job for nearly twelve years, was making good money and still semi-enjoyed what I did.

Adult or not, buying that 1,100-square-foot house with the totem pole in the front yard was definitely my decision. I fell head over heels in love with the quiet neighborhood and the spring-fed creek that ran across the back of the property. The friendly ducks waddling across the street as we waited for the real estate agent sealed the deal with a quack.

Subconsciously, I knew there were only two options for Paul and me. One, we were going to move to the Pacific Northwest. Or two, we would end up moving to Paul's hometown in Indiana to be closer to his parents. He had been too young when I married him, and his mother was the other woman in our relationship. Word of advice: If you're considering marrying a man much younger, make sure you're not closer to his mother's age than his.

That day as we sat in the real estate office, I convinced Paul to join me in a new adventure far from everything and everyone we knew and loved. I was certain that our marriage would never survive if I had to be the third wheel in his relationship with his mom.

As we were getting ready to make the move, I made another big decision: I would try to make a career out of comedy. I had taken a comedy-writing class, and once I realized that everything in life could be viewed through the lens of funny, I wanted nothing to do with the people around me who seemed to be suffering from terminal seriousity. This wasn't an easy or logical decision for a thirty-two-year-old woman who was not voted class clown in high school. Had there been such a category, I might have been voted "Mostly likely to depress people." My role models were Edgar Allan Poe and Sylvia Plath, neither of whom was a laugh riot.

When I shared my plans with people close to me, they looked at me like I had just told them I was planning to run a halfway house for alcoholic porcupines. I could tell they thought I'd come crawling back to the "real world" with my quill-filled tail sooner rather than later.

Imagine arriving in a new place and trying to make a job out of something that was (and still is) mostly a man's field. Worse yet, it was something most people don't even consider to be a real job — something with a failure rate (I now know) of nearly ninety percent. Now imagine doing all of this before the invention of the Internet, so not only could I not job-search online, but I couldn't even watch videos of goats in pajamas to de-stress at the end of the day.

For those first six months, I sent off funny one-liners to greeting card and novelty companies (whose addresses I had to look up in a book at the library). I sent in 100 jokes a month (in an envelope) to a joke-writing service every month; if they bought one, I'd make three dollars. I wrote a funny column for a wellness newsletter for free. I keynoted a wellness conference, again for free. But I did all my writing and phone calls from my office in our new house with its sliding glass door overlooking that wonderful creek.

By the fifth month, it was not looking good. Paul had a badly paying part-time job selling "Crime scene: Do not cross" tape, and we were quickly running through our savings. But then things started to change. I sold a joke to a greeting card company. One of the people at the conference offered me a job speaking for his organization for money. I sold a funny one-liner that ended up on an apron ("My other apron burned in the fire"). I convinced the local community college to hire me to teach continuing education classes in comedy writing and stand-up, something I had only the tiniest bit of knowledge about. By then, I had developed some *chutzpah*.

And here I am, twenty-three years later. Paul is long gone back to the bosom of Indiana. I'm still gazing out on the creek from my office. In 2003, I won the Erma Bombeck Humor Writing Award (for my true story on how my first mammogram caught on fire), and I have published twenty-five funny books. For nine years, I taught academic comedy classes with titles like "Comedy: Hero or Bully" and "Comedy in Media" at a major university. This year, a Hollywood producer asked me to write a screenplay. I teach improv and stand-up, and all of my friends make me giggle myself silly.

I'm still breathless, but mostly from laughing.

~Leigh Anne Jasheway

88

Law and Order

Discrimination is discrimination,
even when people claim it's tradition.
~DaShanne Stokes

fter leaving a crazy and abusive relationship, I decided to change my life. I wrote out my goals and put them on the wall. I enrolled in college at night and took self-improvement courses at work.

As I made steps toward my goals, I started to feel better about myself. My self-esteem increased. My mind became clearer, and I started asking myself, *Where am I headed?* I wanted to do something different and challenging, so I took every job test I found, including one for the Philadelphia Police Department.

The written test was administered at a high school, and I scored ninety-five percent. As part of the interviewing process, I took a lie-detector test and a psychological test at the police academy. After receiving notification in the mail that I had passed both tests, I was required to take the physical exam. When I met with the doctor, he instructed me to stand up to measure my height. After doing so, he said, "Oh, let me measure you again." He did and then said, "You are a quarter of an inch too short."

I asked, "Too short for what?" I didn't know there was a height requirement. A month later, I received a letter informing me I did not get the job.

Disappointed and upset, I returned to my assistant supervisor job at the bank. Three years later, I received a call at work from someone saying she was from the federal government. She asked if I was Kathleen Morris and requested my Social Security number. "I'm not giving my Social Security number over the phone," I responded.

"Can you acknowledge if this is your number?" she asked as she recited my Social Security number. "This is the federal government," she repeated.

"Okay, but I am at work. Can you call me at home?" I asked.

"What time will you be home?" she asked. I said 5:30.

I went home and waited. The phone rang at exactly 5:30 p.m. I answered and asked, "How did you find me?"

She answered, "Your Social Security number."

Then she told me there was a class-action lawsuit against the Philadelphia Police Department for discriminating against women, and my name was on the list. She wanted to confirm I had taken all the tests and my current mailing address. She then asked if I wanted to participate in the lawsuit. I said, "Yes."

> I said, "I want it all."

As part of the settlement, she said, "You will get a job offer, back pay and seniority. What do you want?"

I said, "I want it all."

It would be a couple of years before I received a letter in the mail telling me to report to the police academy within forty-eight hours. This was a shock because I had forgotten completely about it. It also informed me where to go to purchase my cadet uniform and shoes.

I had to cut my shoulder-length hair, which I resisted until the commanding officer threatened that I would not graduate from the academy if I did not cut it. The physical training was intense. I was prepared physically because I was already running four miles a day, but I did not know I would have to climb a ladder up a three-story building. (I am afraid of heights.) The instructors spent thirty minutes coaching and threatening me before I made it to the top. I also did not know how to swim. When the instructor pushed me into the deep end of the pool, I almost drowned. Someone jumped in and pulled me to the ledge. He taught me how to stay afloat by dog paddling.

Two months into training, I was issued a Smith & Wesson Colt 45. I had never seen a real gun or been around a weapon before. The gun was too heavy for me. I had to improve my upper-body strength to be able to handle it, so I started doing chin-ups and push-ups. After all of the additional self-training, I was able to manage my weapon. Four months later, I walked across the stage as one of the five women accepted in the Philadelphia Police Force. After the ceremony, I went to dinner with my family. When I returned to my apartment, a message on my home phone instructed me to report to work that night at midnight.

I reported to the district at 12:00 a.m. with my gun in its holster and wearing the police-issued uniform designed for a man. I was the only woman to stand for roll call. Until that time, women had only worked with juveniles. My new partner and I were assigned to a wagon, and I began my career as a police officer. I had done what most people considered impossible for women. I was now a guardian for the community. I patrolled the streets of Philadelphia for twelve years until an auto accident forced me to retire.

~Kathy Morris

89

Serious Work

Gain control of your time, and you
will gain control of your life.
~John Landis Mason

I am upstairs in my office in the spare bedroom playing solitaire on the computer.

"What are you doing?" my husband asks from the doorway.

"Working," I tell him.

"You can't be serious," he says.

"I am," I tell him.

He shakes his head and walks away.

I can understand his confusion. Playing computer games doesn't command much work respect. Sometimes, he sees me with my feet up on my desk staring absent-mindedly at the birds chirping in the flowering plum tree outside the window. That doesn't look much like work either.

But work comes in many forms. I am a writer. When I'm writing a nonfiction article, I am all business, fact-checking, interviewing, editing. I can be at my computer for hours revising my piece until I get everything just right. When I am writing fiction, I have more leeway. I listen to the voices of my characters, which are not always ready to be heard. So I do other things—have a snack, putter in the garden, take a walk, bake a cake. Eventually, the characters talk to me, and I happily continue writing.

If he catches me when I am having trouble with one of my stories, the doubts can creep in. I think maybe he is right; maybe I am fooling myself about my work. Once, when I was doing an author program at an elementary school, a third-grade boy asked me, "Are you famous?" I had to tell him that I was not, despite all my successes. It was hard to admit; it was certainly not my preference. And when I remember that, it also makes me wonder about what I do.

I drink a cup of green tea as I ponder this idea of serious work. I consider the seventeen books for children I have had published. Some of them came to me easily, letting me write in a fury so that it was obvious I was hard at work. Others took a bit of reflection, more daydreaming, music-listening, window-staring time.

I think about the hundreds of articles I have written for newspapers and magazines over the years, and the poems that have appeared in literary publications. Now I write a weekly nature blog, too. Surely that must count for something.

I take the mug up to my office and lean back in my chair. The screen taunts me. I turn away to look up at the metallic metal sculpture of a gecko crawling on the wall over my bookcase when something clicks. Suddenly, I know how to fix the story. I type furiously until I hear my husband call up, "What's for dinner?"

"Whatever you want to make," I yell down.

I can't take the time to play with pasta, not now. The words are flowing, the characters are interacting, and the plot is building. I have just created a whole world. How much more serious can work get?

~Ferida Wolff

90

Back to School

Aging is not lost youth but a new stage
of opportunity and strength.
~Betty Friedan

s I squirmed in my seat, the professor introduced herself and then looked around the room. "Before we go any further, I'd like to give each of you the chance to introduce yourself. Please tell us a little bit about yourself, including what program you are in, what you've been doing, and why you are pursuing a graduate education."

It had been twenty years since I had last been in a graduate-level course. As I looked around the jam-packed classroom, I realized that most of my classmates would have been mere toddlers back then. Eyeing them, I debated what to say. Honestly, I couldn't help wondering what they were thinking about the student who was twice their age.

When it was my turn, I over-explained:

"My name is Kathleen Plucker, and I've been working as a reading tutor at an elementary school in Glastonbury for the past two years. Before that, I was a kindergarten para-professional there. But I got my M.Ed. in the mid-'90s. At the time, my parents were very opposed to my teaching, so I did not pursue certification then because I felt compelled to respect their wishes. I've since changed my mind about that, but that's another story.

"Anyway, because I was in graduate school when the Internet was really taking off, I ended up developing websites during graduate school and then continued to create more websites and web-based applications in both the educational and corporate worlds. I also taught classes for teachers and librarians and helped them to see ways they could integrate emerging technologies into their workplaces and jobs.

"Over time, I also did some freelance writing and subbed in my children's schools. But I have always wanted to lead my own classroom, and my work these past few years has only increased my desire to do that. Having lost a few friends at this point, I realize that life is short, and I don't want to die not having taught. I'm not getting any younger, so here I am. I am taking classes to obtain certification to teach kindergarten through sixth grade."

It was a mouthful and far more than anyone else had said. But in fairness, everyone else in the room had substantially less life and professional experience on which to comment (other than the professor, who, thankfully, was older than me — but not by much). As soon as I closed my mouth, I was embarrassed by all that I had shared. And yet, it really mattered to me that these younger classmates not dismiss me as unintelligent, uneducated, or outdated — or as someone who had just been sitting around. If I were going to travel this road with them for the next two academic years, I wanted to command respect — and I wanted at least some of my life experiences to count for something in their eyes.

And so began my return to graduate school at age forty-five. I write this over twenty months later, now that my journey has nearly come full circle. Just over a week ago, I completed my student-teaching experience, and two days later, I signed a contract to serve as a long-term substitute for the last two months of the school year. In the interim, I am subbing at various grade levels, which is an interesting challenge. (High school sophomores are quite different from second-graders!) Much of my energy is devoted to securing a full-time position, though given Connecticut's financial troubles, doing so may prove tougher than I'd hoped.

Prior to two years ago, returning to graduate school to take certification classes had seemed impossible. As the mother of two young children and as the spouse of someone who travels for work, I didn't think I could successfully swing classes and motherhood, especially because we had no family living nearby who could help watch our children while I attended class and studied.

But as of two years ago, the kids were finally old enough (ninth and fourth grades) for me to feel more comfortable leaving them home alone occasionally while I was at class. Also, I felt that I could complete my schoolwork while they did theirs (or as they attended practices for their various activities). In other words, I no longer felt that I somehow risked shortchanging them. The downside of waiting so long, though, was that I had grown visibly older with each passing year.

During the past two years, I have learned many teaching methods and classroom-management strategies. But one of my other big takeaways has been how easily we can let our age keep us from doing what interests us.

> *Yes, there have been times when I have felt downright ridiculous.*

Yes, there have been times when I have felt downright ridiculous, wondering how others perceive what I am doing at the ripe old age of forty-seven. As I walked around campus sporting my backpack, I wondered what others concluded about the woman who looked like she should be the professor, not the student. When I was completing my student teaching, introducing myself to colleagues as a student teacher always felt a little ludicrous. And being a student teacher to a host teacher who is fifteen years younger than I am was awkward at times. When I finally host my first open house, introducing myself as a first-year teacher will inevitably feel silly.

Nonetheless, I have pushed forward, motivated by my students. I am looking forward to at least twelve to fifteen years of teaching. In that time, I can positively impact hundreds of students, as well as their parents and my professional peers.

I sincerely hope that my colleagues in my certification program have learned something from me. Perhaps they have benefited from hearing about my experiences as a parent of school-aged children and as a reading tutor at an elementary school.

But I also desire that some who have witnessed my journey have taken something else from it—our age should not deter us from pursuing something that intrigues, interests, or even relentlessly nags us. I hope that other graduate students realized that they, too, can change course if they wish one day. And I hope that my own children will be reminded throughout their lives that their mother, in an effort to be true to herself, reinvented herself. For if there is one thing I do not wish to be, it is stagnant.

Throughout the past two years, I have swallowed my pride regularly, but the payoff has been life-changing and even liberating. I am finally on the cusp of doing what I wanted to do from the very beginning. No longer will I wonder, "What if?"

~Kathleen Whitman Plucker

Chapter 9

The Empowered Woman

Figuring It Out Myself

The First Female

If you want something said, ask a man; if you want something done, ask a woman.
~Margaret Thatcher

ecently, I was awarded the 2017 Distinguished Alumni Award by my high school. This honor gave me the opportunity to speak to the students of Niles West High School. I told my student audience that a big difference between us now is perspective. They were in their seats just beginning their choices. I was standing on stage already knowing where many of my choices had taken me.

I was the founding general manager of WYCC-TV Channel 20, an educational public television station in Chicago. If anyone had told me when I was graduating from Niles West that I would be responsible for putting a television station on the air in Chicago twenty years later, I would have laughed. And, more importantly, I would not have believed it was possible for me to do it.

Time and perspective have given me a belief in myself, my abilities, my capacity to learn as I work, my appropriate use of my determination and energy, and my awareness that being afraid to fail won't kill me.

On a cold November day, the Chancellor of the City Colleges of Chicago asked for a meeting with me. As I sat across from him, I concentrated on the once-in-a-lifetime request he was making. He told me that the City Colleges had purchased the license to put Chicago's second PBS affiliate on the air. He wanted me to build the station and launch it. I would begin as Program Director, and in a couple of months I would be named General Manager of WYCC-TV. This title made me Chicago's first female television GM.

As the eldest of four daughters, one of the greatest gifts my parents gave to each of us was the belief that we could accomplish whatever we wished to do. I always felt I was unlimited by gender. I was ready to work in the male world of television management. I was proud and, at the same time, sad that I was Chicago's first. Happily, more women would follow me into this level of management in television broadcasting.

Much of my energy went toward protecting the station from the whims of those to whom I reported at the City Colleges. Chancellor Shabat became my mentor and always offered a fair ear and productive suggestions. Other males in the college system were not as willing to have a female create and manage the station. There was blatant jealousy, and many attempts were made to block my success. I faced each one with the strength that came from my belief that my young staff and I could do the impossible with the budget we were given. I would make unwavering eye contact with every man who tried to hinder our work. They pushed just so far, in part because of my strength as a manager and also because they knew the boss of all had assigned the station to me. I know many of these men were hoping I would fail. I did not.

Within the three-week window before the station's airdate, my chief engineer came into my office almost in tears. "The console for the master control has not arrived," he said. "I need something to use in the meantime if we are to make our launch deadline! Something like cafeteria tables."

"Go ahead and borrow what you need," I answered.

Shortly after our conversation, I heard drilling. My engineer had made holes in the tables to temporarily place our consoles. Soon afterward, I received a raging call from the President of the College in which the station was being built.

"How dare your staff take tables from our cafeteria without my permission!"

I knew this man had a rather large ego, so I softly and gently thanked him for saving us in our time of dire need. I promised we would always ask his personal permission if we had similar needs in the future. As I left his office, he was smiling.

I wished all confrontations could have been that easy. When the new Chairman for the City Colleges Board of Trustees wanted to broadcast religious services on the station, I sent him a note telling him it was time we spoke in person. This man was a force in the business world and politics and had never been told "no."

I explained that WYCC was a Public Broadcasting station and could not air religious programming. I showed him a letter I had requested from the station's lawyers in Washington. And I said, "No!" He complied, but never spoke directly to me again.

I never felt fear in protecting the station from the bureaucracy in which it was steeped. I believed in myself and my mission. In one decade, my station made the top ten in educational television stations as rated by the Corporation for Public Broadcasting.

Banners throughout Chicago celebrated our first decade on the air. My staff and I felt pride in having built from scratch a beloved and watched station in Chicago. Our city's broadcast historian interviewed me as Chicago's first female television general manager.

On the day after our celebration, a fire alarm went off at the college that housed WYCC-TV. I ordered the entire staff out of the building and stayed with my ship! Sitting in master control, I realized suddenly that if the operators were not back in a half-hour, I had no idea how to change the program to the next one. I was protecting my station, but I was the least useful of anyone. It was a most humbling realization and a wonderful laugh for Chicago's first female TV GM!

~Elynne Chaplik-Aleskow

92

Don't Hammer Afraid

Coming out of your comfort zone is tough in the
beginning, chaotic in the middle, and awesome
in the end... because in the end, it
shows you a whole new world.
~Manoj Arora

I stood in the garage holding a nail in my left hand and a hammer in my right. If I was going to be an independent woman, hanging a dog leash was as good a place to start as any. I didn't want to smash my thumb, so I pecked timidly at the nail until it sank a quarter of an inch into the rough-hewn paneling. But with the next tap, the nail went flying across the garage. "Rats!" I muttered as I searched for it. Second attempt, same result. Ditto for the third.

Was this how my "new" life was going to be? I'd recently filed for divorce from my husband of thirty-five years and had moved to a small house in a quiet neighborhood. Though I'd always considered myself a fairly competent person, I quickly discovered how many things I didn't know. Hammering a nail was only one of them. I sighed and draped the dog leash over the doorknob.

My friends Steve and Lucy stopped by that afternoon to see how I was getting along. "Okay, I guess..." I told them.

"Do you need help with something?" Steve asked. I told him about the hammering fiasco. "Get your hammer and nail and show me how you did it," he said. Steve did an admirable job not laughing when, once again, the nail went flying across the garage when I tapped on it. "The first problem is that you need a real hammer," he said. "This one's more like a toy." But he took it from me and, with just two blows, drove the nail deep into the wood.

"Wow," I said. "How come that didn't work for me?"

"Because you were hammering afraid." He pried the nail out of its hole and handed it to me. "Now you try." It took me four blows, but I hammered with confidence. The nail sank into the paneling, and I didn't smash my fingers. It was a small victory, but a victory nonetheless.

In the coming weeks and months, as I learned to live alone for the first time in my life, I thought often about Steve's advice: Don't hammer afraid.

I remembered it when my toilet stopped up. I didn't have a plunger and wouldn't have known how to use one even if I did. Did I call a plumber? Nope. I watched a YouTube video and

"Because you were hammering afraid."

learned that an accordion plunger works best and how to use one. So off I went to the hardware store. I bought not only a plunger, but also a real hammer and a new furnace filter. Back at home, I unstopped the toilet. Then I turned my attention to the furnace filter. I popped the dirty one out of its slot with no problem. But what was the right way to put the new one in? I turned it this way and that. Lo and behold, I discovered writing on the cardboard frame. THIS END UP, it said, and THIS SIDE FACES OUT. Voilà. Done!

I won't pretend I solved all my problems that easily. Having a husband to do "man things" for most of my life had allowed me to avoid learning some pretty important stuff. It took me several practice runs before I mastered checking the oil and tire pressure in my car. (I certainly didn't know that the mysterious little dashboard light that looks something like a harp is actually a tire pressure warning.) When a horrible smell permeated my guest bathroom, I feared the septic tank needed to be pumped out. As it turns out, the drain trap in the shower was dry, which had allowed sewer gas to back up and cause an odor. Solution? Pour two cups of water down the drain once a week.

Other challenges were much tougher. What was the smartest

way to invest my money? What level of deductible made sense for my health insurance? Did I really need a new water heater or could the old one be repaired? I learned a lot on the Internet, and I wasn't shy about asking friends for advice. And I didn't hesitate to hire a professional for jobs I couldn't handle.

I never imagined I would be starting over as a single woman at age sixty. The road has been rocky at times. Really rocky. But anytime I feel overwhelmed by fears and insecurities, I remember Steve's advice: Don't hammer afraid. And I drive that nail deep into the wood.

~Jennie Ivey

93

Maximillion

Life's challenges are not supposed to paralyze you;
they're supposed to help you discover who you are.
~Bernice Johnson Reagon

Volvos are known for being safe cars, so that's what I looked for when I was buying a used car. What they forgot to tell me was that finding parts or mechanics for them isn't always easy.

When my twenty-five-year-old Volvo started to cut out when I was driving, even without knowing anything about the car, I knew it was a pretty big problem. But it started up again right away, so I ignored it. In hindsight, I might not have made the best choice. And then one day, it just wouldn't start.

I had it towed to a garage that specializes in Volvos, and they got it up and running—for a week or so. Still paying off the first bill, I thought I'd ask a neighbour who fixes cars out of his garage to give it a try. He's a Chevy guy, but a car's a car, right? I soon found out that, in fact, Volvos are Volvos and Chevys are Chevys—and never the twain shall meet!

Given that we lived on an island, I was completely stranded at home with two little kids. I didn't have money to take taxis everywhere, and I certainly didn't have the money to buy another car.

So I finally did what any other fiercely independent—or was it just desperate?—woman would do: I ordered a Haynes manual and started reading.

Just so we're clear, it's not as if my father fixed cars in his spare time when I was growing up or anything so I knew all this stuff. No, I knew nothing about cars. Heck, I am so un-mechanical that I don't even know the difference between a Phillips-head and Robertson screwdriver unless described by shape. (And while I'm sure that I own both kinds, it's rare that I can actually find them.)

After reading through the Haynes manual — okay, I flipped through and looked at the pictures, but it was a start, right? — I searched online. There are Volvo-fixing websites, Volvo boards, and Volvo groups. Who knew? I posted questions, always apologizing for my complete ignorance, and got answers, which usually just led to more questions.

But I made a little bit of progress by checking the fuses (hidden behind the ashtray), siphoning out the cheap gas and replacing it with premium. Then I checked the spark plugs and bought a new fuel-injection relay. The more I learned, the more confident I grew.

That was good because most of the easy things had been ruled out, and my car still wasn't going anywhere. But I felt brave enough to check bigger things, like the fuel pump (another no). Every time I found a new possibility, I felt sure I was going to be able to get my car up and running.

I kept reading the forums and searching through my now well-worn Haynes manual looking for the elusive solution that two trained mechanics before me had missed. I didn't think I knew more than they did, of course, but the difference between us was that I needed my car to work. I needed to go for groceries and get the kids to school if they missed the bus. I missed my freedom. And, I have to admit, I was starting to see my car as more than a car; we were starting to form a bond.

Shortly after realizing that I was not giving up on the car, no matter how frustrated I felt at times, I finally had the breakthrough. After fully understanding how all the parts of the engine work together, I traced the journey from ignition through spark plugs to carburetor (thankfully, that wasn't the problem!) and ended up with distributor — and a new distributor was all it took.

The journey took me a full month and cost me a bit of money in parts that didn't need replacing. But, in the end, it was much cheaper than another mechanic or another car would have been. And even better than getting the car up and running again — which was pretty sweet — was the sense that I really, truly can do anything that I set my mind to. I mean, I fixed a car. I'm still pretty proud.

To celebrate the car being up and running, my kids and I christened it Maximillion. It had already driven half a million kilometres, and we wanted to give it inspiration to get through the next half a million. We've got a long way to go yet, but as everyone knows, the journey is just as much fun as the destination.

~esme mills

94

Doing It My Way

Whatever you are doing, love yourself for doing it.
Whatever you are feeling, love yourself for feeling it.
~Thaddeus Golas

I ticked the items off my list as I loaded the goods into the car: paint, brushes in various sizes, rollers, masking tape... After checking and re-checking, I decided I had all I needed and started for home.

It had been a few months since the divorce. The initial hurt had subsided a little, but my self-esteem had taken a battering. Not only that, it had been so long since I had lived on my own that I had been surprised to find myself struggling to manage the practicalities.

For a time, I had called on friends and family for emotional and practical help, and they had been supportive. One had given me a hand pruning the hedges, which had become so overgrown I thought my garden was about to disappear. Another had introduced me to a good plumber when the boiler failed.

I had been really grateful for this help, but I realised now was the time to become more self-reliant. I knew deep down one of the ways to raise my self-esteem would be to deal with all the practicalities now required by my new status.

The living-room decor was tired to say the least. Two dark patches showed where a couple of paintings had hung that belonged to my other half. *Other half,* I said to myself. *You've got to stop thinking of yourself as half of a couple. You are now a single woman. It's time to be strong, capable, and resilient. You can make that room beautiful again.* While all this was admirable thinking, the other issue was that the divorce settlement had made something of a dent in my finances. The couple of quotes I had received told me I couldn't really afford to pay a decorator.

I had a little experience in painting and hanging wallpaper. My ex and I had always done it together. Okay, so I had been the rookie supporting the skilled artisan, but I wasn't going to dwell on that fact. After all, how hard could it be to paint a couple of walls and hang some paper?

And so it was with a flurry of confidence I had booked a week off work. When my office colleagues asked what I was going to do with the time, I told them I would be transforming my space. They looked suitably impressed, and feeling confident and optimistic, I invited them to a post-decorating party to see the results of my labour. *There's no way you can back down now,* I told myself.

It was, however, with some dismay that as I drew close to the week of the transformation, I started to cough and sneeze. I left the office with aching bones and head. The cold that had been doing the rounds had settled on me. Still, I wasn't going to be daunted. Shivering and coughing as I left work that Friday evening, my last words to my work mates were: "I can't wait to show you all when it's finished." Amidst words of encouragement (and did I detect a little skepticism?), I left the office.

The following morning, I rose early, and after opening all the windows to try to clear my chest, I started to strip the walls. The cold water ran down my arms and formed icy drips under my shirt as I steamed off the old paper. The chill April air seeping in through the windows dampened the room. *I could leave this until I feel better,* I thought to myself, *but is that what a strong, empowered woman would do?* I thought not. I turned up the volume on the radio and sang to the tunes between coughs. I avoided the dampening of my spirits by muttering the words *empowered, resilient, strong*—my new mantra.

For a while, despite the cold and discomfort, I was making progress, but it wasn't too long before I encountered my first problem. The old wallpaper was coming off, but what was this sticky mess it was leaving behind? I pressed my palms against it, and my hands stuck to the wall. Scrubbing harder only increased the slime. Nothing was getting rid of this substance: detergent, household cleaner, bleach. A plethora of cleaning potions were brought out and discarded on the floor around me. Eventually, I remembered a tip from my dad to use sugar soap, and after much rubbing and repeating of the mantra, I was looking at four clean walls. I breathed a sigh of relief. It was time to get out the paintbrushes.

Feeling optimistic once more, I headed to the kitchen to get the paint. However, the optimism was short-lived. Pulling on the door handle, I stood back in amazement as it came away in my hand. Groaning to myself, I remembered I had uncoupled the handle in readiness to paint the doors. "Damn," I hissed. This was punctuated by a clunk on the opposite side of the door as the rest of the handle hit the floor, and it dawned on me that I was locked in. Pulling at the door and sticking a screwdriver under it to try to force it open had no result.

With a sinking feeling, I realised there was only one option. Opening the window wider and standing on the sill, I started to make my undignified exit. *At least there is no one here to witness this,* I thought to myself. *I'll soon be back in and getting on with the job.* But then as I was suspended halfway through the open window, my legs dangling about a foot from the floor, I realised my shirt had caught on the catch. I tried moving left and right, back and forth, but I was well and truly stuck. Another coughing fit ensued as the cold air caught my midriff.

I don't know how long I would have been there, suspended in mid-air, if an old van hadn't come into view around the corner. "Cunliffe and Son, Decorators" was emblazoned on the side. Oh, the irony.

I tugged and tugged but couldn't get loose, by which time Cunliffe and Son had strolled up the path to see what was going on. After some debate during which I reassured them I wasn't trying to break into the property, Cunliffe Senior gave my shirt a sharp tug, and I dropped to the ground. He looked through the window.

"You seem to be doing okay in there, but here's my card in case you need it."

After making sure I had re-entered my property through the door rather than the window, they strolled back down the path.

It's only my pride that is dented, I told myself. *This doesn't mean I'm not strong and independent.* I took myself back to the task at hand, repeating the mantra: *empowered, resilient, strong.*

Carrying on through the rest of the week, I kept repeating this mantra. Each time I climbed the stepladders, my chest heaved and dizziness prevailed. I was so sweaty that the brush slipped through my hands, and my old jeans and shirt became covered in paint.

I felt my self-esteem rise as I admired my work.

At the end of the week, though, despite all odds, the room was looking good. It had taken longer than I expected and hadn't been without event. *But what's a little loss of dignity?* I thought to myself. And this chest infection would soon pass.

Feeling once again optimistic, I skipped off the stepladders for one last time and stood back to admire my work. Unfortunately, I hadn't noticed the can of paint I had left on the floor. As my foot connected with it, I watched in dismay as my cream carpet developed a large patch of "crimson kiss."

Over the weekend, I put the room back together and managed to get a new carpet fitted. It did look great. I had achieved my goal. I felt my self-esteem rise as I admired my work.

My friends came to the post-decorating party and were all in agreement that I had certainly earned the title of empowered and independent woman. For my part, I tried to enjoy my new status as I rubbed pain-relief cream on my back and started the antibiotics for the chest infection that I had neglected all week.

"So, what's the next project?" one of them asked as they left the party that evening. I gave a non-committal "not sure yet" as I waved them off.

Going back into the room, I asked myself, *Well what is the next project to be?* True to my word, the room looked great. Like the empowered woman I had so wanted to be, I had achieved my goal. *Next project,* I thought, but my heart sank at the thought of ever picking up a paintbrush again.

I checked my spending, and when I totaled up how much the room had cost (including the price of a new carpet), a new thought entered my mind. I had to admit, although I had achieved my goal, decorating really wasn't my forte. *In fact,* I thought to myself, *I would rather have been in the office.*

A few months later, I decided that the kitchen was looking ready for a little refurbishment. I knew I could do it. I had learned a lot. It would be an easy job in comparison. However, whenever I thought about doing it, I got that same sinking feeling.

About that same time, an e-mail popped into my account. There were opportunities to do some overtime. I estimated that it would only take a few weekend mornings to pull in enough cash to hire someone. I turned over Cunliffe and Son's card in my hand, and then picked up the phone. The quote wasn't too bad. *I just hope they can do as good a job as I did,* I thought to myself. And at that moment I realised, yes, my self-esteem had risen. I did those few weekends overtime and soon had enough cash to fund the new project.

Mr. Cunliffe and Son came kitted up with plastic sheeting to protect my furniture. Polite, helpful, and courteous, they quietly got on with the work. No paint was spilled, and the only job I had to do was make sure they had plenty of cups of tea. In a couple of days, the kitchen looked brand new. We shook hands, and they went on their way.

My friends at work asked why I had not painted the kitchen myself, as they had been so proud of me. At that point, I decided it was time to tell them the real story of my decorating adventures. They howled with laughter when I told them about my undignified exit through the window.

"I'm giving up this idea of being empowered," I joked. "One way or another, that week nearly killed me."

"You know," one of them said, "I don't believe being empowered is about putting yourself through hell just to prove a point. It's about living life on your terms and achieving your goals in the way that best suits you…"

"…and knowing my limitations," I added wryly.

"No, come on," said another. "You succeeded in completing your challenge. You empowered yourself, but you also found your own way of achieving the same goal. Empowerment, after all, is a learning game, something we are all moving toward in our own way."

I raised a cup of tea to that and settled back down to my computer.

~Michelle Emery

95

My Stand

Invent your world. Surround yourself with people,
color, sounds, and work that nourish you.
~Susan Ariel Rainbow Kennedy

I expected to be many things by the time I was fifty, but alone wasn't one of them. Yet there I stood in a family-sized house that I'd shared with my now-grown children and their father not long ago. My high school sweetheart. My helpmate. My husband of thirty years, who shocked us when he revealed he no longer wanted to be married.

Every room held excruciating reminders of our life together and his hasty departure from it. The master bathroom, for some reason, was the hardest for me to walk into, the place where I still most expected to see him.

One morning, as I made my necessary but almost unbearable way to the bathroom, a divine voice whispered, "Change the shower curtain." And so I did. Funny how such a small step began my journey to healing.

Just days later, when the forecast called for heavy snow, I was reminded how much I'd depended on men my entire life to take care of most home-maintenance responsibilities. *Where,* I wondered, *do I buy bagged salt, and how do I apply it to our long driveway?* I quickly learned from this and similar small challenges in those first weeks that much can be accomplished by simply reading directions, asking others for guidance, and having faith that God will give me the ability to handle whatever lies ahead.

Bolstered by faith and small victories, I began looking for other home-maintenance projects to tackle. Once again, I found myself in the master bathroom. Armed with a wrench and a YouTube video to guide me, I prepared to replace the long-neglected dripping faucet. My daughter stopped by while I was removing the old fixture, and was so impressed with her wrench-wielding mom that she insisted we take and post selfies. My brother was equally impressed when he learned I'd replaced both the faucet and drain with no leaking. Later, he told me I hadn't actually needed to replace the drain. I just laughed. *Oh, well,* I told myself, *extra plumbing practice!*

I was re-energized and ready to prepare the house to sell. Soon, I was caulking cracks, whacking weeds, trimming bushes and mowing the very large property. Any trepidation about buying and caring for a new home on my own faded, and I found myself excited about the fresh start that new home ownership would bring.

There was a bit of a gap between my budget and the darling dream house I was envisioning. With my patient, freshly licensed real estate agent at my side — who happened to also be my uncle — I looked at nearly fifty houses, lost bids on a few, and eventually wondered if maybe I wasn't supposed to buy a house.

And then I looked at a property that didn't come close to checking all the boxes on my list. But as we drove up the driveway — the very steep driveway (so much for a flat lot) — I looked up and whispered to myself, "This is my house."

Since moving in, I've learned to mow that steep lot, stain a deck, secure a fence, commandeer a drill, change a furnace filter, and so much more. When I look at my personal "honey-do" list, I just smile. I know I will be able to check off every task. Sometimes on my own. Sometimes with a little help from a friend or professional. But I can take care of my home. I can take care of me.

While dining recently with a dear friend, she told me I have changed. That I carry myself differently. That I seem more relaxed. At peace. "When life handed you lemons, Dawn, you didn't just make lemonade," she said. "You made the whole stand."

Well, maybe not literally. But, you know, I can if I want to.

~Dawn Belt

96

Opportunity Knocks

*Sometimes if you want to see a change for the better,
you have to take things into your own hands.*
~Clint Eastwood

"The front doors look terrible," I said to my husband. When one's front doors face the afternoon sun in Southern California, there are bound to be problems. Ours was not spared from the intensity of the heat and, over time, the veneer on our oak-stained double front doors began to blister... for the second time. The first time it happened, my father came to our rescue and repaired them, stripping the buckled veneer and painting the doors a bold barn red.

For several years afterward, the doors looked great. But it was as if the sun came back at us with a vengeance, and now the doors looked worse than ever before. Thin strips of red painted wood made hills and valleys on the surface of our front door, taunting me every time I came home and put my key in the lock.

When I complained to my husband that the doors looked awful, I wasn't really expecting a response. Even though he is a very handy partner, able to do almost every home repair himself, I knew his business kept him too occupied for home-maintenance projects. We couldn't afford to pay a contractor to replace or repair them, and asking my father to help again didn't seem right since he was now busy with his own projects. So I had to ask myself, *Is this something you can do yourself?*

Over the years, I have considered myself a handy woman. I still

Figuring It Out Myself | 347

remember the time we were rehabbing our first home, and I was helping to build our fence.

"Hey, Jeff," I heard our neighbor yell from the other side of the yard.

"No, not Jeff," I replied. When I walked out into his view, I could see a look of shock on his face when he saw me and not my husband. I had a hammer in one hand and my son in a baby carrier on my back.

"Oh," he said, "I heard hammering, and I thought..."

"Surprise!" I waved at him with my hammer.

Yes, I knew my way around tools, and more than once they ended up on my Christmas wish list. One of my favorite gifts was a cordless Makita drill that I still use regularly. So I wasn't a complete novice when it came to tackling home-improvement work. I had even recently landscaped our front yard. With some help from my husband, I tore out the entire front lawn and replaced it with California native plants.

> *I had a hammer in one hand and my son in a baby carrier on my back.*

But these were our front doors — the first thing people would see when they came to our home. The project seemed so daunting, and the consequences of a job poorly done seemed high. Even so, I couldn't stand to look at them any longer and decided to look at this as an opportunity to stretch myself.

New tools would be required to strip the buckled veneer. I bought an electric multi-function tool that could scrape and sand in small spots. I also bought a small hand-held electric sander. Even though we had tools that might have done the job, I realized that having tools that were more suitable to a woman's hands was worth the investment.

Learning to use the electric scraper was a challenge. More than once, I thought I was in over my head. If I pushed too hard, it would gouge the wood, which meant more repairs. I wasn't expecting perfection, but I sure was hoping for presentable! And just when I thought I had gotten all the loose veneer scraped off, another piece would start peeling. It was days of scraping, then sanding, then filling with wood putty, and then sanding again. It was tedious work, but I was determined to finish.

Finally, the prep work was done, and I was ready to paint. I chose to go with the same barn red color we had used before. And after several coats of paint and new doorknobs, my work was done. It wasn't a flawless job — if people look closely, they will still see many furrows in the wood and a less-than-smooth finish. But when I stepped back and looked at the doors, I was proud. No more covering them up with Christmas wrap during the holidays. No more cringing when I put my key in the lock. No more embarrassment when friends and family knocked on the door.

Not long after I completed the front-door project, my dad came to visit.

"Hey, Lynne," he said, "the doors look good!"

"Thanks, Dad," I said, stopping to admire them with him. His compliment meant a lot, but the satisfaction of transforming the entrance to our house all on my own was enough.

Finishing the front doors inspired me to tackle some other deferred maintenance projects around our home. I demolished a rotten patio cover, repaired and rehung gutters, and dolled up a dingy backyard enclosure into a cute she-shed that we use for storage. And for Christmas this year, my husband got me a cordless reciprocating saw. I can't wait to find a new project to use it on in the New Year!

~Lynne Leite

97

Take a Man

*You only have control over three things in your
life — the thoughts you think, the images
you visualize, and the actions you take.*
~Jack Canfield

"Take a man," she said, when I announced to an acquaintance at church I was going car shopping the next day. Good advice, I suppose, but I didn't have a man, or any credit, or a down payment, or a stable work history or a co-signer.

What I had was an ancient Chevy Corsica with high mileage, peeling silver paint and a high loan balance. The Chevy broke down at least once a month, leaving me with costly repair bills I couldn't afford and no way to get to work. I did not have a man.

The man had left our twenty-four-year marriage in pursuit of an alternative lifestyle. I was not sure I wanted another man. Even if I had wanted another man someday, it would not be soon enough to help me then — when I needed a new car. I needed a car I could trust to take me and my disabled son at least as far as the county line.

I went to the Chevrolet dealership with my head down and my shoulders hunched. I tried to stroll casually around, looking at all the latest models. Too soon, I was accosted by an eager salesman. He immediately devalued my trade-in by $1,200 because of its high mileage and peeling paint, a manufacturer's defect. He let me fill out a credit application but I didn't think he was taking me seriously.

While I rubbed my hands across the shiny metallic finish of the new cars on display, sat on the plush leather seats and inhaled the seductive new-car aromas, I could see the salesman and his boss drinking coffee at a desk behind a glassed-in cubicle. They were having way too much fun to be seriously trying to get me a loan. "No way," they said when they came out, "unless you get a co-signer. Maybe your ex-husband will co-sign for you."

My brain, previously sharp and focused, failed to see things clearly in its newly dazed, single state. I had left home without a plan. I did not have prepared rebuttals for why I did not qualify for an auto loan.

The next day I was prepared. The largest multi-make auto conglomerate in Portland, Oregon, was having a sales extravaganza at the Portland Expo Center. Every brand would be on display under one roof. I walked in boldly with my shoulders back and my head held high past the Ferraris and Fords, the Mercurys and Mazdas, the Jeeps and Jaguars to the center of the gigantic Quonset-shaped building where the Chevrolets were displayed with their polished hoods propped open.

"What kind of car are you looking for?" the salesman asked.

"I'll be trading in a Corsica, so I guess I'd like another Corsica," I said.

"That doesn't mean you have to buy a Corsica. Of all the cars you see here, which one do you really want?" he asked.

Wow! A trick question! I had never thought beyond a Corsica. I looked around and spotted the car of my son's dreams: a "Polynesian green metallic" Geo Storm. "That one," I said, walking over to it and caressing the sleek lines of its curving fenders.

"Let me see what I can work out for you," he said.

I filled out the loan application and waited. This time, I was prepared. When the dealer wanted to devalue my trade-in because of the peeling paint, I handed them a copy of an article documenting the defects of the factory-applied paint. When the bank questioned my work history, I said, "As you can see, all of my positions have been in my career field, and there have been no lapses in my employment." When the lender questioned my lack of credit history, I explained my recent separation and pending divorce. When they asked for a down payment, I offered to make a balloon payment with my tax refund. When the finance company asked for a co-signer, I said, "I don't need one."

It took several hours. In fact, it was dark, and snow had covered the ground by the time I was ready to leave the Portland Expo Center. It had been several years since I had driven a car with a stick shift. So I took a couple of laps around the nearly empty parking lot to get used to the clutch before I attempted the snowy drive home in my new Geo Storm.

It certainly wasn't a great deal, not even a good deal to most people. But it was a deal. *My* deal! It was the deal that gave me the confidence to begin looking forward instead of back.

~Mason K. Brown

98

Reservation for One

Don't judge too harshly, for if your weaknesses
were to be placed under your footsteps, most
likely you would stumble and fall as well.
~Richelle E. Goodrich

runk drivers are selfish, and mothers who drive drunk with their children in the car should be locked up forever with the other crazy, trashy, drug-addicted, prostitute, thieving women. There is no gray area… period. Even before I had children, I knew what kind of mother I would be: giving, loving, nurturing, safety-conscious — basically perfect.

I would never put my children in harm's way. I dreamt of being that soccer or baseball mom, you know, the kind that drives a minivan and volunteers at her kids' Christmas and Valentine's Day parties. I'd bake fresh oatmeal-raisin cookies (not chocolate-chip because oatmeal and raisins are healthy) and have them waiting, hot out of the oven with ice cold glasses of soy milk when the children got off the school bus. My babies would love me so much and draw pictures of them and me — with hearts for clouds; I'd hang their artwork on the refrigerator door. I'd be Supermom.

But, supermoms don't end up doing time and supermoms' mug shots don't end up on the front page of the local newspaper for driving under the influence with their children in their minivans.

On November 25, 2012 at 5:36 p.m., I was stopped outside the Walgreens on Madison Street in Clarksville, Tennessee.

"Ma'am, have you been drinking?"

"Um… oh… not much. Just a glass of wine or two this afternoon," I mumbled.

"I'm going to need you to step out of the van. Officer Mitchell will stay with the kids."

I obeyed. He asked me to walk in a straight line, heel to toe. I failed. He asked me to say the alphabet backwards. I really failed. My three youngest, ages five, seven, and nine, watched as I was handcuffed, with blue lights flashing behind the maroon Nissan Quest that carried them to and from school, baseball practice, and church on Sunday mornings. They watched as the police officer forced my head down into the patrol car. My children watched as I was driven away to jail, all but my eleven-year-old son who was at a friend's house.

I spent twenty-four hours in the holding tank. I was placed there completely alone. I sat on the cold, concrete floor and cried. Finally, around 5 a.m., I was able to make bail.

I never thought in all my years I would become an alcoholic. After all, I never had a problem with alcohol in college. I even worked at a winery and could take the wine or leave it. Something happened between college, marriage, first baby and fourth baby — something called life.

February 16th, the day I was to find out my fate, quickly came. I was oddly calm, thinking that surely the judge would be lenient. After all, I was a middle school English teacher and Sunday school leader and had never been in trouble in my entire life.

The court hearing whirled by me. It was fast and confusing. My lawyer came back with this proposal: Thirty days in jail — ten days for each child. I would get the child endangerment charges erased from my permanent file if I took the jail time. I decided that if I ever wanted a decent job again, I'd better take the plea, but how in the world would I be able to do jail time and with — those women? I shuddered at the idea.

I had two weeks or so to prepare before I turned myself into the Montgomery County Jail, two weeks to do my shopping for the list of items I could bring: three white shirts, socks, underwear, and three books. There would be no fashion shows in jail.

Those two weeks were just the amount of time I needed to organize my thoughts. I had to imagine that I was going on an unusual journey — a journey most women will never take, especially good, educated mothers. It was going to be a life journey — a time to gain raw experiences that would hopefully fill my personal storybook. I had an opportunity to see how those bad girls lived. Maybe I would pretend I was an undercover journalist or a missionary preparing to go into a war-torn country. Yes, that's what it would be. This would give me a chance to pull purpose out of this tragic situation. I would help those inmates any way I could.

March 1st quickly arrived. I had to turn myself in at 6 a.m. at the intake section with the big window that is just upstairs after you walk into the jail's main doors.

My mother had tears rolling down her cheeks.

"You'll be okay?"

"Yes, of course, Mom. This is going to be fun. Real fun. I am excited, actually. Really excited. Don't worry about me. It's great. It's going to be great. Great fun. Great excitement."

"I will write you and visit you," my mother affirmed.

"You don't have to, Mom. I mean, if it's too hard for you," I said.

"No, I will write every week, and I will visit."

I couldn't look back to tell her, "Okay" or "Goodbye." Knowing the pain she felt and the disappointment I had caused was overwhelming. It put too much of a damper on the pumped up enthusiasm about my upcoming venture, and without that enthusiasm, I think I would have lost it.

"Reservation for one," I said bravely, as I smiled at the shorthaired, hard-faced woman behind the smudged glass window.

"Huh?" she said.

"Oh, um, I'm here to turn myself in — Dana Clark."

"Sit on over there until I call you back," she demanded.

I sat on the cold bench and reminded myself to breathe, that everything was going to be okay, and that I would find hope in this journey by helping those women.

Finally a young male guard opened the heavy metal door that led to the processing area and then guided me to a fairly large room with windows to look out. I felt like I was in there for days before another young woman guard approached the locked door. I knew her from somewhere, but I couldn't put my finger on it. As soon as our eyes met, though, memories flooded me.

"Na'Tisha," I said.

"Uh, yeah," she replied.

For a moment I thought of leaving it at that. I didn't want her to know who I was. She had been one of my seventh-grade language arts students when I taught at Northeast Middle School.

"Aw! Mrs. Clark! I didn't recognize you. Oh, my God! What are you doing in here?"

"Uh… well… I kind of made a bad choice — totally not something I typically do, and um, yeah… that's it."

> *Alcohol was like a really bad friend who gives you really bad advice.*

I lied. It was something I typically did. I had started out just drinking a few glasses of wine on the weekends to help deal with work and laundry and dinner and baths and homework and fighting siblings and baseball practices and soccer practices and dance recitals and on and on. Quickly, I was drinking every day — but not until after the kids were in bed. Soon after that, I was drinking after 4 p.m.; then it moved up to 2 p.m.; then coconut vodka in my morning coffee.

Alcohol was my pick-me-up. It didn't make me tired or lethargic. It eased my back pain. It eased my anxiety. It made me calm and happy and willing to let my girls help me make dinner. Before, I just wanted to do everything on my own. I didn't want the added messes and spills.

But when I drank, I felt like I was a better momma. I had the time and energy to sit on the floor and play Barbies or throw a baseball in the back yard. Alcohol convinced me I was okay to drive. Alcohol was like a really bad friend who gives you really bad advice. *It's no different than some crazy mom who is texting and driving*, I fooled myself. *At least I drive slowly and have my eyes on the road when I drink.*

Na'Tisha stuck her head out of the room, "Hey, you guys, this is Ms. Clark. Man, she was my favorite teacher. She taught me about linking verbs and shit."

My face turned fifty shades of pink. My stomach rolled over and over into a ball of sharp, pinching pain. I didn't think I was going to be able to do this. I remember telling my students to pay attention in school, so they wouldn't end up on the streets some day, or worse — jail — and here I was. The roles had reversed, and I was being checked into jail by my former seventh-grade language arts student.

"Ms. Clark," Na'Tisha shyly said, "I'm gonna need you to strip off all your clothes, and then squat and cough."

"Squat and what?" I said.

"Squat and cough," she repeated, "We gotta make sure you ain't hidin' nothin'… I'm sorry, Ms. Clark, AREN'T hiding anything… up your, uh, well, you know…."

"Like what in the world would I hide up there?" I asked.

"Man, you'd be surprised. Mainly drugs, but sometimes knives and candy and rubber bands."

"I promise you, I have nothing up there," I said as I gave a slight cough.

I couldn't believe this was happening. I stood there buck naked. I was so embarrassed… so ashamed.

After checking me for hidden contraband, Na'Tisha handcuffed my wrists and ankles and escorted me down to the P-Pod. With my one stained flat sheet; a rough blanket that was only the thickness of a sheet; and my thin mat under my arms, I followed her down the long hallway.

The P-Pod was dark and chilly. Ten or so cells were arranged in a circle around a hard cement floor they called the commons area. This is the place where you can walk around freely for one hour a day to shower, get your exercise, and socialize a bit.

"Okay, Ms. Clark, this is where you'll be for a few days until we move you to the M-Pod. It'll be all right. Don't worry."

I could tell she wasn't too convinced that everything would be all right, but her kind words helped a little bit.

As she walked me closer to my cell, a pretty, young black girl with a shaved head shouted through the tiny window of the door, "Hey, she gonna be my celly? Damn, she fine. Look y'all the newbie be wearin' real make-up. Ain't she pretty? She's all mine."

Guard Na'Tisha handed me my bag of clothes and books, and then opened the heavy metal door to my new sardine-box sized home.

"This is Samantha — but they call her 'King X.' She's not too bad," Na'Tisha explained.

Na'Tisha told me to go in and make my bed. She told me at around 7:00 pm., I could go out in the commons area for my one hour of quasi freedom. I asked her what time it was. It was only 7:00 a.m. I jumped when the cell door slammed shut.

"Don't be scared," smirked King X, "I ain't gonna bite you. You gay? I'm gay. You pretty. We gonna get along just fine. You cute for being kinda old. How old are you? I'm twenty-one."

I was overwhelmed with the quick questions spewed at me.

"I'm Dana. I'm not gay. I like men. I'm thirty-eight-years-old," I answered.

"What you in here for?" she asked.

I told her the truth and she said she understood. She had been arrested for a DUI before, too, but this time she was in for domestic violence. She had beaten up her girlfriend, she said. She beat her up because she was flirting with other women. She told me that she didn't know why she got so angry. She said she had a five-year-old daughter that she had with a police officer who used to frequent her neighborhood. She had only been sixteen years old when she got pregnant. She said no one knew it was the police officer's baby. She said that he was good to her at first, but then he ignored her. She didn't care, though, because she liked women better anyway.

She told me I could have the top bunk — that she didn't like being on top. I was wondering how this was going to work since there was no ladder, and I had a lot of lower back problems.

"Hey! For real? Let me show you how we make our beds up in here. That flat sheet ain't gonna stay put if you don't tie the ends up like this."

She took charge. I didn't know how to do this. I had never been in jail before. It seemed there were going to be many tricks I was going to learn along the way during my stay. She grabbed my sheet and began wrapping my mat like a Christmas present, tying each end together in the middle like a bow. I was impressed, and I thought it very kind of her to help a stranger like that.

She went on to show me many other things — like how to keep my whites white.

"Don't ever have these fools wash yo clothes for ya. They'll come back brown. See, now, watcha gotta do is take some of this cheap-ass toothpaste — just use a little bit — and you take some of the shampoo, too. You mix it up with water, and scrub your underwear with it. Turns out really white. See? I did mine last night."

She reached for a T-shirt, a pair of underwear, and a pair of socks and held them up like she was a *The Price Is Right* model. She told me I could borrow some of her toothpaste when I needed it because I wouldn't be getting any sanitary supplies for another week. "They had already come yesterday," she said.

She took out a bag of Skittles that she purchased from the once-a-week mobile commissary cart, picked out the purple and green ones, let them melt in her hand, and then applied the color to her eyelids.

"Now see? This is how we wear make-up. Give me that pencil over there on my bed."

I grabbed the golf-game sized pencil and handed it to her. She used the pencil as eye and lip liner and then filled in her lips with a red Skittle. She told me to remind her later, and she'd show me how to make a permanent tattoo from pencil lead, a staple, and lotion.

I thought it very sweet of her to take me under her wing like that. She knew me from nowhere, and she treated me already like a friend.

The day went by fairly quickly. King X and I talked well into the evening, interrupted only by our tasteless lunch being pushed through a thin slit in our locked door. I learned that she had been abandoned as a child, left in her baby carrier on the front steps of her grandmother's house. She said that her mother was hooked on drugs and couldn't take care of her.

Figuring It Out Myself | 359

She does remember seeing her mother from time to time at Thanksgiving and Christmas. She said she didn't know who her father was, and that her grandmother, while she provided well for her, wasn't very nurturing. She told me that her uncle had sexually abused her when she was just three. She told me how badly she wanted to be a good role model for her own daughter, but things weren't working out that way. Her grandmother had custody of her daughter. She prayed that God would keep her daughter safe from sexual predators. The topic of her daughter brought tears to her sad and weary eyes.

"I never wanted this to happen to my daughter — you know, not be raised by her own mother," she said, "I swear when I get outta here, I'm gonna do better."

I began to think about my own children — how I had abandoned them, too, over the last few months, not physically, but emotionally, because of my drinking. The thought of me putting them in grave danger took my breath away. In that moment, I realized we are all capable of the unthinkable, given the right set of life circumstances.

King X told me that she would introduce me to the other women when we got out at 7 p.m. for our one-hour rec time. I was a bit nervous to meet them, not sure what to expect, but I felt that with King X on my side, everything would be okay.

Seven o'clock came and the cell door popped open like a jack-in-the-box makes a sudden jump. The noise was sharp and startling.

"Come on. Let's do this," King X said.

I cautiously followed her out into the commons area. There I was introduced to about fifteen women, many of whom looked just like me or looked just like my younger sister.

"Hey, y'all, this Mrs. Clark. She's my new celly. She cool. She gonna teach us some Shakespeare."

I met little Lily, a delicate longhaired redhead with freckles. She had been caught manufacturing meth. She said that she never thought she'd get hooked on that stuff, but she started using it when she began college. She said it helped her study better, plus it helped her lose weight, and because she had always been made fun of as a child for her pudgy figure, it was hard to give up. I told her that I had a daughter named Lily — my youngest, in fact. I shared with her how I had made up songs for each of my children that I sang when I rocked them to sleep. I sang my Lily song: *Lily, Lily, I love you. Lily, Lily, yes, it's true. I love my Lily. Of her I'm very fond. She's my little lily pad just a floatin' 'round the pond.*

"Awww, Mrs. Clark. I love that song. Will you make me a song?"

"Yeah, Mrs. Clark," chimed in Eureka, a very thin black girl with long braids, "will you write me a baby song with my name in it?"

I was overwhelmed with tenderness for these two young ladies. Everything I had thought about women in jail was slowly being chipped away. They weren't mean; they weren't evil; they weren't selfish and trashy. They were simply broken women with broken pasts, just like my own.

Eventually, I was moved up to the M-Pod where we were given a few more hours of social time a day. We were able to go out in the commons area from 10 a.m. to 12 p.m.; 2 p.m. to 4 p.m.; and 6 p.m. to 8 p.m. During these hours I met Stacey, an older lady who was a former physician's assistant. She became addicted to pain pills and was caught writing false prescriptions. She was sentenced to one year in jail.

I met Lori, Tabitha, and Lydia, all heroin addicts and who sold their bodies to support their addictions. I met a precious Latino lady named Maria. She led Bible studies during the 2 p.m. to 4 p.m. rec time. She also drew beautiful greeting cards and traded them with the others for candy or shampoo. I met Muffin and Tee-Tee who often were in competition for their unique hair-braiding abilities and showed me how to give myself a pedicure with water, lotion, and the top of a deodorant bottle. I met Sara who was caught shoplifting diapers. Sara had the voice of an angel and would often serenade us to sleep.

At least 90% of the women with whom I was in jail were addicted to either drugs or alcohol. I resolved to seek treatment when I was released.

"You ain't gonna forget me? Are you?" King X said as I walked out the cell door for the last time.

"No, King X, I will never forget you," I cried, "You are a beautiful woman with a beautiful heart. Go be a Supermom to that baby girl of yours. She needs you."

From there, I spent nine months at The Bethany House II, a restoration home for women where I learned to implement the 12-Step Program, learned to deal with depression and anxiety in a healthy way, and most importantly, I learned to love and forgive myself.

Those women changed my world. I had been living in bondage for years trying to be the perfect mom. I finally understood that just because we *make* mistakes does not mean we *are* mistakes. I learned to abandon my presumptuous judgments and began to see the beauty and potential of every woman no matter what her past. It was in these lessons that I found true liberty for the very first time.

~Dana D. Clark

99

Two in the Morning

Tears are words that need to be written.
~Paulo Coelho

I woke drenched in sweat, the kind only abject fear or chemotherapy could cause. I looked at the clock: 2:13 a.m. I sat up.

Or, well, half sat up. The radiation site throbbed, my skin felt brittle, and my muscles stabbed me when I moved. Slumping to the side, I sighed, squinting down at a package my friend Jeff sent. It sat on top of three other packages, and beside five more stacked near the bed. Therein nestled the fear.

Yes, I had stage three cancer. Yes, my tumor was the size of a mouse. Not a single doctor told me I might live through this. But that wasn't what woke me up and drenched me with sweat. It was my mother.

My ninety-four-year-old mother knew only the basics of my diagnosis. She didn't live with me and didn't own a spy satellite. Yet somehow, I felt she knew I'd received all these packages, but I hadn't written one thank-you card. Not one. In her book, that was inexcusable.

I needed to make some thank-you notes, but my imagination had died on the day of my diagnosis. Radiation, chemo and the constant threat of death crushed my tiny natural courage. I'd not drawn, written or painted. I'd done nothing creative for two and a half months. It felt like being held underwater for ten and a half weeks.

With the death of both my imagination and courage, I felt my body would soon follow. Without the energy to move much, I sat still and waited to die.

My friends sent presents, but absent my usual tools, I could not thank them. According to my mother and etiquette guidelines, thank-you notes, like sushi, were best served fresh.

I'd saved a few reserve cards for my mother's weekly mail, but if I used them as thank-yous, then I would have nothing for her since I lacked the ability to move. That would be unforgivable.

That dilemma left me in a sweat at two in the morning.

Maybe, I thought, *if I just draw something, anything, I could make copies. I could color them later, between naps.* I opened the bedroom door to get pen and paper.

Two gingery cats greeted me, meowing, prancing and somersaulting. Collectively, I referred to them as "The Princelings." They loved to see me in the middle of the night when I hobbled between the bedroom and the bathroom, sometimes collapsing on the floor in between. They always snuggled in, finding it fun.

Now, they attacked my slippers. I sighed, wishing I had their energy, courage and *joie de vivre.*

"Okay," I said, shuffling over to the chair. I picked up a pen and a notebook. "How do we write a thank-you note that explains my chemo and keeps your Grandma from disowning me?"

Exhausted from walking ten feet, I rested. They jumped into my lap. One sat on the notebook. The other sat on the hand that held the pen.

"As much as I'd love to," I grumbled, trying to retrieve my notebook from under a kitty, "I can't send you along to explain."

The Princelings stared up at me with their bright eyes, as if to ask, "Why not?"

And then, in that cold, silent February nighttime, a long absent sensation scratched deep in the back of my head. An imaginative thought began to hatch.

"Okay," I said, wriggling my pen free from a set of paws. "Okay, we'll try it your way."

Then, at 2:58, I started something I'd never attempted: I drew a comic-book page. I drew it in four panels and gave the cats all the dialogue bubbles. The squiggly line that was supposed to be me lay with her back to the readers, too weak to move. The cats did the talking for me. They explained, said "thank you," made jokes, and then went back to napping. In short, my cartoon Princelings did all the things I wished I could.

I kept drawing.

At 4:59, I heard my alarm go off in the other room. Time to eat before I took my morning chemo dose. Usually, I dreaded the eating as much as the horse pills, but this morning, after all that bravery, I felt the glimmering of an appetite. I ate twice my usual breakfast amount: two crackers, instead of one.

A few hours later, when I felt strong enough to think, I continued to sketch. Two days later, I had a first draft. Two days after that, I got dressed, put a seat cover and a bucket in the car, and drove six blocks to the copy shop. The round-trip drive took forty minutes. Exhausted, I napped until I could manage to color in my cartoons.

Within a week, I'd drawn three more. By the next round of chemo, I was up to ten, although not all of them were funny. Some made fun of the boredom of being sick, but some demonstrated the terror of not knowing the ultimate outcome.

Finally, on the last day allowed by etiquette to mail a thank-you note, I sent all ten cartoons to Jeff. If he hated them, I could blame the psychosis on chemo.

Two days later, he messaged me. He said he loved the cartoons. They touched his heart. They helped him understand what I felt.

They did? I stared at the screen. That was a weird thing to say. It helped *him*?

The weeks slowly passed, day by day. The more cartoons I made, the less I felt like I was drowning. The cartoon Princelings could say things on paper that I could never say in real life.

I showed the cartoons to more people. Like Jeff, they also said weird things, like: "These taught me something."

Finally, knowing the news of my activities would eventually get back to my mother, I sat on the porch and painted a card with an iris on it. I folded in the first five cartoons and added an extra stamp to her envelope. I didn't write any explanation.

Figuring It Out Myself |

The next week, when I called at my appointed time, she said hello, and then added: "I read your comics."

Well, crud, I thought. I'd hoped we'd start with small talk before we plunged into the topic of my cancer and how I coped with it. But no. "You did?"

"I did," she said. "They are very much like you."

My stomach dropped. What did that mean? Did she think my cartoons were afraid of spiders? Cried loudly and often? Were inept at crosswords? With too many choices and none of them flattering, I cleared my throat and decided to plunge ahead. "How so?"

She breathed a little, gentle laugh. "I find them remarkably brave."

When those words in my mother's voice vibrated against my eardrums, the earth slowed. Time paused and reversed itself. Gravity changed. I no longer felt like I was drowning.

My mother thought I, of all people, was both remarkable and brave.

I closed my eyes. I pressed the phone, and by extension, my mother, to my cheek.

~Virginia Elizabeth Hayes

100

My Obsession with a Cold Case

The difference between the difficult and the impossible is that the impossible takes a little longer time.
~Lady Aberdeen

L ast year on Holy Saturday, I was visiting my grandparents' grave. It was always quiet, which I appreciated. Lilies were everywhere, along with stuffed bunny rabbits at the children's graves. In the distance an owl was hooting. I sat in silence for a while, then began to walk on the grass barefoot when a man approached me. He looked a little younger than me, with black curly hair.

"Do you have a pen?" he asked.

I was a little startled. First because he disrupted my quiet, second because the request was so odd. "No, sorry," I said.

"Would the office have a pen?"

"I think so," I said.

He headed toward the office, and being nosy, I wandered to look at the grave he was visiting.

She was a young girl, aged fourteen. From the picture on her gravestone, I could see that she had long blond hair, blue eyes. She was a stunner.

When I saw the man coming back, I walked away. I didn't want to intrude.

But I was haunted by our strange intersection. What was the story there? Was he a family member? An old boyfriend?

On the Day of the Dead, I visited my grandparents' grave again. This time, I looked closer at the grave where the man had been standing, and I took note of the girl's name: Suzanne Arlene Bombardier. Born on March 14, 1966. Died on June 22, 1980. Etched on her grave were the words: you're in my heart. I Googled her name on my cell. As I read her story, my eyes filled with tears.

Suzanne Bombardier was babysitting her nieces while her sister Stephanie was at work. It was the first day of summer in 1980. They lived in Antioch, California. These days, it's known as the city where Phillip Garrido held Jaycee Dugard hostage for eighteen years.

When Suzanne's sister Stephanie got home that night, the house looked fine. There were no signs of a struggle or forced entry. Suzanne wasn't on the couch, but her sister figured she had fallen asleep with her nieces while putting them to bed.

It wasn't until the next day when their mother called looking for Suzanne that they both began to worry. The only trace of her was her suitcase still near the couch. There were no signs of a forced struggle or entry. They called the police.

On June 27, her report card arrived in the mail. She had received straight A's and made the honor roll. The same day a body was spotted by a fisherman in the San Joaquin River near Antioch.

Suzanne's stepfather identified the body. She had been stabbed through the heart. Her killer was never found.

Standing near her grave, I covered my mouth. I put down my phone.

"Oh, I am so sorry!" I said. I wasn't even sure why I was apologizing — the fact that she endured such a horrible crime, or the fact that her killer was still out there. I didn't know what to do.

I placed a flower on her grave, and then I went home. I did what I often do when I am trying to make sense of an experience. I wrote about it in a blog, which I called "The Lost Girl." The story was tugging at me. Yet what was I going to do — find her killer? I wasn't an investigative reporter. I wrote about Muppets and not finding the right purse. How was I going to track down the story? But the story started to find me.

After the holidays, a woman named Leesa wrote to me. She had been friends with Suzanne (known to family and friends as Suzie) and thanked me for writing about her. In 1979, they had bonded at thirteen — two recent transplants to Antioch, talking about boys and families. Leesa told me there was next to nothing about Suzie online.

I decided to find someone to write the story. A "real journalist" had to write this story. I wrote several people at local newspapers. One was interested; however, there was no new evidence so there was nothing new to report. I asked other writers, no luck. I pitched the story to *This American Life*. No response. Was it possible that I could write this story? Was that crazy?

The one good thing about working part-time was I had time to do research. I went to the Pleasant Hill Library's microfilm machines and found articles in the *Contra Costa Times* and *The San Francisco Chronicle*.

When I told people the new story I was working on, they looked surprised. *What about your Jonestown novel? Or a collection of pop culture essays?* I had been working on both projects, but they had stalled. I wanted to write about Suzie. I kept on being pulled by the story. Part of it was sheer fascination; when I was sixteen, four girls were kidnapped in the space of six months near where I lived. One was found dead. The other girls — Amber Swartz-Garcia, Michaela Garecht and Ilene Misheloff — were still missing.

I remember that I always had to be careful. Don't talk to strangers. Always make sure you're around people. Walk home as fast as you can, then lock the door behind you. I always had this fear that something bad could happen if I wasn't vigilant. But what if being vigilant wasn't enough?

The other part was that I needed to be a hero, to succeed at something during this low period in my career. I wanted to find closure in a story that had no closure. It seemed like the world forgot about this girl. Maybe if I found a happy ending for Suzie, I could find one for myself.

I pitched the story to a site called Defrosting Cold Cases. Alice, the site's owner, wanted the story but wanted it fast. I wrote it quickly. It was accepted the next morning and was June's Case of the Month — fitting because June was the 34th anniversary of Susie's death.

I made the usual rounds sharing the story on social media. Friends of mine shared the story as well. Susie was profiled on sfgate.com, *San Francisco Chronicle's* online outlet. A writer friend interviewed me. I wanted so much to get results, but I was realizing how naïve I had been. I guess I was thinking the police would magically find evidence that said so-and-so did it. Case closed.

Awful thoughts invaded my head: *You can be working on something better. You honestly think you can solve a thirty-four year old crime? All you know about detective work you learned from Nancy Drew, soap operas and* Law & Order *reruns.*

I was contacted for an interview by a webcast that specialized in aliens. I declined.

Meanwhile, fear crept back into my life. One night after my story went live, I missed my local commuter train after work. I was in nearby Walnut Creek, which was safe. Yet I felt so nervous. It was the same old fear: something bad could happen if I wasn't careful. I saw a man staring at me. He looked normal. Then I remembered how normal Ted Bundy looked, even handsome. I quickly walked to another bench near the station agent's phone. My cell phone hadn't been charged, so it was dead.

I considered my options. I knew a little karate. I could fight my way to safety. Did Suzie fight? Yes, I knew she put up a hell of a fight. When the train finally came, I sought shelter near a group of women.

Fear had always been part of the world, but something about working on Suzie's tale made it feel more intimate, closer. When I told my father I was working on this story, he became alarmed. "What are you thinking? This guy is still out there. What if he comes after you?"

"If you're that concerned, buy me a stun gun," I responded. I didn't want to live my life in fear. I was always careful when I left the house. But I also knew terrible things could happen, even to careful people.

Meanwhile, I was starting to grow discouraged. I reposted the "lost girl" blog again on my new website, along with the Defrosting Cold Cases link. One night I got an e-mail from a man named Gregory Glod, who wanted to talk to me about Suzie. He had been the junior detective assigned to the case, then left the police force to work in the Secret Service agency, where he'd been for twenty-six years. Now he was deputy director of the Pentagon Force Protection Agency. We set up a time to talk.

He was a junior detective when Suzie disappeared. He still remembered the day they found the body. He rushed to the area where police divers had pulled a girl out of the water. He decided right then and there he was going to find out who killed her and bring the person to justice. They'd gotten a few leads, but each one fizzled out. It was the first big case he ever worked on. It was a case he couldn't forget.

A month later, I met Greg and retired police detective Ron Rackley for lunch in Antioch. Greg, Ron and I talked about Suzie. It was clear they were still haunted by the story. I made copies of the microfilm articles for them. They studied something I found randomly in the *Antioch Herald*: the list of students who made the honor roll for spring 1980, including Suzie. Greg decided to set up a scholarship in her name at the local high school, and then showed me possible areas where he wanted to build a memorial to her in Antioch.

When I started working on this story, my goal was to find out who killed Suzanne Bombardier. The case had been in limbo way too long. My other goal was that Suzie wouldn't be forgotten.

I wanted people to know that for fourteen years, Suzanne Arlene Bombardier was here on this earth. She loved Gilda Radner, Rod Stewart's "You're in My Heart" and her family. She was smart and beautiful.

The new interest I created in this cold case ended up solving it. On December 11, 2017, Mitchell Lynn Bacom was arrested at his home in Antioch, California for the rape and murder of Suzanne Arlene Bombardier. A DNA sample taken from Suzanne was a perfect match with Bacom, thanks to updated DNA testing. As of February 2018, he had pled not guilty and was awaiting trial.

Someday when I go back to the cemetery where my grandparents and Suzie are buried, I hope to see that man at the grave again. I want to be brave enough to approach him. I want to tell him, "Thank you. You helped light the spark."

~Jennifer Kathleen Gibbons

This article first appeared in Salon.com, at http://www.Salon.com. An online version remains in the Salon archives. Reprinted with permission.

Wow, You're So Lucky!

Luck is not chance, it's toil;
fortune's expensive smile is earned.
~Emily Dickinson

"**W**ow, you're so lucky!" a friend exclaimed. I cocked my head. *That's an odd reaction to front-page news that I had helped launch a new investment bank as a Partner and CFO.* Then three other people said the same thing. *Why are they saying that? Sure, I'm fortunate to have the opportunity, but it's not like I got the job through a scratch-off lottery ticket or Publishers Clearing House unexpectedly showed up at my door.*

I knew that people said odd things unwittingly and I couldn't let their insinuations make me second-guess myself. Maybe I didn't fit the bill of what they envisioned. My varied career background? Or that I was a mom with a husband, two kids, and lots of pets? Who knows.

At the time, I was publisher of a leading technical industry magazine. A former colleague (I had been his client when I worked in finance at an oil and gas company) approached me with his vision for starting an investment bank. "I'd follow you into a fire," I quipped, as I had always had tremendous respect for his capabilities, values and leadership. "Besides, how hard could it be?"

Actually, I knew it was going to be really hard. At that point, I had been working nearly twenty-five years, so I had an appreciation of the scope of the tasks ahead of us. Of course, there was also the bliss (or anxiety) of the phenomenon of "not knowing what you don't know." What I did know, though, was this was a great strategy and I wasn't going to pass up the opportunity to try and build something new. No time like the present.

And so, with the full faith that we would succeed, I quit my job and we opened shop in his pool house. Day one, we floundered and poked the non-responsive fax machine. I quickly realized we needed severe administrative intervention. And that first hire was indicative of all subsequent hires: recognizing that each of us brought something to the table and no one person knows everything. Nothing is more rewarding — from my perspective — than team problem solving.

I was committed to working with the best and brightest to serve corporations in the energy industry. Our clients needed capital, strategy and guidance in how to build their businesses. Culture trumped everything, and finding the best "athletes" was our guiding rule.

As planned, within months, we combined with a leading equity research firm and moved out of the pool house. We quickly grew to more than two dozen folks, and within a few years we had nearly 200 employees. Each day I worked with colleagues tackling new issues even more daunting than unresponsive fax machines: raising a private equity fund in the midst of the Global Financial Crisis; navigating the regulatory maze of foreign banking requirements to open overseas offices; developing processes for our growing team while maintaining an industry-leading culture and entrepreneurial spirit.

And whenever I hit an emotional roadblock because I was frustrated or unheard or battling doubts — I would pause. *You can do this.* Luck wasn't the driving force; it was conviction and commitment.

A decade after our founding, we combined with a global financial services firm and we are still building. Today our combined organization has offices in eleven cities and more than 600 of the best people in the industry.

Okay, so maybe I am really lucky.

~Alexandra Pruner

Meet Our Contributors

A graduate of the University of Maryland at College Park, **Tonya Abari** is a teacher turned freelance editor and writer. To supplement multi-passionate endeavors, she has also worked as a web moderator, Zumba instructor, and traveling set teacher. She enjoys reading and traveling with her husband and exuberant toddler.

Kristi Adams is a travel writer who's written about llamas in Europe, the trials of using German GPS, adventure caves, and more. She lives in Germany with her husband, who's serving on active duty, and a grumpy rescue cat. She is a proud seven-time contributor to the *Chicken Soup for the Soul* series. Learn more at www.kristiadamsmedia.com.

Lucy Alexander received her marketing degree from Villanova University. After spending ten years in Europe in the fashion industry, she now lives outside Philadelphia. In addition to raising her son, she runs a consulting business for individuals looking to reinvent themselves after life has thrown them a curveball.

Esther M. Bailey writes to inspire others through the written word. Bailey enjoys dining out and hosting guests in her Scottsdale, AZ home.

Linda Barbosa is the author of *How Can I Smile at a Time Like This?* She also writes under a pen name for a popular advice website. When not jumping out of perfectly good airplanes, Linda enjoys the retired life with her husband Joe in their quiet, two-horse town.

Diana Bauder has been a blogger since 2013 and recently started pursing a freelance writing career. She previously worked with special needs children and adults, and as a caregiver. Diana raised a family and now treasures her role as "Amma" to three adorable granddaughters.

Dawn Belt is a paralegal in the Midwest. She is a mother of two wonderful children and one delightful granddaughter. Dawn is enjoying learning to become a very handy woman who takes pride in her successes and her attempts at success. She plans to continue on this journey with her head held high.

Crystal Birmingham-Overmeyer grew up in California, fell in love in Sonora and lives in Central California with her two puppies and husband, Brandon. She began her love affair with poetry at thirteen and hasn't looked back since.

Jan Bono writes a cozy mystery series set on the southwest Washington coast. She's also published five collections of humorous personal experience, two poetry chapbooks, nine one-act plays, a dinner theater play, and has written for magazines ranging from *Guideposts* to *Woman's World*. Learn more at www.JanBonoBooks.com.

Miranda Boyer is a substitute teacher, aspiring YA author, and an active member of her local writers' group. She reads copious amounts of books every year and blogs about them on her webpage MirandaBoyer.com.

Ellie Braun-Haley is a regular contributor to the *Chicken Soup for the Soul* series with stories translated into a number of languages. She is frequently asked to write or speak about miracles. When not writing she enjoys time with her children, grandchildren and great-grandchildren. She teaches and designs greeting cards. E-mail her at milady@evrcanada.com.

Mason K. Brown lives between homes in Seaside and Forest Grove, OR with her rescue dog, Wicket. An author, speaker and storyteller, she writes primarily inspirational nonfiction and humor. She is widely published in anthologies and devotionals. Learn more at www.masonkbrown.com.

Michelle Bruce is a busy wife and mother of four children. In her free time, she enjoys her children's many sporting events, spending time with her numerous pets, antiquing with her husband, refinishing vintage furniture, and writing both fiction and nonfiction stories. E-mail her at brucefamily6@gmail.com.

Eva Carter is a freelance writer and photographer. This is her twentieth story published in the *Chicken Soup for the Soul* series. She has a twenty-three-year background in the telecommunications industry. She enjoys going out to dinner and travelling with her husband, Larry.

Elynne Chaplik-Aleskow, a Pushcart Prize-nominated writer, is founding general manager of WYCC-TV/PBS and distinguished professor emeritus of Wright College. Her stories have been performed throughout the U.S. and Canada and are published in anthologies and her book, *My Gift of Now*, which *Conversations Magazine* named an inspired book.

Jane McBride Choate has been writing since she was a child. Being published in the *Chicken Soup for the Soul* series is a dream come true for her.

Dana D. Clark received her B.A. in English (1996) and M.A. in education (1999) from Austin Peay State University, both with honors. She has four children (two boys/two girls). Currently, she works as a regional monitor for the State of Tennessee. Dana enjoys thrift-shopping, home decorating, and mentoring those afflicted with addiction.

Christine Clarke-Johnsen is a retired teacher who has had several short stories published in magazines. As a storyteller, she enjoys telling stories that touch people's hearts or make them laugh. She is currently writing and illustrating a children's picture book. She also is in two choirs and enjoys badminton and kayaking.

Darcy Daniels is a historian and mom of two daughters, one of whom is chronically ill. She is the author of the blog *Brave Fragile Warriors: Caring for Kids with Chronic Illness*, and serves on the Family Advisory Council at Massachusetts General Hospital for Children.

NancyLee Davis was writing before starting school. She wrote a column in a weekly newspaper, taught Special Education, raised four children, Angus cattle, and show dogs on a farm, and drove racecars before retiring to the beach. She enjoys kayaking, growing orchids, and racecars.

Aimee DuFresne is a Joy Catalyst and soul-shifting creator, writer, traveler, and latte-lover. She is the author of *Keep Going: From Grief to Growth*, a memoir about love, loss, living in the moment and the power of perseverance. Learn more at www.aimeedufresne.com.

Pascale Duguay is a freelance writer, translator (French/English), high school librarian, and founder of ThePartTimeWriter.com. She lives in the lively bilingual community of the Quebec Eastern Townships where she enjoys baking, gardening, jogging, reading and writing in the sun. E-mail her at pascaleduguay@hotmail.com.

Mindi Susman Ellis is a writer, artist and adventurer who lives in the Midwest. She adores her two adult-ish children. She owns a marketing and communications business. Mindi loves yoga, hiking, water sports, and almost anything outdoors. Her next adventure will be in Europe. E-mail her at mindicreates@gmail.com.

Michelle Emery lives in a small village in northern England. She works for the National Health Service and enjoys writing in the evening. Graduating with a first class honours degree in English and History, she has always had an interest in the written word.

Molly England perpetually attempts to simplify her life. She aspires to be a decent mother, wife, daughter, and friend. Meanwhile, she processes life's daily chaos and beauty by jotting down her thoughts. Molly's writing is featured in *The Washington Post*, *HuffPost*, *Scary Mommy*, *Babble*, *Salon*, and more.

Holly English is the author of several novels. She is the mother of three grown children who are practically perfect and the grandmother of four grandchildren who are definitely perfect. She is currently writing a western novel titled, *Regret*.

Malinda Dunlap Fillingim is a recent widow, trying to navigate the hard road of grief. Writing, along with prayer and good chocolate, empowers her and helps her heal. For scheduling her to speak at your church or women's group, e-mail her at fillingam@ec.rr.com. She lives near Wilmington, NC.

Patricia Fish is a social media writer and a frequent contributor to the *Chicken Soup for the Soul* series. She blogs at patfish.blogspot.com and patfish.wordpress.com. Pat has written five books: *Attention, Please!*, *Mystery & Mirth*, *Everything You Need to Know About Being a Woman Can Be Learned in the Garden*, *The Memoirs of Josephine Fish* and *Clarion Call*.

Mother to six, **Jeneva Ford** earned her B.A. in English in middle age. Travel, including to Thailand, a summer in Europe, and visiting forty-nine states, has left great memories. A novel simmers and if time and energy hold out, this essay, her first published work, may lead to bigger things! Now retired, she still reads and dreams.

Erin E. Forson has been an educator, social worker and librarian. She loves to read, write, spend time exploring the world with her family, and learn! She is currently working on an MBA so she can explore more opportunities in her world.

Jennifer Kathleen Gibbons has been published in *Salon*, *Stereo Embers*, *Bird's Thumb* and *Hunger Mountain*. She lives in Central California and

Vermont and will be getting her MFA in Writing and Publishing at Vermont College of Fine Arts in May 2018. She is currently working on a memoir about her involvement in the Suzanne Bombardier cold case.

Annette Gulati is a freelance writer and children's author living in Seattle, WA. She's published stories, articles, essays, poems, crafts, and activities in numerous magazines, newspapers, and anthologies. She also writes books for children's educational publishers. Learn more at www.annettegulati.com.

Marilyn Haight survived domestic abuse and lived long enough to be willing to talk about it, though it is always uncomfortable to remember. She is a retired businesswoman, and the author of four self-help books and one book of poetry, which you may read about on her website at www.marilynhaight.com.

Virginia Elizabeth Hayes was born the youngest of nine girls and grew up to be a writer. Calling Missouri home, she lives with her husband and two cats. Her cartoon-memoir is called: *The Princeling Papers: Or, How to Fight Cancer with Colored-Pencils and Kittens*.

Christy Heitger-Ewing, an award-winning writer who pens human interest stories for national and local magazines, has contributed to twenty anthologies (ten for the *Chicken Soup for the Soul* series) and is the author of *Cabin Glory: Amusing Tales of Time Spent at the Family Retreat* (www.cabinglory.com). She lives in Indiana with her husband and two sons.

Lorne Holden is an artist, choreographer, and writer. Her book, *Make It Happen in 10 Minutes a Day: The Simple, Lifesaving Method for Getting Things Done*, is an Amazon bestseller.

Linda Hoff Irvin is a psychotherapist in private practice who has been practicing for more years than she cares to admit. She is happily re-married and her son is doing well. E-mail her at lhofflcsw@gmail.com.

Jennie Ivey lives and writes in Tennessee. She is the author of many works of fiction and nonfiction, including numerous stories in the *Chicken Soup for the Soul* series. Learn more at jennieivey.com.

Sarah James is a licensed mental health and addictions therapist. She was born and raised in Charleston, WV. She completed her solo thru-hike of the Colorado Trail in 2017 at age twenty-four. She now lives in Asheville, NC where she enjoys hiking, rafting, eating, and being a cat mom. E-mail her at smjames67@gmail.com.

Leigh Anne Jasheway is a humor columnist, author, stand-up comic, and humorous motivational speaker. She won the Erma Bombeck Humor Writing Award in 2003 with her true story of the time her first mammogram caught on fire. She also teaches comedy writing and improv, and wrangles wiener dogs.

Home-front mom **Linda Jewell** supports our troops, veterans, and their families. She's involved in Cookie Deployments and writes about patriotism, parenting, and prayer. Linda provides practical tips, inspiration, and encouragement to strengthen moms of those in the military during tough times. E-mail her at Linda.Jewell@icloud.com.

Susan A. Karas has spent years perfecting her craft, graduating proudly from many writing programs. She won the national Guideposts Writing Contest, and has gone on to be published many times in the magazine, as well as in the *Chicken Soup for the Soul* series, and various other publications. She is currently working on her first novel.

Ruth Kephart is a retired RN, lives in Pennsylvania and writes poetry in her spare time. She makes jewelry and crafts to support her mission trips to Haiti and has been to Haiti six times. She has had poetry published in several journals and anthologies including the *Chicken Soup for the Soul* series. E-mail her at hootowlrn@windstream.net.

April Knight is a freelance writer and artist. She began writing stories when she was twelve years old and had her first story published when she was thirteen. She is happiest when she is horseback riding or beachcombing.

Nancy Julien Kopp lives in the Flint Hills of Kansas where she writes creative nonfiction, children's fiction, poetry and articles on writing. She has been published in many ezines, magazines, newspapers and anthologies. Nancy blogs with tips for writers at www.writergrannysworld.blogspot.com.

Cathi LaMarche is an essayist, novelist, poet, and writing coach. Her work has appeared in over thirty anthologies. When not immersed in the written word, she is helping to spread awareness about the devastating effects of Lyme disease.

Lynne Leite is a storyteller at heart who loves faith, family, fun, and friends. She recently published her first novel, a Christian thriller entitled *All the Days Ordained*. She lives in Southern California with her husband and loves spending time with her grown kids and grandbabies. Learn more at LynneLeite.com.

Ilana Long is a writer, actress, stand-up comic, English teacher and mom of teen twins. She is the author of *Ziggy's Big Idea* (Kar-Ben Publishing 2014) and recently completed her first science-fiction novel.

B.B. Loyd received her BFA through the University of Maryland in 1974 while living in Germany. She completed her Teaching Certificate at Sam Houston State University and taught art and English during her career to students in grades 1-12. A studio artist, poet, and writer, B.B. and her husband enjoy living in Texas.

L.M. Lush is an inspirational writer and teacher. After retiring from her career in IT, she started a spiritual business in New York and hopes to have her first book published soon. She enjoys playing the piano and cello, photography, and hiking with her dogs, Sadie and Oreo. Learn more at LMLush.com.

Debra Mayhew is a pastor's wife, mom to seven, teacher, editor, and writer. She loves small town living, stormy weather, good books, and family time. Learn more at debramayhew.com.

A former lay missionary, **Claire McGarry** now freelances for magazines, contributes to CatholicMom.com, and posts at ShiftingMyPerspective. com. She's also the founder of MOSAIC of Faith, a ministry with several different programs for mothers and children. She lives with her husband and three children in New Hampshire.

Kristine McGovern is a former journalist and award-winning playwright whose short plays have been performed across the country. She has a degree in Philosophy and is a winner of the T F Evans Award presented by the Shaw Society of the United Kingdom.

Amy Mermelstein is a writer from Cabin John, MD. She has been published in *The Washington Post Magazine* and *Bethesda Magazine*. Amy is married and has two teenage boys who play a lot of baseball. When Amy is not on a baseball field cheering, she enjoys hiking, biking, yoga, and gardening. She is working on her first novel.

Marie-Therese Miller is the author of nonfiction books for children, including the *Dog Tales* series, *Managing Responsibilities*, and *Rachel Carson*. Her stories appear in multiple *Chicken Soup for the Soul* books. She holds a Ph.D. from St. John's University, where her dissertation focus was James Thurber and humor.

esme mills loves to create change through story, because story has the power like no other to connect and transform. She holds a Bachelor of Arts in Professional Communications and a Master of Letters in Creative Writing. Read more about her at esmemills.com.

Marya Morin is a freelance writer. Her stories have appeared in publications such as *Woman's World* and Hallmark. Marya also penned a weekly humorous column for an online newsletter, and writes custom poetry on request. She lives in the country with her husband. E-mail her at Akushla514@hotmail.com.

Kathy Morris is a natural creative channel who shares her gifts with the world through poetry, writing, and energy work. She is also the founder of the Inner Journeys Natural Healing Center. Her memoir, *Up From the Ashes*, includes her healing journey and poetry. E-mail her at innerjourney@att.net or learn more at innerjourneys-heals.com.

Nicole L.V. Mullis is the author of the novel *A Teacher Named Faith*. Her work has appeared in newspapers, magazines, and anthologies, including the *Chicken Soup for the Soul* series. Her plays have been produced in festivals across the United States. She lives in Michigan with her husband and children.

Nell Musolf is a freelance writer living in the Upper Midwest with her husband, three cats and rescue dog. Nell is the mother of two adult sons. Nell enjoys reading, drinking coffee, visiting thrift shops, and taking her dog on long walks. She writes creative nonfiction, romance and mysteries.

Giulietta Nardone lives in Massachusetts with her husband, two cats and four pinball machines. Her stories have been published in books, newspapers and broadcast on the radio. In addition to writing, Giulietta paints, sings, bikes, acts, hikes, travels, and saves the wild things. E-mail her at giuliettan@gmail.com.

Phyllis Bird Nordstrom enjoys speaking and writing, both of which came about later in life. This is her second story published in the *Chicken Soup for the Soul* series. This summer she also became a member of The Write Team for her local newspaper. She and her husband of fifty-nine years live in the Midwest.

Judy O'Kelley's work appears in magazines, newspapers, greeting cards, and musicals from the Midwest to Beijing. A passionate tutor, Judy finds inspiration in her insightful students. She enjoys sunrises, storm chasing, midnight board games, and any time she spends with her adult kids. E-mail her at judyokelleycards@gmail.com.

Jenny Pavlovic has written several published stories and two books, including *8 State Hurricane Kate: The Journey and Legacy of a Katrina Cattle Dog*. She lives in Wisconsin with dogs Chase and Cayenne and cat Junipurr. She enjoys walking her dogs, swimming, kayaking, and gardening, and has a Ph.D. in biomedical engineering.

A writer since she could hold a pen, **Ronda Payne** is passionate about words. She is a full-time copywriter, freelancer, and storyteller. Ronda joyfully lives in Maple Ridge, B.C. in yet another renovation project home with her husband and their pets.

Kristen Mai Pham is a screenwriter and an author. She is a refugee of the Vietnam War, but her stories are not about war. They are about inspiration, healing, hope, and ultimately, joy. She lives in California with her husband, Paul. Follow her on Instagram at kristenmaipham or e-mail her at kristenmaipham3@gmail.com.

Rebecca J. Platt received her Bachelor of Arts in Theology in 2012 and her Master's of Education in 2016 from Southeastern University. She has been married for twenty-two years and has two children. Rebecca enjoys camping, woodworking, beach trips, and serving as an Academic Success Coordinator at Southeastern University.

Kathleen Whitman Plucker spends most days teaching kindergarten in Windsor, CT. She loves planning activities for her students and hopes she is inspiring them to be lifelong readers and writers. Outside of the classroom, Kathleen enjoys traveling with her husband and two teenaged children.

Marsha Porter got her writing start with the 500-word essay, the punishment du jour at her Catholic grade school. Later, she co-authored an annual movie review guide, wrote for local newspapers, and dabbled in fiction. Her cats are an inspiration for her writing and the joy of her life.

Alexandra Pruner is Partner and CFO of Perella Weinberg Partners (PWP), a leading global independent investment bank and asset management firm. She helped co-found Tudor, Pickering, Holt & Co., the energy investment bank. She's a 1983 grad of Brown University (Economics) and is lucky to have had a long career spanning many roles, a supportive husband and two grown children.

Kelly Rae spent years as an elementary and middle school teacher. She has a daughter and loads of nieces and nephews. Besides writing, Kelly enjoys traveling, knitting, stories, and good company. She plans to write books that inspire girls to find and use their voices.

Sarah Reece received her Bachelor of Science of Business from California State University, East Bay in 2015. She has her own yarn-dyeing business. Sarah loves traveling, scuba diving, hiking, and reading. She plans to write science-fiction and fantasy novels.

Wendy Ann Rich can't decorate walls with her pedigree papers. Graduating "off the wall" is her best self. She loves to cocoon snippets of life, writing about them with a peculiar magnifying glass. Wendy's world has rescue dogs, seniors, and toddlers who know how to live life with envious ease. Picture books are next for her.

Nicole Rook-McAlister studied Journalism in college. A wife and mother of two, her home is a beautiful three-floor log cabin in the Pine Barrens where books overflow shelves, tables, and rafters. Her time is spent pursuing dreams of urban homesteading, self-learning art, and delving into local and world folklore.

Rachel E. Ryan, editor and writer for Gospel Advocate Co., holds a bachelor's and master's in English. She and her daughter, Olivia, live in Mount Juliet, TN, where they worship with the Church of Christ. Rachel enjoys quiet mornings with her journal, traveling with her family, and reading books with her daughter.

Sandi Schwartz is a freelance writer and blogger specializing in parenting, wellness, environmental issues, and human behavior. She enjoys analyzing everyday life using science, humor, and a passion to improve the world. Her blog, *Happy Science Mom*, is a parenting toolkit for raising happy, balanced children.

Julieann Selden is a writer, speaker, mom, wife, graduate student, and nonprofit volunteer. Her husband, Ken, is recently in remission from sarcoma cancer. On her blog, contemplatingcancer.com, she examines the thoughts and emotions of life through the lens of an aggressive cancer diagnosis.

Lesley Jane Seymour is Founder of CoveyClub, an online/offline platform for lifelong learners. She is an award-winning journalist and former editor-in-chief of *YM*, *Redbook*, *Marie Claire* and *MORE* magazines. A mother of two, her goal is to connect women around the country and the world.

Tami Shaikh is a mom, author, activist, and a storyteller. She has written three books and numerous articles in *The Huffington Post* and the *MindBodyNetwork*. She currently lives in Orange County, CA and is a mother of three children. Tami is currently a student at Chapman University, working on her MFA in Creative Writing.

Deborah Shouse's latest book, *Connecting in the Land of Dementia: Creative Activities to Explore Together*, offers meaningful ways to stay connected from dozens of innovators worldwide. The book is filled with action-oriented ideas that increase the quality moments for people who are living with dementia and their care partners. Learn more at DementiaJourney.org.

Diane Stark is a wife, mother of five, and freelance writer. She is a frequent contributor to the *Chicken Soup for the Soul* series. Her work has also been published in *Guideposts*, *Focus on the Family*, and dozens of other magazines. Diane loves to write about the important things in life: her family and her faith.

Virginia Stark is the author of many short stories and several novels. Her books are widely available internationally. Virginia's writing spans many genres from inspirational to dystopian. Her love and passion for life is her common theme. Connect with her via Facebook or e-mail her at virginiaseastark@gmail.com.

L.A. Strucke, a graduate of Rowan University, is a frequent contributor to the *Chicken Soup for the Soul* series, *Guideposts*, *Highlights for Children* and other publications. Her interests are songwriting, art, and visiting her four children and their families. She dedicates this story to Zoon, Jadzia, Hermione and Geneviève.

JC Sullivan continues to prove that it's never too late to hit that reset button. Now a bicoastal actor/director, she credits surfing for making her even more fearless. She's learned no matter who you are, everyone achieves their dreams the same way: by taking that first step… then the next!

Sheila Taylor-Clark is a CPA, author, two-time breast cancer survivor, and motivational speaker. A graduate of JSU, she lives in Lewisville, TX and is married to Nathaniel Clark, Jr. They have adult twin sons and an eight-year-old daughter (McKenzie). E-mail her at shaycpa@msn.com.

Happy to be part of the *Chicken Soup for the Soul* series, **Jodi Renee Thomas** is a freelance writer who is constantly striving to better her craft and reach for the stars. She lives happily in Florida with her husband and daughter, and dogs who like to bother her while she is trying to type.

Deon Toban has been writing short stories and poems for the last twenty years, as writing is one of her passions. When she's not writing, she's enjoying her other passions, such as traveling, reading, and interior design. She is currently working on her first novel.

Mirna Valerio is an ultramarathoner, mom, educator, motivational speaker and adventurer. She is the author of *A Beautiful Work in Progress*, a running memoir, and a 2018 National Geographic Adventurer of the Year.

Melissa Valks is addicted to travel and has visited almost seventy countries, many as solo adventures off the beaten path. Melissa has had numerous writings published, including a book about living and teaching in Korea, and has contributed to three *Chicken Soup for the Soul* books. E-mail her at melissavalks@yahoo.ca.

Nancy G. Villalobos is a retired elementary school educator who lives in Southern California with her Cavalier King Charles Spaniel, Coco. She has finished her first memoir, *Peru, My Other Country*, and is working on a second about the enduring power of women's friendships. E-mail her at nancyvillalobos603@gmail.com.

Mary T. Wagner is a former journalist and soccer mom who changed direction at forty by entering law school and becoming a prosecuting attorney. She counts wearing spike heels and learning to use a cordless drill among her "late blooming" discoveries, and authored *When the Shoe Fits… Essays of Love, Life and Second Chances*.

Diana L. Walters is the administrator of an assisted living facility in Chattanooga. She and her husband develop multi-sensory material to help people with dementia remember their faith, and train groups for ministry in care facilities. E-mail her at dianalwalters@comcast.net.

Ferida Wolff is the author of seventeen books for children and three essay books for children. Her essays have appeared in anthologies, newspapers, and magazines. She writes *Ferida's Backyard*, a blog that looks at the nature/human connection. E-mail her at feridawolff@msn.com.

D.B. Zane is a teacher, writer and mother of three, and has been married for nearly thirty years. In addition to reading and writing, she enjoys knitting.

Sheri Zeck writes stories that encourage, inspire, and entertain others. Her freelance works include stories for *Guideposts*, *Angels on Earth*, *Farm & Ranch Living* and many *Chicken Soup for the Soul* books. Sheri writes about her faith, family, and adventures of raising three girls. Visit her at www.sherizeck.com.

Luanne Tovey Zuccari lives in Western New York with her husband, Paul. Fortunate to live near her two grown children, she has plenty of opportunity to enjoy her eight grandchildren. As the mother of a child who was killed by a drunk driver, she found an outlet for her grief as well as a lifelong friend as part of MADD.

Meet Amy Newmark

Amy Newmark is the bestselling author, editor-in-chief, and publisher of the *Chicken Soup for the Soul* book series. Since 2008, she has published more than 150 new books, most of them national bestsellers in the U.S. and Canada, more than doubling the number of Chicken Soup for the Soul titles in print today. She is also the author of *Simply Happy*, a crash course in Chicken Soup for the Soul advice and wisdom that is filled with easy-to-implement, practical tips for enjoying a better life.

Amy is credited with revitalizing the Chicken Soup for the Soul brand, which has been a publishing industry phenomenon since the first book came out in 1993. By compiling inspirational and aspirational true stories curated from ordinary people who have had extraordinary experiences, Amy has kept the twenty-five-year-old Chicken Soup for the Soul brand fresh and relevant.

Amy graduated *magna cum laude* from Harvard University where she majored in Portuguese and minored in French. She then embarked on a three-decade career as a Wall Street analyst, a hedge fund manager, and a corporate executive in the technology field. She is a Chartered Financial Analyst.

Her return to literary pursuits was inevitable, as her honors thesis in college involved traveling throughout Brazil's impoverished northeast region, collecting stories from regular people. She is delighted to have come full circle in her writing career — from collecting stories "from the people" in Brazil as a twenty-year-old to, three decades later, collecting stories "from the people" for Chicken Soup for the Soul.

When Amy and her husband Bill, the CEO of Chicken Soup for the Soul, are not working, they are visiting their four grown children and their first grandchild.

Follow Amy on Twitter @amynewmark. Listen to her free podcast, The Chicken Soup for the Soul Podcast, at www.chickensoup.podbean. com, or find it at Apple Podcasts, Google Play, the Podcasts app on iPhone, or using your favorite podcast app on other devices.

Meet Joi Gordon

Joi Gordon joined the team at Dress for Success in 1999 and three years later, took over the leadership helm at Dress for Success Worldwide. Under Joi's leadership, the organization has expanded from a singular brick and mortar location in Manhattan to a global entity, spanning across 160 cities in thirty countries and serving over one million women by giving them the tools they need to achieve lifelong economic independence.

Joi has been dedicated to ensuring that Dress for Success is recognized as a global leader in empowering women in their economic and social development and to expand the organization's reach — so that more women across the globe will have access to the resources and tools they need to succeed in the workplace. Not only has she expanded the organization geographically, but programmatically as well, providing women with a plethora of programming at all points of their employment development cycle.

Beyond her efforts at Dress for Success, Joi is actively engaged in numerous community engagement initiatives, serving as a member of the Women's Forum of New York and an executive board member of the Greater Queens Chapter of the Links, Inc. Joi has received an Ellis Island Medal of Honor, been named among *Working Mother* magazine's "Most Powerful Moms in Non-profit," and has been recognized as one of the "25 Most Influential Black Women in Business" by *Network*

Journal Magazine. Additionally, over the span of her nineteen years at Dress for Success, Joi has been honored with numerous civic and community service awards.

Joi received her Bachelor of Arts degree in Radio/Television Broadcasting from the University of Oklahoma and juris doctorate also from the University of Oklahoma's College of Law. She lives with her husband Errol in Queens. Her greatest joys are her two children, Sydney and Nicholas.

DRESS FOR SUCCESS®
Going Places. Going Strong.

About Dress
for Success

ress for Success is an international not-for-profit organization that empowers women to achieve economic independence by providing a network of support, professional attire and the development tools to help women thrive in work and in life.

Since its founding in 1997, Dress for Success has expanded to more than 160 cities in thirty countries. To date, Dress for Success has helped more than one million women work towards self-sufficiency. Three-quarters of the participants in its workforce development program find jobs within ninety days after completing the ten-week program.

Over the years Dress for Success has expanded beyond providing suits and professional attire to women and now provides women with mock interview training, résumé building, job retention and advancement skill building, networking and mentoring opportunities, financial education, health and wellness courses and leadership development.

To learn more about Dress for Success, or to find one of its local affiliates, please visit www.dressforsuccess.org.

Thank You

This project started back in 2012 when our senior editor, Barbara LoMonaco, suggested we collect stories for a book called *Chicken Soup for the Soul: The Independent Woman*. Years passed while we thought about it, and then as we watched the news, and the Women's March, and the increased number of women running for political office, we realized it was time for Barbara's book to come out, but as Empowered Woman instead of Independent Woman. So first thanks go to Barbara for getting the ball rolling on this book, and for reading most of the thousands of stories that were submitted. She was joined in this effort by Susan Heim and Elaine Kimbler.

Susan Heim did the preliminary round of editing after Amy chose the stories from several hundred semifinalists, and Associate Publisher D'ette Corona continued to be Amy's right-hand woman in creating the final manuscript and working with all our wonderful writers. Barbara LoMonaco and Kristiana Pastir, along with outside proofreader Elaine Kimbler, jumped in at the end to proof, proof, proof. And yes, there will always be typos anyway, so feel free to let us know about them at webmaster@chickensoupforthesoul.com, and we will correct them in future printings.

The whole publishing team deserves a hand, including Senior Director of Marketing Maureen Peltier, Senior Director of Production Victor Cataldo, executive assistant Mary Fisher, editor Ronelle Frankel, and graphic designer Daniel Zaccari who turned our manuscript into this beautiful book.

Share with Us

We all have had Chicken Soup for the Soul moments in our lives. If you would like to share your story or poem with millions of people around the world, go to chickensoup.com and click on "Submit Your Story." You may be able to help another reader and become a published author at the same time. Some of our past contributors have launched writing and speaking careers from the publication of their stories in our books!

We only accept story submissions via our website. They are no longer accepted via mail or fax. Visit our website, www.chickensoup.com, and click on Submit Your Story for our writing guidelines and a list of topics we are working on.

To contact us regarding other matters, please send us an e-mail through webmaster@chickensoupforthesoul.com, or fax or write us at:

Chicken Soup for the Soul
P.O. Box 700
Cos Cob, CT 06807-0700
Fax: 203-861-7194

One more note from your friends at Chicken Soup for the Soul: Occasionally, we receive an unsolicited book manuscript from one of our readers, and we would like to respectfully inform you that we do not accept unsolicited manuscripts, and we must discard the ones that appear.

Chicken Soup for the Soul

Changing the world one story at a time®
www.chickensoup.com